BLACK HISTORY EVERYDAY
PART TWO
BLACK HISTORY EVERYDAY

NKISI SARABANDA
Signature of the Spirit

PART TWO
FREDERICK MONDERSON

SUMON PUBLISHERS

FREDERICK MONDERSON

Black History Everyday – Part Two Photo. At the "Tribute to Prof. George Simmonds" at the Victoria 5 Theater in Harlem, "Young" Fred Monderson sat at the feet of his heroes Dr. Ben-Jochannan and with Prof. George Simmonds in full-chiefly regalia, among others.

ISBN 978-1-61023-060-5
LCCN – 201-7907788

Black History Everyday Part Two Photo. Marcus Garvey's Red, Black and Green, symbol of the African-American experience.

BLACK HISTORY EVERYDAY
PART TWO
ABOUT THE AUTHOR

Frederick Monderson is a retired college professor and school teacher who taught African History in the City University of New York and American History and Government in the New York public schools. He has written more than 1000 articles in the New York Black Press, *Daily Challenge*, *Afro Times* and *New American* newspapers. In this venture, Monderson lends his expertise as a historian, Egyptologist, journalist and author of several books including *When is a "Gangster Government" a "Gangster Government?"* *Ladies in the House*; *Michael Jackson: The Last Dance*; *50 on Point*; *Barack Obama: Ready, Fit to Lead*; *Barack Obama: Master of Washington D.C.*; *Obama: Master and Commander*; *Sonny Carson: The Final Triumph*; *Black Nationalism: Alive and Well*; *Black Nationalism: Still Alive and Well*; *African Nationalist: Poetry and Prose*; and on ancient Egypt *Seven Letters to Mike Tyson on Egyptian Temples*; *10 Poems Praising Great Blacks for Mike Tyson*; *Research Essays on Ancient Egypt*; *Temple of Karnak: The Majestic Architecture of Ancient Kemet*; *Where are the Kamite Kings?*; *Abydos and Osiris*; *Temple of Luxor*; *Medinet Habu: Mortuary Temple of Rameses III*; *The Quintessential Book on Ancient Egypt*: *"Holy Land"* (A Novel on Egypt); *Hatshepsut's Temple at Deir el Bahari*; *The Majesty of Egyptian Gods and* Temples (a book of *Egyptian* Poems); *Egypt Essays on Ancient Kemet*; *The*

FREDERICK MONDERSON

Ramesseum: *Mortuary Temple of Rameses II; The Colonnade: Then and Now; Reflections on Ancient Kemet; Grassroots View of Ancient Egypt; Into the Egyptian Mind; Glory of the Ancestors: 19 Letters to O.J. Simpson on Ancient African History;* and (*a Trilogy on Dr. Ben*) *as Celebrating Dr. Ben-Jochannan; Black History Extravaganza; and Let's Liberate the Temple.* A student of the esteemed Dr. Yosef ben-Jochannan, Dr. Monderson conducts tours to Egypt.

For Tour information: Please contact Orleane Brooks-Williams at Nostrand Travel, 730 Nostrand Avenue, Brooklyn, New York 11216. Phone Number 718-756-5300. **Next Tour of Egypt** - July 24-August 7, 2020.

Black History Everyday - Part Two Photo. "Mother Africa" in colorful splendor.

BLACK HISTORY EVERYDAY
PART TWO

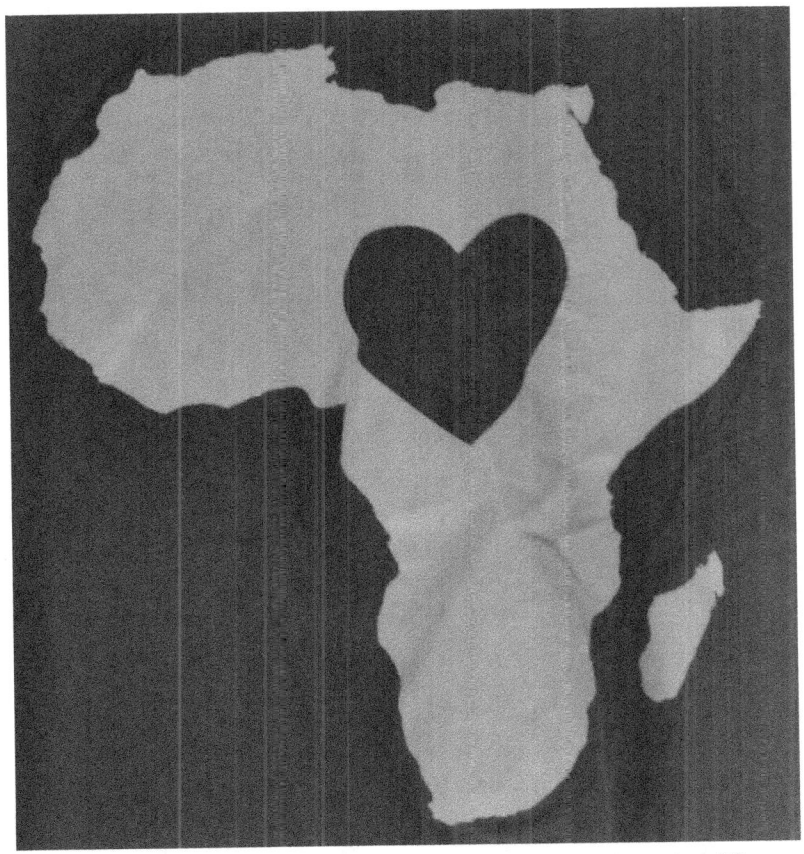

Black History Everyday – Part Two
Photo. A heart of love in "Mother Africa."

FREDERICK MONDERSON

Black History Everyday - Part Two Photo.
"Justice or Else" is the **MESSAGE**!

TABLE OF CONTENTS

1. **PRAISING THE GREAT TEACHER DR. JOHN HENRIK CLARKE**   10
2. **PRESIDENT OBAMA IN AFRICA**   28
3. **OBAMA'S DIVINE MISSION**   64

BLACK HISTORY EVERYDAY
PART TWO

4. ODE TO KWAME TURE — 73
5. MA'AT VERSUS ISFIT IN PRESIDENTIAL POLITICS — 78
6. POWER OF ECONOMIC BOYCOTT — 84
7. QUEEN OF SHEBA IN RACIAL PORTRAYAL AS HISTORICAL DISTORTION — 96
8. SHARPTON, TODAY — 118
9. SONNY CARSON: BORN VISIONARY — 124
10. THAT MISSOURI COMPROMISE — 138
11. THE SUPREME COURT AND ITS JUSTICES — 153
12. THE WHITE HOUSE CONTRADICTION — 182
13. VOTING RIGHTS AND REDISTRICTING — 192
14. "WE BE MARCHING" — 205
15. OBAMA: WORSE PRESIDENT? — 266
16. BEN CARSON, SERIOUSLY? — 284
17. THE SLAVE TRADE TO THE AMERICAS — 311
18. PROF. GEORGE SIMMONDS, "UNSUNG HERO" — 412

19.	DICK GREGORY'S CALLUS ON MY SOUL	415
20.	MARCUS MOZIAH GARVEY	430
21.	OFFICIAL VIEW OF CIVIL RIGHTS	444
22.	MARCUS GARVEY AND THE UNIA	466
23.	HAVE WE FORGOTTEN SONNY CARSON?	489
24.	REFLECTIONS ON BLACK HISTORY IN BROOKLYN - A DECADE AGO	498
25.	SHAMELESS "ANTE BELLUM" LEGISLATORS	516
26.	THE SCOURGE OF RACIAL HATRED	526
27.	MOOD OF THE COUNTRY	538
28.	HATERS WILL HATE	544
29.	"HONORING A GIANT"	552
30.	ABOUT THAT 96 PERCENT	563
31.	KILLING DR. KING AGAIN	575
32.	COUP VERSUS CONSPIRAY	582
33.	THE RISING TIDE OF COLOR	592
34.	THE VOTING RIGHTS ACT	603
35.	MARCUS MOZIAH GARVEY	613

BLACK HISTORY EVERYDAY
PART TWO

Black History Everyday - Part Two Photo. The **"Immortals!"** Dr. Yosef A.A. ben-Jochannan; Chancellor Williams; Cheikh Anta Diop; and John Henrik Clarke.

Black History Everyday - Part Two Photo. Dr. Roscoe Brown (right) and a fellow Tuskegee Airman associate stand proudly as iconic Harlemite and Americans.

"History tells a people where they have been and what they have been, where they are and what they

FREDERICK MONDERSON

are. Most important, an understanding of history tells a people where they still must go and what they still must be." *African People in World History* [1993]

"It is a story that can never be told in all is gruesome details. Of the countless number of Africans ripped from the villages of Africa – from the Senegal River to northern Angola – during the nearly four centuries of the slave trade, approximately one third of them died on the torturous march to the ships and on third died in the holding stations on both sides of the Atlantic or on the ships. It is estimated that ten to twenty million arrived in the New World alive, to be then committed to bondage. If the Atlantic were to dry up, it would reveal a scattered pathway of human bones. African bones marking the various routes of the Middle Passage. From Tom Feelings, *The Middle Passage* [1995] introduction.

1. PRAISING THE GREAT TEACHER DR. JOHN HENRIK CLARKE BY DR. FRED MONDERSON

The Board of Education of People of African Ancestry (**BEEPA**) sponsored its annual tribute to Dr. John H. Clarke at Rev. Johnny Youngblood's **Mount Pisgah Church** on Nostrand and

BLACK HISTORY EVERYDAY
PART TWO

DeKalb Avenues where the Dr. John H. Clarke and Dr. Yosef Ben-Jochannan Lecture Series was conducted, Thursday 7:00-9:00 PM. In a powerful oration aided by an informative **Power Point Presentation**, the Keynote Speaker **Dr. Marimba Ani**, in praising her "spiritual and intellectual father" made the case that Dr. Clarke was an internationally respected **Pan-African Sovereignist**. Her praise of this scholar extraordinaire was punctuated by direct quotes from the Master-Teacher's works as gadfly not simply in education, equally defending and elevating African people worldwide, but incessantly challenging the oppressor while equally pointing out African people's shortfalls and simultaneously making recommendations on what needs to be done to achieve their independence and sustain nationhood viability in a challenging 21st Century global environment.

Elsewhere, a respected gentleman recounted the master educator asking of the audience in a lecture, "How many of you took a bath this morning?" In a moment of astonished consternation and eye-brow raising, everyone raised their hand, to which Dr. Clarke responded, "Can you imagine our economic strength if we made soap?" This was an example of how and consistently Dr. Clarke challenged his students, audience, African people, to address the realities of nation-building to win sustainable respect in a harsh and competitive world that offers no quarter. To underscore this consistent admonition of Dr. Clarke, at the end of Dr. Ani's presentation Dr. Adelaide Sanford informed of the establishment of a black company that manufactures and markets paper products. Strange, but this indispensable product so widely used by African people is very consistent with Dr. Clarke's idea and admonition that we make and wear everything we use and consume as a way of establishing economic independence.

Speaker after speaker preceding Dr. Ani spoke of the influence the great man had in steering their academic career, intellectual development and activist state of mind. A student of Hunter College long influenced by Dr. Clarke, Chairman of the Black and Puerto Rican Department, New York State Assemblyman Charles Baron and his NYC Councilwoman wife Inez, a power-couple consistently on the ubiquitous firing line, showered praises on Dr. Clarke, one of the greatest African activists, intellectually and socially, of the 20th Century.

Basir Mchawy, while confessing of not being a Hunter College Student, yet praising Dr. Clarke for the symbolism he represented as an Africanist on the level of and one who himself praised Marcus Moziah Garvey for his admonitions that Africans "do-for-self." That is, cherish the practice of ownership from farming to property, to manufacturing to banking, a reality stressed by Kwame Nkrumah, the Pan-Africanist President of Ghana, West Africa, "Seek ye

BLACK HISTORY EVERYDAY
PART TWO

first the economic power" and all others will be added, he consistently advocated.

Black History Everyday - Part Two Photo. Faces and signs in the crowd for the 50th Anniversary March on Washington.

FREDERICK MONDERSON

Black History Everyday - Part Two Photo. Faces and signs in the crowd for the 50th Anniversary March on Washington.

BLACK HISTORY EVERYDAY
PART TWO

The Garvey example is recounted as related by Dr. Duguay also in the audience, for when Marcus Garvey looked at the ancient Egyptian Pyramids, he did not ask, "How were they built?" but, "How were they paid for?" Underscoring the significance of economics/finances, in nation building and state sponsored projects of significance, he insisted Blacks buy Black, pool their money in order to become independent economically.

Black History Everyday - Part Two Photo. We Shall Not be Moved March. Faces in the Crowd.

The Master of Ceremonies Dr. James McIntosh, in the effective "traffic cop" mode moved the program along expeditiously. Next it was Omowale Clay's turn representing Sister Viola Plummer of the **December 12 Movement** in which he

FREDERICK MONDERSON

emphasized a sad reality, "Our children are being killed in the streets. We are being drowned in drugs," and this is really a wake-up call for Black people. He insisted, "We must have a plebiscite to determine what our relationship with the USA is." Strange, yet "Dr. Mac" called upon the audience to "Pray that Brother Gil Noble would come here." Lo and behold, his son Chris Noble arrived with the greeting, "Good evening family!" Saluting the freedom fighters, warriors and soldiers in the room, many spoke on their behalf.

Chris Noble reminded the audience, Dr. McIntosh, Sister Betty Dopson and **CEMOTAP** "Never forget great men like Dr. Clarke." Presenting a painting made by **Gil Noble**, a painter, artist and sculptor himself, Chris recalled it was made in his **LIKE IT IS** office because Betty Dopson, Dr. McIntosh and **CEMOTAP** "stand up for Black People." In which Sister Betty reminded, "We loved your father and he loved us." Turning to Dr. Clarke, Chris, a musician in his own right, extolled the Master Teacher as the "Sarah Vaughn, Oscar Peterson and Errol Garner of history all rolled up in one." Dr. Clarke was a "genius that must be celebrated over and over" as the Charlie Parker "who gave an abundance of knowledge to our people."

Praising the audience in attendance and emphasizing a quote from Kwame Ture, "It is the duty of the conscious to make the conscious who think they are

BLACK HISTORY EVERYDAY
PART TWO

conscious realize they are not really conscious but should become conscious." Mr. Noble insisted, "Our existence in this country has never been an American story, it been an African story."

Called from the Mike, Bob Law and Bernard White did not respond.

Emphasizing everyone knew who Robin Hood was and that "When he rescued Maid Marian" he was a hero; Dr. Mac called upon Dr. Sidiqi Odinga leading the Movement to recall the names and struggles of political prisoners in the USA, this freedom fighter in her own right, sought as Chukwe Lumumba insisted, "To restore the balance of the universe." In introducing her husband Sekou Odinga "Who talk the talk and walk the walk" and like Sonny Carson who also "talk the walk and walk the talk," Mr. Odinga reminded, "Dr. Clarke wrote letters to Parole Boards on behalf of many insisting 'We must support political prisoners who fought for us, who died for us. Many of their colleagues died for us.'" Even further, in these struggles and praising the efforts of Dr. Clarke who pointedly state, "As an African people we came enmasse as political prisoners."

"We have to say the names of these Brothers."
"Freedom ain't cheap and don't come easy."

Jericho Movement - "Freedom is a constant struggle inside and outside the walls."

FREDERICK MONDERSON

Dr. Mac insisted, "Communications is one of the first things that gets attacked in war."

"You walk it like you talk it."

Persons recognized in the audience included Abdul Haqq, Brother Shepherd and Sister Veronica Nikki and Kimberly Edwards. Brother John King, Brother Abdul Hafiz Mohammed's name was called but he had another engagement, so he sent a representative.

Thanking **CEMOTAP** for inviting her to be their **Keynote Speaker**, the scholar, cultural scientist and teacher, **Dr. Marimba Ani** began her address by emphasizing the need to go beyond teaching. "If you want to honor someone, you must do what they want you to do. It is very important we be consistent in the work. It is not enough to simply say the rhetoric, we must put words into action, and so, **I say to Nana Dr. John Henrik Clarke, Thank you**."

Dr. Clarke loved us! The political organization we champion comes from love, the deep love we have for African people. Nana is one of the highest terms or praises we can give our heroes. We must understand the African spiritual warfare being waged and equally the need for victory for our people. The political spiritual ancestor community connectedness and connection to fulfilling my spiritual quest is

BLACK HISTORY EVERYDAY PART TWO

manifest in organizational activism. One of the greatest voices of African liberation, a teacher, my teacher, historian, consultant, Dr. John Clarke was a **Pan-African Sovereignist**. One of the things of being a warrior is that we constantly confront the enemy. Confront the hard issues. As a warrior you can't be comfortable. You can't be safe. You have to say things that shake people up. Dr. Clarke is one such leader. Dr. Ani confessed, "He is my ideological father. He taught me much."

Black History Everyday - Part Two Photo. We Shall Not be Moved March. Faces in the Crowd.

"I'm pushing this envelope where it needs to go in the direction of **African Sovereignty**. We must understand resistance plus freedom, plus liberation plus government, equals sovereignty. This is a national concept. It requires land that is our base in

FREDERICK MONDERSON

our homeland. We must have total control of our resources. There must be self-reliance, self-determination, **UJAMAA**, African family-hood.

Black History Everyday - Part Two Photo. Faces and signs in the crowd for the 50th Anniversary March on Washington.

That is, an African spiritual system based on our ancestral connection. There is the need for an African defined future. We must have self-defense, a powerful African army. There is the need for an ancestral connection to our ancestors that inspires liberation from something. We must organize for self-defense, we must recognize and struggle against the confusion in our political system.

Dr. John Clarke taught us to think carefully, politically. He pushed us to think about what we should be doing. He taught us, "African sovereignty is black power. Why? Because power gives you the

BLACK HISTORY EVERYDAY
PART TWO

ability to exact sanctions, be they rewards or punishment. Only through African sovereignty can we guarantee that we will not be re-enslaved. We must have governance to do **Ma'at**. Only with African consciousness can we guarantee we will win. Our conscious people have never heard of the **Citadel in Haiti**. It is a bastion of defense created to defy any attempt to re-enslave Haiti, after the **Haitian Revolution**.

One of Dr. Clarke's classic pronouncements is that, **"Everything that touches your lives should be an instrument of your liberation or you must throw it into the trash heap of history."** **"Education has but one honored purpose. That is, to train the student to be a proper handler of power."** Nana Clarke was uncompromising on education and power. Let's do it. Let's get to work.

THE EXERCISE OF POWER

We must look into education for nation building and management. Nation management is our only hope. We must pursue African education for self-reliance. The **UNIA** and the **ACL** preached self-reliance.

Every form of true education prepares the student for the real challenges of life. "Black money, black

FREDERICK MONDERSON

brains and black energy must rule the world. There must be African education for African power. Powerful people never educate powerless people (in how) to take their power away from them."

Black History Everyday - Part Two Photo. Dorothy Height, President of **The Conference of Negro Women**.

BLACK HISTORY EVERYDAY PART TWO

MEANINGLESS RHETORIC

"We shouted 'Nation Time' too soon. African people need to stop shouting nation time until they are clear about the responsibilities of running a nation."

Black History Everyday - Part Two Photo. We Shall Not be Moved March. Faces in the Crowd.

Dr. Clarke asked the question, "Who owns the resources of Africa?" "Foreign entities own the resources of Africa by virtue of their control of the method of extraction."

Foreign engineers do not train African engineers in the intricacies of the technology they use. With all the resources they possess, no one is building cars, trucks, locomotives in Africa. They are certainly not making armaments in Africa. This must change if Africa is to be truly free.

ANALYSIS

There must be a sharing of deep thought to expand the realm of our thinking. We are a world people. The total liberation of Africa must involve a commitment of all the Africans on the face of the earth. This kind of thinking, Dr. Ani insisted, was being articulated in the 1950s in a hundred-year project. Now that we are in the 21st Century, instead of nearing completion of bringing these ideas into fruition, we are far from such an achievement. However, we must never forget, "Each generation must assume the responsibility of securing their manhood. The definition, their being of this earth."

We must question every person that calls themselves a leader, a preacher, a policy maker, whether they are indeed such.

Again, Dr. Clarke asked, "How will my people stay on this earth? How will they be educated? How will they be housed? How will they be fed? And, how will they be defended?"

BLACK HISTORY EVERYDAY
PART TWO

Black History Everyday - Part Two Photo. Faces and signs in the crowd for the 50th Anniversary March on Washington.

Black History Everyday - Part Two Photo. Faces and signs in the crowd for the 50th Anniversary March on Washington.

FREDERICK MONDERSON

African people must be ready for the 21st Century. The **African Sovereignist Movement** insists we must have our own homes. Dr. Clarke recommended we must not sell what we own but buy property. Being in charge of our own destiny, nation, is our own responsibility.

And so, whether during **Black History Month** or all year long, **WE MUST BUY BLACK 365!**

Black History Everyday - Part Two Photo. We Shall Not be Moved March. Faces in the Crowd.

BLACK HISTORY EVERYDAY
PART TWO

Black History Everyday - Part Two Photo. Stalwarts at **CEMOTAP's** Celebration.

"Slavery has been fruitful in giving itself names. It has been called "the peculiar institution," the social system" and the (impediment." ... It has been called by a great many names, and it will call itself by yet another name, you and I and all of us had better wait and see what new form the old monster will assume, in what new skin this old snake will next come forth." Frederick Douglass. *Speech at the American Anti-Slavery Society, Boston* [May 10. 1865]

"In the forts and factories of Royal African Company, a distinction was made between 'sale slaves' and 'castle slaves' or 'factory slaves.' Both were acquired in the same way, but, while the former were destined to face the Middle Passage, the latter were retained around the forts and factories in the conduct of trade.

FREDERICK MONDERSON

The directors took some interest in these 'castle slaves.' Perhaps the most important from the company's point of view was 'castle slaves' should be taught skills to enhance their value and utility. Such workers were not to be sold or transported overseas except for great crimes." Walter Rodney. *African Slavery in the Context of the Atlantic Slave Trade*, in Seth M. Schneider and Tilden G. Edelstein. *The Black Americans*: *Interpretative Readings*.

2. PRESIDENT OBAMA IN AFRICA AND SLAVE TRADE PART ONE BY DR. FRED MONDERSON

After successfully attending a Summit establishing a new chapter in American-Russian relations, then on to Italy for a G-8 Economic Conference where he and the first family had an audience with Pope Benedict, President Obama arrived in Ghana, West Africa, for a one-day visit charged with more significance and electricity than that of all past Presidents combined who have visited Africa. To recall, as a Senator from Illinois, Barack Obama visited Kenya, his father's homeland, which provided a tremendous welcome to this son of a son. Elders dressed Obama in the traditional garb and this provided a firestorm in the 2008 Presidential Elections at home as opponents sought to paint him as so many things. However, this

BLACK HISTORY EVERYDAY
PART TWO

time as the first African-American President, rather than return to his "roots" in Kenya, President Obama chose Ghana because of its symbolism as a thriving and vibrant democracy, as evident from a recent election and peaceful transfer of power.

In a historic address to the Ghanaian Parliament, carried by CNN and equally broadcast across the African continent, Mr. Obama was pragmatic, stuck to his guns and delivered a "tough love" speech outlining America's new relationship with African nations. He emphasized the simple and unmistakable fact, "we must start with the simple premise that Africa's future is up to Africans" and recognizing Europe's imperial role on the continent insisted, "a colonial map that made little sense bred conflict and the West has often approached Africa as a patron, rather than a partner, but the West is not responsible for the destruction of the Zimbabwean economy over the last decade, or wars in which children are enlisted as combatants." No but the west was responsible for centuries of rape and pillage of the African landmass, population and minerals.

FREDERICK MONDERSON

Black History Everyday - Part Two Photo. Faces and signs in the crowd for the 50th Anniversary March on Washington.

Black History Everyday - Part Two Photo. Faces and signs in the crowd for the 50th Anniversary March on Washington.

Five hundred years after the discovery of the Americas and the subsequent efforts to conquer this

BLACK HISTORY EVERYDAY
PART TWO

hemisphere, the European Slave Trade in Africans, and plantation slavery with psychological and physical emasculation of the victims of such barbarism, we see the legacy of slavery still functioning institutionally in many guises even though we have crossed the bridge to the next century. This forces us to remember (in this emerging great nation of America), English colonials under Britain fought the French, in the **French and Indian Wars** (1756-1763) and fought the British in the **War of Independence** (1776-1783). This new nation then fought the British again in the **War of 1812**. Then we fought the Spanish in the **Spanish-American War** (1898-1900); the Germans and their allies in **World War I** (1914-1918) though we practically entered the conflict in 1917; again, the Germans, Italians and Japan in **World War II** (1939-1945) entering that conflict on December 7, 1941; the **Korean War** (1950-1953); and against the Chinese, Russians and their allies in the **anti-Communist Cold War**. Yet again, particularly the Russians, who have atomic weapons, still aimed at us that can devastate this nation, their people can all come to these shores, blend in with the population and with some effort particularly aided by their cultural organizations, begin moving up the ladder towards realization of the American Dream. However, the ravages and devastation of slavery and its legacy still identify sons and daughters of Africa in America and make us victims of racism that was born out of this dehumanizing experience.

Black History Everyday - Part Two Photo. Sharpton and Crump's March on Liberty Square. The People United will never be defeated!

Therefore, we need to never forget as we ended the Twentieth Century and crossed the bridge to the Twenty-First Century; it was W.E.B. DuBois who said the question of the "color bar" would dominate these past hundred years. All people must move away from this odious conception and practice that is very much alive and well in the world in today's 21st Century! Fordham in *Geography of African Affairs* (1965: 58-59) recounted how Africans worldwide are viewed in the most disdainful manner and supplied an example that indicated, "As late as 1928 a distinguished Englishman" could write, "The Negroes of Tropical Africa specialized in their

BLACK HISTORY EVERYDAY
PART TWO

isolation and stagnation in utter savagery. They may even have been drifting away from the human standard back towards the brute when migratory impulses drew the Caucasian, the world's redeemer, to enter Tropical Africa ... mingle his blood with that of the pristine Negroes and raise the mental status of these dark skinned, wooly haired, prognathous retrograded men ...."

Fordham continued: "Echoes of this attitude were still to be heard in the British House of Lords in 1961" when he quoted Lord Barbizon of Tara, on March 23, 1961, in *Hansard* Vol. 229, No. 57, Cols. 1277-9. "As I went to it [the United Nations] I really got the impression that there was a convention of Nigger minstrels going on ... the Commonwealth is a piebald set-up, and a pie-bald set-up is a poor form of organization that will never last." Of course, that is not to say, some of African people have not progressed despite difficult odds, as they struggled with and without bootstraps.

However, in reflection, as we celebrated another Martin Luther King Birthday and head towards Black History Month in February, 1998, the voices of such commentators as Julian Bond, Leonard James, Kwame Mfume, Leonard Jeffries, Tony Martin, Sonny Carson and a whole host of others, all pointed to the disparities and difficulties of high unemployment, police brutality, racial discrimination, poverty, lack of proper medical care, drug infestation, crime, poor education, etc., that

FREDERICK MONDERSON

plague African-American. This odious legacy is principally because of the African heritage of Black people that seems anathema to many in this nation. Even though we now have a Black President many people still harbor odious sentiments towards him and other Blacks, particularly because of their skin color. But it must be remembered, Black people paid the ultimate sacrifice to build America, and having earned their place, they intend to take a seat at the table of this nation, under the philosophic and humanistic banner believing in the "fatherhood of God and the brotherhood of man."

Black History Everyday - Part Two Photo. Congressman Major Owens and another distinguished gentleman, mathematician.

With that, we need to understand the forced removal of Africans, called the Atlantic Slave Trade, began soon after the Portuguese landed in West Africa in

BLACK HISTORY EVERYDAY
PART TWO

1441. That year, a trickle of Africans was first taken to Lisbon, Portugal. Lloyd (1972: 51) has shown early contacts by the Portuguese along the West African coast was beginning to clear the way for the later onslaught.

"In 1434 Portuguese ships passed Cape Bojador in Mauretania; by 1475 Fernando Po had been reached, and in 1483 Portuguese sailors visited the capital of Benin, probably the most highly organized coastal kingdom at this period. The Portuguese were impressed by it and established a trading port at Ughoton (Gwatto) in 1486, but their main attention was directed to the Gold Coast with its more valuable exports; the castle of San Jorge da Mina was erected at Elmina in 1482. Gold apart, the West African coast offered little to attract European trade until the discovery of the Americas provided a demand for slaves."

Black History Everyday - Part Two Photo. Faces and signs in the crowd for the 50th Anniversary March on Washington.

FREDERICK MONDERSON

Black History Everyday - Part Two Photo. Faces and signs in the crowd for the 50th Anniversary March on Washington.

However, from 1485 onward observers witness a number of significant events in Europe. First there was the unification of Spain and the defeat of the Moors at the "Fall Granada" and in 1492 Columbus' first expedition was underway. Decades thereafter, Africans began to be shipped to the Americas to cultivate plantations. By the end of the century, they were producing sugar cane and derivative products; particularly in the British West Indies, e.g., Barbados, Trinidad; Slavery came after 1814 in Cape Town, South Africa; and after the Dutch in Guiana now Guyana, enslaved Africans were harnessed to exploit this sweet product with its derivative industries.

BLACK HISTORY EVERYDAY
PART TWO

Black History Everyday - Part Two Photo. We Shall Not be Moved March. Faces in the Crowd.

Iliffe (1995: 127-128) explained: "The Atlantic slave trade began in 1441 when a young Portuguese sea-captain Antam Goncalvez, kidnapped a man and woman on the Western Saharan coast to please his employer, Prince Henry the Navigator-successfully, for Goncalvez was knighted. Four years later the Portuguese built a fort on Arguin Island, off the Mauritanian coast, from which to purchase slaves and, more particularly, gold, which was especially scarce at this time. After failing in 1415 to capture the gold trade by occupying Ceuta on the Moroccan coast, Portuguese mariners groped down the West African coast towards the gold sources. Arguin was designed to lure gold caravans away from the journey to Morocco. Yet slaves were not merely by-products, for a lively market in African slaves had existed since the mid-fourteenth century in southern Europe, where labor was scarce after the "Black Death" and slavery had survived since Roman times in domestic service and pockets of intensive agriculture, especially the production of sugar, which Europeans had learned from Muslims during the Crusade. As sugar plantation spread westwards through the Mediterranean to Atlantic islands like Madeira and eventually to the Americas, they depended increasingly on slave labor. The Atlantic slave trade was largely a response to their demand."

Significantly, by 1505 or thereabouts, exploration of the "New World" had become ingrained. The result was systematic and widespread destruction of indigenous cultures, viz., the Incas, Mayas, Aztecs, etc., that were flourishing in this hemisphere. Commenting on the people who followed Columbus into North, Central and South America at the end of Fifteenth Century, Davidson (1996: 202) wrote: "These others, who were Spanish soldiers and adventurers, ruined the [native] American peoples whom they found. Their intention was not trade, but loot; not peace, but war; not partnership, but enslavement. They fell upon these lands with greed and the fury of destruction. And the [native] American peoples, unlike the Africans, were unable to defend themselves. Being at an earlier stage of social and technical development than the Africans, they fell easy victims to Spanish violence. Along the coast of Guinea, the Portuguese and other Europeans

BLACK HISTORY EVERYDAY
PART TWO

had begun by trying their hand at violence. But they had given that up. The Africans they met were too strong for them. In the Americas it was different."

Even further, Davidson (1996: 203) continued: "There was terrible destruction of the 'Indians,' the name that was mistakenly given by these raiders to the native-born American people. A Spanish report of 1518, only twenty-six years after the first voyage of Columbus across the Atlantic, says that when the island of Cuba was discovered it was reckoned to contain more than a million 'Indians,' but today their number does not exceed 11,000. And judging from what has happened, there will be none of them left in three - or four-years' time, unless some remedy is applied."

That unfortunate state of affairs, forced Bishop Bartholomew De Las Casas to petition the papacy. He requested that Africans be brought into the Americas for labor purposes, to replace the rapidly disappearing indigenous population. Losing the battle to "save the Indians," he unleashed an even greater tragedy that lasted for centuries, and claimed many, many more lives. This stain on humanity's integrity was Europe's Slave Trade in Africans to America.

The Age of Exploration created new opportunities for discovery and transformation of the new lands, introduced by Columbus and the other explorers, for which they sought official sanction. The "Papal

FREDERICK MONDERSON

Division of the World" in 1492 gave half to Portugal and the other half to Spain, Christian nations and ardent defenders of their religion and the papacy. Two years later in 1494, the "demarcation" was enshrined in the "Treaty of Tordesillas," moving the boundary line 300-leagues to the west. The new official pronouncement now gave most of the New World to Spain. That determination excluded the Portuguese foothold in Brazil that is today the largest country in South America. As such, this Papal beneficence prohibited the Spanish from involvement in the trade in enslaved persons from Africa. The Portuguese, however, did have a free hand there. Iliffe (1995: 130) continued, recounting: "The first West African slaves went mainly to Portugal, then to Madeira, and then to Sao Tome. Direct shipments from Africa to the Americas began in 1532. As European and African diseases destroyed the Amerindian peoples, African slaves replaced them, because Africans alone were available in the required numbers, and then were cheaper than white indentured laborers, and they had the unique degree of immunity to both European and African diseases which came from living in the tropical periphery of the Old World."

By the late sixteenth century nearly 80 per cent of all exported West African slaves went to the Americas, especially to Brazil, where plantation sugar took root during the 1540s.

BLACK HISTORY EVERYDAY
PART TWO

Black History Everyday - Part Two Photo. **We Shall Not be Moved March**. Faces in the Crowd.

The Spanish "Hacienda Treaty" was agreed to in 1713. Whom-so-ever held it had permission to supply the Spanish possessions in America with enslaved persons from Africa. In fact, Moore and Dunbar (1968: 110) have written: "The British took a leading part in this trade from the middle of the seventeenth century, with the development of the plantation colonies. New impetus was given when at the Peace of Utrecht in 1713 [Britain] obtained the Asiento." This Spanish contract was to supply cargo to and from the New World. For the African victims involved, this dreaded official instrument, yet, provoked many wars at sea among slaving European nations. Dreaded, in the sense that, the Spanish could not get slaves in Africa, so they had them brought to their New World plantation. For Africans, it provided death and hopelessness of Slave Trade and Slavery. Oliver and Fage (1970: 120) argued, Spanish territory was very lucrative and: "The early Spanish colonies there had been supplied with African slaves, mainly through the Portuguese, from about 1510. But it was not until the competitive irruption into the West Indies of the Dutch, French and English in the seventeenth century, when there was a rapidly growing European demand for sugar - a crop making heavy demands on labor - that the transatlantic slave trade began to dominate European activities in West Africa. Compared with an estimate of some 275,000 Negro slaves landed overseas by 1600, the seventeenth-century figure is thought to be about 1,340,000; the figures of the eighteenth and nineteenth centuries seem to have been about 6,050,000 and 1,900,000 respectively. The new development ousted the Portuguese from the Gold Coast. For a short time, the trans-Atlantic trade was almost a Dutch monopoly, but their success provoked English and French hostility, and by the eighteenth century it was the traders of these two nations who were the principal competitors in the international trade, thought the Portuguese continued with a private slave trade of their own, from Angola and San Thome to Brazil. In terms of the trade alone, victory went to Britain. By the end of the eighteenth century her ships were carrying nearly half the slaves taken to America."

And so, it continued for centuries. But that is not to say, though scholars have mentioned the Portuguese,

BLACK HISTORY EVERYDAY
PART TWO

English, French and Dutch, that these were the only nations involved. We must remember, colonial America was also an active participant in Slave Trade development. This systematic and undeniable holocaust, which Merimba Ani termed the **GREAT MAAFA**, provided an inexhaustible supply of free labor required by slave trading nations then transforming the American landscape. Those other nations involved included the Brandenbergers or Germans, the Danes, and Swedes. Still, though not involved in carrying Africans to the "new world," the Spanish, because of the needs of empire, helped maintain a system of slavery in America, for three centuries after Columbus, that encouraged the perpetuation of this ghastly free and cruel labor-supply phenomenon.

From the Atlantic Slave Trade's inception, it would appear that few of the traders worried or were concerned about carrying conditions aboard their ships. As a result, the terms "tight packers" and "loose packers" came to characterize how enslaved Africans were transported to the Americas.

FREDERICK MONDERSON

Black History Everyday - Part Two Photo. Jitu Weusi, iconic educator and activist, lends his support to another demonstration for change.

As Malcolm X said, "We did not land on Plymouth Rock, Plymouth Rock landed on us." In this, the "Triangular Trade" and "Middle Passage" treatment promised nothing but death, hopeless melancholy and despair.

Relative to mortality and in view of this situation, in 1788 and again in 1792, the **House of Commons of the British Parliament** conducted inquiries on the Slave Trade. They found that "persons transported from Africa to the West Indies are kidnapped, solely for the purpose of selling them to the traders." Alexander Falconbridge (1788: 13), a surgeon in the Slave Trade, had written there is "great reason to believe that most of the Negroes shipped from the coast of Africa are kidnapped."

BLACK HISTORY EVERYDAY
PART TWO

Sold to European slavers, the enslaved Africans faced a difficult journey. It took some fifty-two days to cross the Atlantic from Africa to America. At times the voyage was longer. However, it was seldom shorter!

Black History Everyday - Part Two Photo. We Shall Not be Moved March. Faces in the Crowd.

Significantly, a constant problem of the Slave Trade was overcrowding. The famous slave ship **BROOKES**, out of Liverpool, sailed to the West Coast of Africa in 1783. This 320-ton frigate was built without forecastle and pierced for 20 guns that enabled every square foot of the vessel to be used to store its human cargo. **Minutes of the Evidence on the Slave Trade to Parliament** (1789: 43) indicated calculations

FREDERICK MONDERSON

were made of the men's room, boys' room, women's room, the gun-room, cabin, half-deck and a number of platforms.

Black History Everyday - Part Two Photo. Faces and signs in the crowd for the 50th Anniversary March on Washington.

Black History Everyday - Part Two Photo. Faces and signs in the crowd for the 50th Anniversary March on Washington.

BLACK HISTORY EVERYDAY
PART TWO

A. Stuart-Brown (1932: 48-49) described some carrying logistics of this famous vessel: "The slaves were lodged on the lower deck, the men in a room 46 feet by 25 feet 4 inches and 5 feet 8 inches high, the women in a smaller room 28 feet 6 inches by 23 feet 6 inches and the boy's room was 13 feet 9 inches by 25 feet."

In one instance, this slaving ship spent 10 months on the coast and collected 609 enslaved Africans. Those who boarded first experienced the horrors of "holding" before the "Middle Passage."

Dr. Thomas Trotter, the **BROOKES'** surgeon, according to *Evidence of Robert Stokes Esq., Before the Select Committee of the House of Lords* in 1948, reported seeing Africans all over the ship. In testimony to the Committee of Parliament, Stokes (1849: 5) describing his observations, on the ship and states that the "slaves in the passage was so crowded below, it is impossible to walk through them without treading on them." These conditions existed in the "pre-regulation period" when "tight packers" was the rule. "Tight packers" meant purchase and carry as many enslaved persons without concern about safety and mortality. Some ships carried as many as 800 persons. Imagine! In the **Frontispiece** of this same source, Charles Fox, an abolitionist had stated: "True humanity consists not in a squeamish ear; it consists not in staring or shrinking at tales such as these, but in a disposition of heart to relieve misery.

FREDERICK MONDERSON

True humanity appertains rather to the mind than to the nerves, and prompts men to use real and active endeavors to execute the measures which it suggests."

After regulation in 1789, **BROOKES** was restricted to carry only 454 enslaved Africans. The ship was still crowded with 450 aboard. One could only wonder how it managed to transport 609. After regulation, "loose packing" or carry fewer based on ship's tonnage, helped reduce the mortality rate aboard this and many other British slavers. While in this essay the British example is often used, the practice applies for colonial America and other slave-trading European nations, making Britain the "best of a bad lot." Some have disagreed and believe they were the worst during the 1700s-1800s. Fact is, British regulation was not a pre-requisite of other nations. Business operated on the conscience of the monetary unit whether pound, frank, mark, or dollar. The stark inhumanity of the trade victimized and physically dehumanized the African man, woman and child.

According to **An Historical Account of the Liverpool African Slave Trade** (1884: iii) there was an old saying in the City of Liverpool: "Get slaves honestly, if you can, and if you cannot get them honestly, get them!" Of course, a colleague of mine, Stanley Simpson, reviewing this comment asked: "What is meant by the term 'honestly' in this context during the 1700s?" Does it mean pay first for

BLACK HISTORY EVERYDAY
PART TWO

the merchandise? Or, pay a good price for what you got. If so, what would be the true value of a human being? That is the question. In fact, it forces us to wonder what is the true value of an African man, woman or child, then as well as today? When we apply this context to the present state of relations among African people, it does not matter if persons are killed by their own or by others, a human life should not be regarded as being without value. That is why more than a dozen years ago, the Theme of 1997 (2016) **Black Solidarity Day** was: "No (Black) one should die at the hands of another." This was Sonny Carson's idea and should apply equally today across this nation, whether in Chicago, New York, or Los Angeles!

Black History Everyday - Part Two Photo. We Shall Not be Moved March. Faces in the Crowd.

FREDERICK MONDERSON

In those Atlantic Slave Trade times, in the principal British trading city of Liverpool and elsewhere, it was a popular belief, notes *An Historical Account* ... (1884: 14) that: "Slavery was right; it was supported by the Bible, and strenuously advocated by the clergy of the time; as well as the politicians. They asserted it was divine right that the blacks were of an inferior race and were to be bought and sold by the white man, with his brand on them .... How many crimes have been committed in the name of the book?" Perhaps, however, it was not in the name of the Book but in the name of profits!

We are told further in the same source (1884: 16) of George Franklin Cook, tragedian, who was born April 17, 1756 and died September 26, 1812. While drunk at a performance in the Liverpool Theater, he is quoted as saying to his critics: "I have not come here to be insulted by a set of wretches, of which every brick in your infernal town is cemented with an African's blood." We are also informed in *Edinburgh Review* (1908: 26) that the "chief center of the African trade Liverpool, [was] remarkable in the commercial history of the United Kingdom." *Even further, the same source, Edinburgh* Review (1908: 33) states: "Of all English communities, Liverpool derived the most wealth from the debasing trade." More, in the *Illustrated London News* (1957: 18) we are again reminded of descriptions of the city's investment in the Slave Trade as an "impressive array of commercial institutions, banking houses, insurance companies, trading

BLACK HISTORY EVERYDAY
PART TWO

associations and produce exchanges." In addition, *Illustrated London News* (1957: 18) informed further, "Liverpool merchants performed a variety of economic functions incorporating the means for financing and insuring the commodities they bought and sold, and controlling the ships which carried the commodities overseas." Even more, that the "Liverpool merchant body exerted a powerful influence over Parliament through the Liverpool Parliamentary Office." This was probably because the prosperity of the port was tied to the import of raw cotton, sugar, wheat, flour, rum, and tobacco, and to the export of cotton piece goods, woolens, salt, coal, iron products, chemicals, glass and soap. However, this profit motive notwithstanding, things have an uncanny way of working themselves out, for there were individuals whose conscience and high moral standards dictated that they resist and challenge this plague perpetuated by their countrymen. One such instance can be cited of James Fox, an abolitionist quoted as saying during the English Parliament's attempt to regulate the Slave Trade, that: "There can be no regulation of robbery and murder."

We know the Atlantic Slave Trade began after Bishop De Las Casas sought papal approval to ship Africans to the Americas to save lives of Amerindians. Foxburn (1932: 56) has shown: "Las Casas, ... saw no harm in subjecting African Negroes to the treatment from which he sought earnestly to save the aborigines of the new world." However, some have argued that de Las Casas thought this the

FREDERICK MONDERSON

lesser of two evils. Perhaps he never thought it would escalate as it did. Yet and arguably, the trade was continued under religious sanction through the belief that Africans were not Christians, not Europeans, had an "exotic culture" and easily definable by skin color. Therefore, official policy held it was okay to enslave them. Thereafter, in 1562-63, Sir John Hawkins, the first Englishman to trade in enslaved Africans, sailed to Africa in the slave ship Solomon. Two years later in 1564-65, he sailed in the slave ship Jesus, blazing a trail for his countrymen.

Black History Everyday - Part Two Photo. Faces and signs in the crowd for the 50th Anniversary March on Washington.

Harris (1972: 72-73) has argued, "it was a combination of European attitudes about blacks and the demand for cheap labor that sired the Atlantic slave trade and New World black slavery." When the

BLACK HISTORY EVERYDAY
PART TWO

Portuguese arrived in Africa, they began seizing Africans to take to Europe as 'curiosity pieces' which confirmed that a "new land had been reached." The early African victims were honored in Portugal, taught Portuguese, and used as informants and guides for future Portuguese voyages to Africa.

Black History Everyday - Part Two Photo. **"In the Beginning"** there was **AFRICA!**

However, as the number of Africans increased in Lisbon they gradually were relegated to menial tasks, and by the middle of the fifteenth century, a lively trade in African labor (slaves) developed. Thus, even

FREDERICK MONDERSON

before the Americas were settled by Europeans, Europe witnessed the development of black slavery, especially in Portugal, Spain, Italy, and Sicily. It has been estimated, for example, that between 1458 and 1460, from 700 to 800 slaves were exported annually from Africa to Europe, with an estimate of 35,000 for 1450-1500.

Some authorities have calculated that from 50,000 to 100,000 Africans were taken to Europe during the whole course of the trade. Whatever the numbers, the point to emphasize here is that a half century prior to their settlement in the Americas, many Europeans (especially the inhabitants of Spain and Portugal, the two countries that spearheaded American settlement) had become accustomed to the enslavement of the Africans.

BLACK HISTORY EVERYDAY
PART TWO

Black History Everyday - Part Two Photo. This lady has a Problem. She says: "**I Can't Breathe!**"

Yet, and conversely, by the 18th century, a religious

conviction motivated men of good will to lead the fight to outlaw the slave trade. In Britain, many important abolitionists were involved including Granville Sharpe, Thomas Clarkson, Charles Fox, Wilberforce, Macaulay, and the Reverend John Newton, a reformed slave dealer. Reverend Newton authored the hymn "How Sweet the Name of Jesus Sounds," after a religious conversion, while aboard a slave ship, he operated off the coast of West Africa.

In 1849, evidence was presented by *Robert Stokes before the Committee of the House of Lords*, as previously stated. This body, following inquiries of six decades earlier, reflected on the high mortality rate of English seamen in the trade before regulation. Their results revealed the following percentage of mortality rates: 50, 20, 20, 30, 33, 25, 30 and 50. This showed an average of 32 per cent death rate for seamen on board some English slavers. Well, if the slavers were experiencing such high rates of mortality, imagine what it was among their cargo!

John Latimer (1893: 474-75) in *The Annals of Bristol in the 18th Century* recounted the view of "one captain from the port of the slave trade who did not deserve long ago to be hanged."

Slaving methods of procuring sailors were notorious. In the slaving business, these seamen were: "Dreadfully ill-treated .... drugged with liquor until impotent to offer resistance... sailors ... encouraged to run into debt, and then offered the alternative of a

BLACK HISTORY EVERYDAY
PART TWO

slaving voyage or a goal [jail] ... never permitted to read the articles they signed on entering a ship, and by the insertion in these documents of iniquitous clauses.... wages in the slave trade (30 s per month) though nominally higher, were actually higher in other trades."

Nonetheless, in his *Essay on the Impolicy of the Slave Trade*, Thomas Clarkson (1785: 35) mentioned the "difficulty of procuring seamen for the slave trade is well known at the ports where it is carried on." Again, Clarkson (1788: 57) notes, "in the year 1786, 1,125 seamen will be found upon the dead list in consequence of this execrable trade." That same year recalled, Clarkson (1788: 60) among West India Seamen, "1470 deserted or were discharged .... Only 610 seamen out of the whole number deserted or were discharged yet found their way out of the colonies... that 860 yet remain to be accounted for in the expenditure of the year 1786." These figures, reinforced the view that mortality rates were high aboard these frigates of death, and, once tricked, sailors seemed to want to get out of the business themselves. Still, and also important, not all sailors were shanghaied and money was being made by the investors, whose mantra was "Buy low, sell high." Imagine!

More importantly, however, was the high incidence of deaths among the Africans, victimized in this Atlantic Slave Trade's forced migration, being the subject of centuries of psychological and physical

FREDERICK MONDERSON

assaults. In 1788, Clarkson called for "Efficiency of Regulation of the Slave Trade" because of its effects on both victims in the trade, Africans and Europeans. He supplied particularly interesting data on the subject of mortality. In his evidence, sailors' testimony show, "we purchased 350 slaves and buried 61; in a second voyage, in the same ship, we purchased 350, and buried 200; and in ... we purchased 370 and buried 100 .... We purchased 700 slaves and lost 250 ... we purchased 300, out of which we buried 17 ... 350 were purchased, and 25 were lost as before.... about 500 were purchased, and 150 buried."

Black History Everyday - Part Two Photo. We Shall Not be Moved March. Faces in the Crowd.

Most deaths were due to overcrowding and the intolerable conditions of the voyage. Practically, the physical and psychological cruelty of slavers were significant factors Africans had to reckon with. Victimizers also became victims of conditions they created.

BLACK HISTORY EVERYDAY
PART TWO

In the end, the African personality was denuded and broken from this experience. Or, as the Afrocentrists would say, the Africans were "detached, isolated, de-centered." Arriving in the West Indies the African was again debased. There, a final merciless legislative act transformed him into chattel or property. For example, *Report of the Lords' Committee of* Council... 1789, Part III, in Jamaica, slaves were considered as property as indicated *Anno 1696 Act 38: XL....* "That no slave shall be free by becoming Christian; and for payment of debts and legacies, all slaves shall be deemed and taken as all other goods and chattels are in the hands of executors or administrators; all children of slaves, born in the possession of tenant for life or years, shall remain or revert."

Black History Everyday – Part Two Photo. "No Justice, No Peace! We Will Not go Back!"

FREDERICK MONDERSON

Black History Everyday - Part Two Photo. Faces and signs in the crowd for the 50th Anniversary March on Washington.

Black History Everyday - Part Two Photo. Faces and signs in the crowd for the 50th Anniversary March on Washington.

BLACK HISTORY EVERYDAY PART TWO

Again, in Jamaica, Anno 1719, Act 67: V... no Negro, mulatto, or Indian slave shall hire themselves out to work, either ashore or on board any ship or vessel, boat, ferry, canoe ... every such slave so offending, shall be whipped at the discretion of any magistrate in the parish or precinct where such slave or slaves shall offer themselves for hire.

In Barbados, slaves were also considered as property, for according to Act No. 94 of April 29, 1668, the "Negro slaves of this island shall be real estate .... all Negro slaves, in all courts of judicature and other places within this island, shall be held, taken, and adjudged to be estate real ... and shall descend unto the heirs and widow of any person dying intestate."

Again, in Barbados, January 1672, Act No. 178 was considered "A declarative Act upon the act making Negroes real estate" and "that Negroes shall be deemed real estate and not chattel ... Negroes may be sued for and recovered by action personal ... Negroes continue chattel for the payment of debts.'

Even further, on August 8, 1688, Act No. 329 states, 'where any Negro or other slave ... shall suffer death then shall such justices and freeholders, colonels and field officers who adjudged such Negro or other slave to suffer death, immediately after sentence thereof given inquire by the best means they are able of the value of such Negro or other slave, in which value they shall not exceed the sum of five and twenty pound sterling .... tempt or persuade any Negroes or other slaves to leave their masters and mistresses... adjudged to pay the master of the said Negro or other slave five and twenty pounds.'

On November 28, 1705, Act No. 516 read: "... for all Negroes and other slaves that shall be imported to this island and landed there, an importation or duty shall be paid, that the merchant or merchants ... pay into the treasurer of this island ... five shillings current money for each and every Negro or other slave imported, whether male or female, young or old ....'

Finally, a *Supplemental Act* was passed on February 7, 1715, No. 593 that read as follows: 'Be it therefore enacted ... that no Negroes or other slaves whatsoever, which shall for the future be once imported into this island shall be exempted from paying the duty of five shillings a head, but such only which shall be within 48 hours exported in the same ship or vessel.'

Therefore, the psycho-social ramifications of the century's old experience seemed to, and still, so significantly plague the survivors of the greatest of all tragedies, that Prof. Donna Richards/Merimba Ani of Hunter College called **The Maafa** or "Great Enslavement" as "the basis of the Western World's Economic Development on the Backs of African people!"

Now, when President Obama refers to "mismanagement of the Zimbabwean economy" let

BLACK HISTORY EVERYDAY
PART TWO

us not forget the history that underlay the independence of that nation and the resistance to its independence that were instrumental in forcing President Mugabe into that direction of Zimbabwean financial hopelessness.

Black History Everyday - Part Two Photo. Herman Ferguson, a significant nationalist and a key figure behind Malcolm X Day in Harlem.

"And we have done more in the two and a half years that I've been in here than the previous 43 Presidents to uphold that principle, whether it's ending "don't ask, don't tell," making sure that gay and lesbian partners can visit each other in hospitals, making sure that federal benefits can be provided to same-sex couples." **Barack Obama**

"We don't begrudge financial success in this country. We admire it. When Americans talk about folks like me paying my fair share of taxes, it's not because they envy the rich. It's because they understand that when I get a tax break I don't need and the country can't afford, it either adds to the deficit, or somebody else has to make up the difference – like a senior on a fixed income, or a student trying to get through school or a family trying to make ends meet. That's not right. Americans know that's not right. They know that this generation's success is only possible because past generations felt a responsibility to each other, and to the future of their country, and they know our way of life will only endure if we feel the same sense of shared responsibility. That's how we'll reduce our deficit. That's an America built to last."
Barack Obama, *State of the Union Address, January* 2012

3. OBAMA'S DIVINE MISSION BY DR. FRED MONDERSON

That Barack Obama's mission was "divinely inspired" and guided should be evident to all even those purposely wearing blindfolds. In so many ways, this has been demonstrated as; first, in the

BLACK HISTORY EVERYDAY
PART TWO

rescue of the American Auto Industry so many have decried because of their short-sidedness. If this truly indigenous American enterprise employing millions of workers failed, it would have signaled the beginning of America's precipitous decline. What a laughing stock the nation would have become. Even our fighting forces abroad would have begun questioning their own defense of the nation from distant shores. Let's be serious, if Jerry Falwell, Tammy Fay Baker and husband as well as Pat Robertson could talk to God and more modern Michele Bachmann could claim "God told me to run" for president it is not farfetched to see the significance of Barack Obama's meteoric rise, his impact on the world and particularly his defense of America, as divinely inspired. Perhaps it was written in destiny as foretold in 1922 by Caseley Hayford of Ghana, West Africa, who decried the mechanical, calculating and inhuman relations of modern man. He predicted only the human nature of the African can save humanity from its impending destruction. Thus, the African can come in many forms and sizes, but the divine mission remains undoubted.

FREDERICK MONDERSON

Black History Everyday - Part Two Photo. **We Shall Not be Moved March**. Faces in the Crowd.

The interesting thing about Michele Bachmann claim "God told me to run for the Presidency" is purely a political ploy playing to a particular base. If god wanted her to run for the Presidency, all that was missing was the actual handing over of the keys. He would have provided the wherewithal and resources, a plan of what to say and do, to distance her from Republican contenders and then she would have mopped-up Obama. There is a failure in there somewhere. Obama on the other hand, continues to successfully "do god's work," does good in the name of humanity, gets good grades and seems to be riding on an express elevator to heaven. Thus, I ask you, "Whose side is God on?"

BLACK HISTORY EVERYDAY PART TWO

The *Ancient Egyptian Book of Coming Forth By Day* or Book of the Dead speaks of the challenge of **Ma'at** - goodness, right, truth, balance, against **Isfet** - evil, wrong, disequilibrium. Many contemporary Republican presidential contenders question Mr. Obama's leadership but unfortunately their cataract clouded vision preclude their understanding of true leadership as the president struggles to move the nation from the mist and morass of recent moral, social and economic failures. A typical example of questioned leadership can be seen in the withdrawing of American forces from Iraq where Obama's critics saw weaknesses in this strategy. History teaches, George Washington crossed the Delaware to "winter his forces" before successfully attacking the British. Napoleon invaded Egypt also to "winter" and "lick his wounds" following a British defeat; and though he later lost the "Battle of the Nile" he unleashed the wonders of ancient Egyptian discovery. Again, Osama bin Laden was evil and in President Obama's quick dispatch of the evil mastermind, many Republican contenders wanted to see the body; like Barnabas they wanted to "See the wounds and put their fingers therein." Well, they could dispatch divers to the deep to recover what's left!

FREDERICK MONDERSON

Black History Everyday - Part Two Photo. Faces and signs in the crowd for the 50th Anniversary March on Washington.

Black History Everyday - Part Two Photo. Faces and signs in the crowd for the 50th Anniversary March on Washington.

BLACK HISTORY EVERYDAY
PART TWO

The loss of the US Drone in Iran is another example of vision diametrically opposed to sound leadership. Remember Kosovo or whatever, John McCain said "Let's go in!" Obama, on the other hand, said. "I consulted with my advisers. Let's proceed with caution." The Joint Chiefs and other advisers at the President's disposal are the best in the world. Many of these said minds, military and otherwise, are the same personnel who will advise any Republican presidential victor in the upcoming 2012 election. Many proffered that Mr. Obama bomb the drone or send in a team to recover it. Mr. Obama cautioned, No! This was a violation of that nation's sovereignty. Bombing was an act of war! Hurried rescue of a minuscule objective is risky; remember Carter's Iran rescue. So, President Obama politely asked Iran to return the drone to which they said No! He knew this would be their reply.

Demonstrating his studied leadership, Mr. Obama realized loss of the drone is a casualty of war! In Iran's position, we have to at least assume they photographed and possibly dismantled it and not-inconceivable they shopped it around to interested parties. Fact is, upon the request which Iran refused, therein lies a major error on their part. Like Ra's defeat of the evil Apepi monster; St. Michael vanquishing the Devil; and even **Blade** telling the Vampire, "I'll Catch You Later;" President Obama knows Ahmenijhdad and his cohorts are evil and is planning to "Catch them later." The problem is that

FREDERICK MONDERSON

he won't tell the Republican blowhards what his plans are for such "bad boys!"

Black History Everyday - Part Two Photo. **We Shall Not be Moved March**. Faces in the Crowd.

In his *The Book of Coming Forth By Day: The Declaration of Innocence*, Maulana Karenga elucidates on "The Essentiality of Moral Social Practice." While Obama is concerned with the many, Republicans are only interested in protecting the few, their base, the rich one percent. In essence, in this respect, we could see President Obama practicing Ma'at and Republicans, in vigorous opposition, practicing its opposite, Isfit! This philosophic concept of "Ma'at" Karenga writes, "Is the essentiality of moral social practice in human development." He defines Ma'at (1990: 31) as "that which endures and raises a person and people up, but Isfit leads to destruction. Ma'at, as social practice,

BLACK HISTORY EVERYDAY
PART TWO

serves several functions in human development. First, it is the basic means by which the affinity of God and humans is expressed. Ma'at is the essential substance and sustenance of God and humans as expressed in earlier Kemetic anthropology which equated God and King .... Ma'at, then is both the nourishment and essence of God and to practice it is to share in his essence and be in harmony with his desire for the world. Therefore, Ma'at is the grounds for ontological unity and affinity of God and humans and again the grounds of human potential for perfectibility, i.e., moral and spiritual development which leads to assimilation with God."

When Congresswoman Michele Bachmann in her misguided innocence said, President Obama has changed history, she was probably right in a wrong but really right sense of the thought. Perhaps, unknowingly, she is referring to, championing, Mr. Obama's divine task of maintaining Ma'at in the world. This, in turn, means "maintaining the creation and righteousness of the order this implies and necessitates." For as leader or ruler, he must remain "committed" to "restoring, establishing and expanding Ma'at." As the *Book of Rising and Transformation* affirms, in his divine mission Obama seeks to set "Heaven ... at peace and earth ... in joy, for they have heard that [he] will set Ma'at in the place of Isfet, i.e., right in the place of wrong, order in the place of disorder." Mid-course correction is useful in any journey for the long duration and America can certainly benefit from such a course of

FREDERICK MONDERSON

action, if as it's claimed to be the last hope for humanity.

Black History Everyday - Part Two Photo. "… and Justice for All!

"We must recognize that black people, whether we are in Durham, North Carolina; San Francisco, California; Jamaica, Trinidad, Brazil, Europe, or on the "mother continent," that we are all an African people, we are Africans, there can be no question about that. **Kwame Ture** [Stokely Carmichael]. *Speech* [October 1969]

"Black power … is a call for black people in this country to unite, to recognize their heritage, to build a sense of community. It is a call for black people to begin to define their own goals, to lead their own organizations and to support their organizations. It is

BLACK HISTORY EVERYDAY
PART TWO

a call to reject the racist institutions and values of this society." **Kwame Toure** [Stokely Carmichael] and **Chares Vernon Hamilton**. *Black Power* [1972]

4. ODE TO KWAME TURE (STOKELY CARMICHAEL) BY DR. FRED MONDERSON

O great Black mountain of a man
Your name will forever echo
Among the great heroes
In the Black Pantheon.

When white power was evident
You sounded the bell demanding Black Power
How fortunate you are to pass
Within the bosom of beloved "Mother Africa."

You were a child of the Fifties
A warrior of the Sixties
More than anything, a Pan-African nationalist in the Seventies
A statesman of the Eighties and
A revered and respected elder in the Nineties.

Your indomitable spirit created
An unquenchable fire to see
Africa's sons and daughters free

FREDERICK MONDERSON

Your ideas brought us to the end of this century
Now, the new Millennium will bear
The fruits of your earned victory.

In the clarion call
You helped all to see
Whether economic, politic, culture or history
There's no turning back now
The demands for Black Power
Will set us all Free.

O great and noble warrior,
Now go take your rightful place among revered ancestors
Whose efforts have been similarly Noble
Good Brother, your place is assured
You fought the good fight
Now join your namesakes
Kwame Nkrumah and Sekou Ture.

How easy it is to see
Marcus, Malcolm, Martin
Elijah, Robeson, DuBois
Fannie Lou, Mary Bethune
Sojourner and Harriet.

BLACK HISTORY EVERYDAY
PART TWO

Black History Everyday - Part Two Photo.
We Shall Not be Moved March. Faces in the Crowd.

All standing at the stairway
Of your ascent into Africa's paradise
Marvin, Duke and Gillespie
Singing and playing sweet music
Welcoming you into their Blessed Company.

FREDERICK MONDERSON

Black History Everyday - Part Two Photo. Faces and signs in the crowd for the 50th Anniversary March on Washington.

Black History Everyday - Part Two Photo. Faces and signs in the crowd for the 50th Anniversary March on Washington.

BLACK HISTORY EVERYDAY
PART TWO

"In the philosophy of pharaonic Egypt, Maat is a concept of central importance. It implies order, universal balance, cosmic regulation, justice, truth, truth-in-justice, rectitude and moral uprightness. The concept of balanced order is the permanent basis of pharaonic civilization. Balanced order brings peace (*htp*), condemns crime (*d3yt*) and evil (*bin dwt*). Whoever breaks the law (*hpw, hepw*, plural of hp, hep, law) is punished (*hsf*), as a matter of course." Theophile Obenga. *African Philosophy: The Pharaonic Period – 2780-330 B.C.* (2004)

"The social order secretes benevolence and loving kindness, without stifling personal initiative and work: *ir sk3.k*, 'If you cultivate a farm...'" *Maat* castigates slander, lying, defamation, boastfulness and flattery. All persons, great or humble, rich or poor, deserve respect; such are the unequivocal prescriptions of *Maat*. Order is a categorical imperative *ndr m3ct m sni.s*. 'Stick to the truth; do not exaggerate. In the last analysis, what prevails is justice, Maat." **Theophile Obenga**. *African Philosophy: The Pharaonic Period – 2780-330 B.C.* (2004)

FREDERICK MONDERSON

Black History Everyday - Part Two Photo. And a child shall lead them...."

5. MA'AT VERSUS ISFIT IN PRESIDENTIAL POLITICS BY DR. FRED MONDERSON

History has shown any movement for the better is always met with opposition and skepticism. Take the case of all great reformers, Osiris, Buddha, Jesus, Joan of Arc, even George Washington with all his faults, not excluding Martin Luther King, Malcolm X and Medgar Evers, as change agents of their time. In that mountain of a man, Mr. Obama is no different as he struggled to defend what is right, doing Ma'at even to his opponents while ignoring the stone throwers. Subscribing to the higher mission, President Obama realizes, as Maulana Karenga (1990: 32) says, "Creation, then, is constantly threatened by chaos, disorder or Isfet, and humans are morally compelled to share the responsibility with God of defending the

BLACK HISTORY EVERYDAY PART TWO

boundaries of good, right and order, and expanding them. In this activity humans become like God."

Black History Everyday - Part Two Photo. **We Shall Not be Moved March.** Faces in the Crowd.

"The Ma'atian stress on moral social practice is rooted in the assumption that self-actualization of humans is best achieved in morally grounded relations with others." "The operative principle here is self-realization and grounding in moral relations with others. It is at this point that the ethic of care and responsibility or rather of love in the most human sense [*merut*] and service [*wenut*] are evident and required in *Ma'at*. To serve is to benefit not only others but also oneself.

For example, the *Book of Ankhsheshonqi* teaches "Service is righteous action towards and for God, humans and by extension, nature which in some meaningful and moral way returns a reciprocal benefit." This moral responsibility to respect and protect the earth is what Karenga preached in his **Kwanza Message** at Boys and Girls High school in Brooklyn, New York, on December 27, 2011. Now, contrary to past deregulation, as per his mission, the president insists the Environmental Protection Agency must enforce strict regulation to play its part in saving the earth from becoming another mars. Therefore, when Republican contenders tout "abolish the EPS" they are acting as agents of *Isfet*.

Again, Ankhsheshonqi cautions, "The only real good deed is the one done for one who needs it." Perhaps that proponent of ancient "African deep thought" foresaw and foretold of the conflict of the one and the ninety-nine percent. Within this same prophetic construct can be placed the "Millionaires Tax Cut" for those who do not need it; and the Health Care Reform Act that benefits the fifty million Americans who need its protection. Can we thrown in the Lilly Ledbetter Act for women certainly need to earn the same as men? Last but not least, President Obama's insistence on and support for educational initiatives, upgrade of school facilities, repair of roads, ports, airports, rail lines not only improves performance and infrastructure of the American landscape but also puts Americans back to work, helping to improve their economic and social positions.

BLACK HISTORY EVERYDAY
PART TWO

Now to contrast the "highly intellectual," "smartest guy in the room," "I'm going to be the nominee" arrogance of Newt Gingrich with the deep-thinking Barack Obama, the vision is like night and day and so too the thanklessness for a well-done job. Nevertheless, Ankhsheshonqi admonishes as Karenga has pointed out, "One should not be disappointed for not being recognized or thanked by everyone for whom one does good."

Antedating the wisdom of the *Book of Ecclesiastes* which urges, as we all sometimes do, "Cast your bread upon the waters and after many days it will return to you;" Ankhsheshonqi admonishes, "If you do good by a hundred persons and just one of them acknowledges it, no part of it is lost." His optimism is reflected in the law of reciprocity in that, "Do a good deed and throw it in the water and when the water dries up, you will find it." Again, we see in the ancient Egyptian/African reservoir of deep thought wisdom many paraphrased modern wise sayings such as "It's better to give than to receive." In Ankhsheshonqi's original thought, "Sweeter is the water of one who has given than the wine of one who has received."

Today we recognize Republicans have borrowed Jesse Jackson's "Big Tent" idea that should shelter great diversity among its presidential candidates and supporters. This pastor, however, is not the case for we have the "Black protester with guns;" his "praying for Obama's death" pastor; the "Koran burning"

FREDERICK MONDERSON

Florida pastor declaring his intention to run for the Presidency as a Republican; Ring-master Donald Trump with his magnetic attraction for clowns; illegal immigrant chasing Sheriff Arapaio; "Waterloo" DeMint; "You lie" Wilson; "Poisoning the well" Santorum; "Gangster government" Bachmann; "Corporations are people" Romney; "I'll be the nominee" Newt; "I can't remember which Department I will abolish" Perry; "Blacks are brainwashed for voting Democratic" Herman Cain; and hopefully, "Converted on the Road to Damascus" Paul. All these jokers have been chosen to play a key role in effectuating the divine mission of Barack Obama. As such, they mirror the antithesis of Ma'at; or put in Christian historical parlance, they exhibit the "Petrine Syndrome" of denial, viz., Bachmann, Trump, Santorum, McConnell; and "Judas Escariot Syndrome," Cain, Allen West, "Black Protester with Guns, not excluding Cornell West, Tavis Smiley and so many others.

Now, as many of these players fade into oblivion and President Obama pursues his platform of better educational opportunities and practices, particularly with greater emphasis on the role of Community Colleges in retraining especially in the industrial arts; emphasizing the need for clean energy and a more vigorous enforcement of environmental use, paying greater attention to overhauling the nation's physical infrastructure and as the economy continues to improve, the American people will see the wisdom of Obama's leadership and play their part in his re-

BLACK HISTORY EVERYDAY
PART TWO

election and in fulfilling his divine mission designed for their betterment.

Black History Everyday - Part Two Photo. Faces and signs in the crowd for the 50th Anniversary March on Washington.

Black History Everyday - Part Two Photo. Faces and signs in the crowd for the 50th Anniversary March on Washington.

FREDERICK MONDERSON

"The condition of Negro labor is inseparable from that of white labor; the immediate crisis confronting black labor grows out of the unresolved crisis in the national economy. Bayard Rustin. *Preamble to the March on Washington* [1963]

"Our continent has been carved up by the great powers; alien governments have been forced upon the African people by military conquest and by economic domination; strivings for nationhood and national dignity have been beaten down by force; traditional economics and ancient customs have been disrupted, and human skills and energy have been harnessed for the advantage of our conquerors. In these times there has been no peace; there could be no brotherhood between men." Albert Luthuli. Noble Speech.

6. POWER OF ECONOMIC BOYCOTT BY DR. FRED MONDERSON

On Tuesday August 6, 2013, the noted radio personality Bob Law, joined by Rev. Calvin Butts moderated a program at First Church of God in Christ on Kingston Avenue and Park Place in Brooklyn, regarding black earning power, the potentialities of their spending practices and the capabilities of an organized economic effort that maximizes this

BLACK HISTORY EVERYDAY
PART TWO

spending potential as well as where to invest with the greatest economic benefit to African people.

Mr. Law pointed out; this new movement is a national effort supported by Rev. Ben Chavis, Conrad Mohammed, Sister Souljah, Rev. Dr. Calvin Butts of Abyssinian Baptist Church in Harlem and a number of politically and economically conscious individuals across the national spectrum. Reminding that "Jesus came specifically to his own," Bob Law told the nearly three hundred individuals gathered to receive his usually highly informative message; he wanted them to join his effort because a great deal was at stake. He wanted them to assess the situation and redirect their spending habits to really get the most "bank for their buck."

Black History Everyday - Part Two Photo. The Message is crystal clear, they want Mutula Shakur home, its long beyond his parole time!

FREDERICK MONDERSON

For one thing, a plague has infested the Black community that beyond economic considerations has implications for health concerns with a tremendous impact on the family structure. This is exacerbated because many families, individuals, are struggling in the bowels of our community and they don't even realize the true impact of this "sweet tasting plague." Even more important, they are at a disadvantage because of the inability to control their spending habits, then as an analogy he delved into the impact of the Montgomery Bus Boycott of which Rev. Augustus Jones and Rev. Wyatt Tee Walker were a part and how that strategy undergirded the effectiveness of the Civil Rights Movement within the context of Adam Clayton Powell's admonition, "Don't buy where you do not or cannot work!" As such, Mr. Law spoke to the "preponderance of fast food joints" that "saturate the Black Community" and create a moral and social dilemma of dependence with lasting implications not simply for economic matters of spending, but health and the inability to pay full attention to one's own eating habits, food choices, preparation, etc. This is especially so because of the lack of fruits and vegetables in the African-American diet, given to unavailability in the Black Community. This in turn has given way to that preponderance of Fast Foods establishments which call into question health issues as diabetes, cancer, heart attacks, strokes plaguing Blacks at a time when health care is more and more expensive and hospitals that serve the Black community are being closed en masse. Case in point in Central Brooklyn alone we

BLACK HISTORY EVERYDAY
PART TWO

can show many hospitals are closed or closing. Brooklyn Women's Hospital, Caledonian, Brooklyn Jewish, St. Mary's, while Long Island College and Interfaith are on "life support."

Black History Everyday - Part Two Photo. Sharpton and Crump's March on Liberty Square, Washington, DC. "We want to live!"

This "Fast Foods state of affairs" prompted this reporter to investigate this matter further. As such, I chose the "Nostrand Avenue Corridor from Fulton Street to Eastern Parkway in Brooklyn." This is a good representative sample, of the Black Community, and while the results are not exactly a duplicate elsewhere, they can, however, serve as a pretty good barometer to assess the significance of the problem posed. Well, what did this inquiry find?

There are "23 Fast Food Establishments" not counting the nearly 12 or so Delis in this 12-block

FREDERICK MONDERSON

stretch along Nostrand Ave from Fulton Street to Eastern Parkway. There are 4 at Fulton Street and Nostrand Avenue alone and 1 or sometimes up to 3 on each block as you approach Eastern Parkway. As such, in this and other instances, Bob Law wanted to redirect spending habits, because "we represent these businesses' margin of profit." When "they lose that margin of profit" they respond to the demands of the Black Community. One way to get this nation to respond to African people's concerns is the economic boycott and it becomes more effective if conducted on a national level across city after city, state after state, with religious institutions playing a significant role.

Next Reverend Butts began to elaborate on the problem. Reminding that "We represent the margin of profit" then if "We stop buying a product" the makers suffer and begin to listen to our concerns! This strategy has had the greatest success backed by the Black Church, whether it's the African Methodist Episcopal, the Christian Methodist Episcopalian, or the Church of God In Christ. The Montgomery Bus Boycott was effective because of the role of the church! Adam Clayton Powell's mantra, "Don't buy where you can't work" was not "Burn, Baby Burn" but "Economics, Baby Economics." We must remember Marcus Garvey and Elijah Mohammed encouraged Black people to "Do for self!" The Black Churches were built by people pooling their money. Bishop McCulloh and Sweet Daddy Jones were able to establish banks, insurance companies, foundations

BLACK HISTORY EVERYDAY
PART TWO

with people pooling their money. "When you begin to amass economic strength, you gain respect in this nation. We can focus our economic strength."

Black History Everyday - Part Two Photo. We Shall Not be Moved March. Faces in the Crowd.

"We have the right to read, own property, save our money. We spend crazy with people who really don't care about us. They don't employ us and take our monies out of our community. We can make a difference." Remember, "a little bit of salt changes the flavor of food. When we buy, we must ask, 'Where are the Black people who work here?' So, we must shop at Black establishments. We must respect ourselves and we must spread the word! We must remember radio stations such as **KISS** and **WLIB** do not program in our best interest. TV is not of any

FREDERICK MONDERSON

substance. We must spread the word through our churches, civic organizations, and fraternities. We must become disciples of an economic gospel that puts our community first." Dr. Butts confessed, "I am a devotee of this methodology. We must remember the effectiveness of the "Principles of Kwanza." We must Remember Trayvon Martin. Finally, I want you to pay attention to 3 movies, **Fruitvale Station**, **The Butler** and **12 Years a Slave** for they chronicle our experiences.

Bob Law again addressed the gathering. He introduced Bishop Jerry Seabrook. The Bishop referenced a recent episode. Today the streets of Detroit look like a war zone. The City is in default. Yet, poor folks raised $18,000.00 in a free-will offering for a pressing cause. This was pocket money understandably. People protesting and marching were outraged because of Zimmerman, Randy Evans shot by Officer Torsney who was declared not guilty because of a "temporary insanity" plea. Then there was Eleanor Bumpers in the Bronx. These all claimed police feared for their lives when they shot these people. It is clear from *Dred Scott's 1857 Decision* to now; we are still denied justice! A national coalition is formed around this issue. Let us begin to use the leverage we have in our community which is our economic strength in our spending habits.

BLACK HISTORY EVERYDAY
PART TWO

Black History Everyday - Part Two Photo. Faces and signs in the crowd for the 50th Anniversary March on Washington.

Annually we spend nearly one trillion dollars! Blacks outspend everyone else. We spend more money on everything than everyone else! Revlon! Nobody respects us! Everybody takes us for granted! When the Russian Prime Minister said something derogatory about Gays, these people called in the "Vodka lords" and told them "We will stop buying your Vodka unless you say and do something!" That is clout! "Economics is one of the ways we have power." Remember Emmett Till. It was not "Stand your ground" in St. Louis, New York, Mississippi or Florida. It is the institution of racism. Institutional Racism. "What's in your hand?" "Over One Trillion Dollars!" "Hold on to your dollars! Instead, give to constructive organizations that are working in our

FREDERICK MONDERSON

best interest." Give your "Burger and Fries" monies to Sankofa Academy or the Learning Tree School.

Black History Everyday - Part Two Photo. Brooklyn Boro-President Eric A. Adams greets an admirer at Rev. Sharpton's "Power and Policy forum" on MLK's Holiday, 1-20-2020.

States is already banned in other nations because of the preservatives put in them to extend shelf life. Burger King, Wendy, Kentucky Fried Chicken all take out money from our community but don't support anything we do for social justice. The Fast Food industry depends on our money! We must push back and not allow our community to be systematically pulled from under us. We must never forget police lynch mobs murder our people and are acquitted. The Cola industry and Craft and Mac and Cheese are making millions. We must be a part of this national movement. Remember, John Killins, Lorraine Hansberry, James Baldwin all, for the

BLACK HISTORY EVERYDAY
PART TWO

longest, spoke out against this issue. Yet, we are still denied justice and freedom.

Then Mr. Law mentioned Rev. Leon Sullivan in Detroit. He was trying to get to some big-wig in the auto industry to say we need jobs. The man outright said "I don't have time to speak with you." That was Wednesday afternoon. Rev. Sullivan got the word out to 72 pastors. On Sunday morning word went out from these church pulpits "Don't Buy his product!" By Tuesday morning, the man called Rev. Sullivan stating, "When are you available to meet with me!" This shows leadership has traditionally come from the church. Systemic racism is condoning and supporting institutional racism. They are closing hospitals, close over one hundred schools. So, "We Must Stand Our Ground: Turn Black Spending into Political Power!" We must use our money to influence policy! We must have an intelligent policy that is used effectively.

We don't have to stop all Black folks from buying fast food. Just 8 percent need stop buying fast food. This is indeed a national movement. Chukwe Lumumba in Mississippi and Maulana Karenga in Los Angeles are part of this movement. Then he admonished, "Can you hold back some of your Fast Food Spending. Your Burger and Fries Money."

Bishop Seabrook called for a self-assessment. These fast food establishments are not hiring anyone from our community. Chinese, Hispanics, Koreans not

FREDERICK MONDERSON

hiring anyone from our community! Someone offered, "Have you seen a Chinese restaurant go out of business?" Then he addressed "Black on Black" crime.

"We rally around other people killing us but not rally around us killing us. If we come together in unity, we could stop some of this injustice. Burger King is a Florida Based Fast Food company."

We must remember we spend between 900 billion and one trillion dollars. 321 billion on books, 714 billion on beauty and hair products. All the while 24 schools were closed with 19 more on the block. 34 schools must be replaced. 23 Schools closed in Philadelphia. All the while 420 billion are spent on prisons.

Ollie McClean, Founder and principal of the Sankofa Academy, nearly 30 years in existence, next related the positive curriculum taught in that school. She delved into some of the activities the young people are a part of and the percentage who go on to college. This, then, is a good example why Bob Law suggested, "Hold Back the Burger and Fries" small change and give to such positive organizations as Sankofa and the Learning Tree. Meanwhile we will continue to coordinate economic strategy boycott across the country!

BLACK HISTORY EVERYDAY
PART TWO

Black History Everyday - Part Two Photo. Sharpton and Crump's March on Washington, DC. Two young men showing support!

"When the Queen of Sheba heard of the fame of Solomon, she came to prove him with hard questions." *The Second Book of the Kings*. 2: 11 [Bible]

FREDERICK MONDERSON

Black History Everyday - Part Two Photo. Arrangement of the Planks showcasing the results of lynching Africans in America.

"I am Black and Comely." Queen of Sheba.

7. QUEEN OF SHEBA IN RACIAL PORTRAYAL AS HISTORICAL DISTORTION
BY
DR. FRED MONDERSON

Standing in line for the cashier at a local supermarket chain, some years ago. my eye caught one of the customary tabloids with headlines that read "World's Mysteries Solved." Like any enthusiastic of any such esoteric phenomenon, I purchased the paper and took it home. Such topics as a new "Discovery of Noah Ark's" are recurring historical themes, and "Vatican Confirms the Existence of Angels," were some of the

BLACK HISTORY EVERYDAY
PART TWO

articles in this issue. Turning to the centerfold, my eyes caught the main story, "Scientists Discover the Home of the Queen of Sheba." This was a short story, juxtaposed to a large picture of the Queen of Sheba. It was a picture of a beautiful woman, white! What's wrong with this picture?

Just then a friend, Rodolfo was visiting my home. When I brought this to his attention and having some familiarity with my work, he admonished: "You should write an article on this distortion." Finally, I agreed, looking at the article again it read: "British Archaeologists have discovered the home of the Queen of Sheba, located in the southern Nigerian forest region." Often times the general reading public would overlook such a report.

Many times, readers have questioned the veracity of the tabloids to sensationalize, fabricating their stories that in a number of instances are outright distortions of fact. Too often, Gary Byrd on WLIB, New York radio has commented: "The information you don't have could kill you." Equally too, Malcolm X admonished his listeners to be skillful readers, for newspapers have a tendency to put things in a manner that denigrates Blacks, and generally distorts the truth. "They" also "hide information" in "their" papers placing it somewhere on page 96, where most people hardly get to. Malcolm X referred to this and other reporting aspects, "They know how to put it!"

FREDERICK MONDERSON

Black History Everyday - Part Two Photo. Faces and signs in the crowd for the 50th Anniversary March on Washington.

Black History Everyday - Part Two Photo. Faces and signs in the crowd for the 50th Anniversary March on Washington.

BLACK HISTORY EVERYDAY
PART TWO

In this 21st Century and new millennium, Blacks in America and worldwide must be concerned about the ever-present problems of racism that distorts the image of African people whether politically, historically, culturally, psychologically or simply let's say, as human beings.

The fact is, in a general sense, the information presented to Blacks and whites, pertaining to the same issue are colored differently and there should be more concerted efforts to synchronize what both groups are being taught. Equally too, there needs to be more systematic analysis of every issue. That is why the problem solving skills inherent in intellectual autonomy is an effective tool.

Black History Everyday - Part Two Photo. **We Shall Not be Moved March**. Faces in the Crowd.

Now to present my case, I will document a few examples to show that historical truths are perennially distorted and to set the record straight,

FREDERICK MONDERSON

men and women of objective scholarship must constantly challenge distortions.

As a student of Professor Ben-Jochannan, I have often listened to his debates and observed the ink spilled discussing a line in the Bible. Depending on the versions one consults, the question is always did the Queen of Sheba say, 'I am Black and comely.' Or, 'I am Black but comely.' In the first instance she is saying "I'm Black and beautiful," and being proud of it. In the second instance, in saying "I'm Black but beautiful," she is, if you will, denigrating her Blackness but affirming her beauty. People on a pejorative bent towards Blacks flaunt the latter affirming she was not proud of her Blackness, though they would concede she was beautiful. Did the editor of the tabloid know this or was he simply uncaring and determined to distort in the belief it would go unnoticed. Of course, if Solomon had married the Queen of Sheba and made an 'honest woman' out of her, this matter would probably have been solved. Now, in an extension of this argument, a more potent social issue is raised. Still, in the heart of Southern Nigeria, the picture presented of the Queen is that of a white woman! Some scholars have asserted that contrary to popular opinion, though Sheba was beautiful, and this is not mistaken, Solomon pursued her more because her empire was greater than his! And, if we accept the Southern Nigeria origins, then her empire extended clear across the Sudan to Ethiopia, with the potential to send trading ventures well into Asia. Given he already had a harem of some

BLACK HISTORY EVERYDAY
PART TWO

600 women, Sheba's empire, not her beauty may have been a more credible attraction.

Historical distortions like forgeries are nothing new. The "**Donation of Constantine**" is one such example of a forgery.

People with historical consciousness know, after the decline of Egyptian/Kemetic civilization, and the rise of Greece and Rome, Jesus the Christ came, was crucified, died, buried and rose again. In the centuries right after, early Christians were martyred through fear of the Roman rulers that the promised heavenly kingdom was a threat to the Roman Empire. After the games and the mauling by "African lions," there were martyrdoms, etc. Of course, the African had nothing to do with this. It was the Romans who took lions from Africa and had them devour Christians!

Constantine the Great became Emperor of Rome. On the eve of a major military engagement he had a dream or vision that involved religious matters, priestly paraphernalia, the Bishop's Miter, and insignia of his vestments, etc. Succeeding in battle the next day, Constantine credited his dream with being part of his good fortune. He declared 'We killed enough Christians;' 'Let us cage the lions;' 'Stop eating Christians for lunch;' and 'End the crucifixion.' He declared Christianity would be recognized as a legitimate religion in the Roman

Empire. The Church could get equal footing with the state, Christians would be respected. He called the Council of Nicaea in 325 AD and invited all the Bishops of the Christian church to hammer out the glitches in the fundamental tenets of Christianity. Constantine was hailed as the first Christian Emperor of the Roman Empire.

A document entitled "The Donation of Constantine" later showed the Emperor had donated extensive tracts of land to the church that were tax-exempt, etc. A thousand years later, an Italian Lorenzo Valla, a linguist, while doing research made a remarkable discovery. As anyone familiar with linguistics would know language constantly changes. New words are added and old words dropped from non-use. Remember, 'where's the beef?'

Lorenzo Valla (1518) showed that the document contained words that did not come into the vernacular until centuries after Constantine; therefore, he declared the document 'Donation of Constantine' a forgery. The Bishop of Chichester and Baronius in his *"Annales Ecclesiastici"* (ad an. 324) admitted that the "Donatio" was a forgery. As an example, using the same "Where's the Beef" analogy, a 1920s document purports something of significance and the above line used, when it was not yet "Born." Thus, it is considered historical fraud or misrepresentation.

The search for Prester John was one of those monumental failures that remained a perennial

BLACK HISTORY EVERYDAY PART TWO

success for Europeans. Perhaps as equally important as the riches of the East, the search for Prester John in Africa motivated Portuguese explorers for centuries. Since he was never found, it is not inconceivable that the thought of finding his kingdom is not a moot issue.

Following the decline of the Roman Empire and Rise of Islam, the Moors or Shakespeare's "Blackamoors" invaded Southern Europe. They occupied that land from 711 to 1485 A.D. providing the "Arab conduit" of ancient African intellectualism, developed in the Nile Valley. Perhaps in that age the myth of Prester John was born, yet it fueled particularly Portuguese aspirations of exploration and colonization. The notion of Prester John, a white king ruling a Black kingdom in Africa represented a "phalanx of global white supremacy" on that continent. Everyone came, searching, yet to find this individual.

As Professor Clarke liked to say "The Africans invited Europeans for lunch and we became the meal." The result was "naked imperialism" "enlightened imperialism" and then later "intellectual imperialism." Of course, the missionaries were a vanguard in colonial strategy. We can thank Jomo Kenyatta for his insightful assessment of this aftermath in Facing Mount Kenya. "When the missionaries came" he wrote, "they gave us the Bible and taught us to close our eyes and pray. When we opened our eyes, we were holding the Bible and the Europeans the land."

FREDERICK MONDERSON

As a youngster growing up in Guyana, reading was an enjoyable past time. There was no "Black History," these were not yet "born." Even though they have been manifestly evolving from time immemorial. We were taught **English History** 1066-1485, from the Norman Invasion to the War of the Roses and Ascension of the Tudors. We read about the "Phantom in Africa." He was a masked crusader who single-handedly subdued all comers in the heart of Africa. As if that was not enough, Edgar Rice Burroughs gave us Tarzan and Hollywood had a field day in its systematic and well-choreographed denigration of the African persona. And, we all laughed heartily as one white man defeated and made fools of "tribes of Africans" portrayed and degraded as "savages." A recent article indicated "there were no Africans" in Walt Disney's new movie, 'Tarzan.' That's taking it to the next level!

Black History Everyday – Part Two
Photo. The People United will never be Defeated!

BLACK HISTORY EVERYDAY
PART TWO

Black History Everyday - Part Two Photo. Faces and signs in the crowd for the 50th Anniversary March on Washington.

Black History Everyday - Part Two Photo. Faces and signs in the crowd for the 50th Anniversary March on Washington.

FREDERICK MONDERSON

Black History Everyday - Part Two Photo. Faces and signs in the crowd for the 50th Anniversary March on Washington.

The Western literary traditions began with Homer's *Iliad* and Odyssey. It is believed he visited Egypt/Kemet. The description of Thebes with its "palaces" and "hundred gates" refers to the City of Thebes in the time of Rameses III of the XXth Dynasty. However, the erudite Cheikh Anta Diop in *The African origin of Civilization: Myth or Reality* argued: "If Homer visited Egypt and this fact is attested to by Greek tradition - it was probably during the time of the XXVth Sudanese Dynasty, under Piankhi or Shabaka, around 750 B.C." Then again, much controversy surrounds the Greeks in Egypt. Modern scholars have accepted some of these classical writers' views on the Egyptians but they reject salient parts particularly of an ethnological nature. Herodotus visited Egypt around 450 B.C.

BLACK HISTORY EVERYDAY
PART TWO

and, his *Histories,* Book II, *Euterpe* is devoted to that land. Granted he traveled the land seeking information from priests who guarded their history and culture very well. Yet he secured information from them. He also observed much but he was right about their color!

Black History Everyday – Part Two Photo. Sharpton and Crump's March on Liberty Square, Washington, DC. "We Can't Breathe!"

FREDERICK MONDERSON

Black History Everyday - Part Two Photo. Hands Up!

In the era of the 18th Century, the American, French and a little later the Haitian Revolutions, when men aspired to the nobility of freedom, of spirit and of body, Africans in American were enslaved. In that era of *les philosophes'* and free thinking, Count Volney wrote his *Ruins of Empire,* and postulated the

BLACK HISTORY EVERYDAY PART TWO

view, 'men and women of sable skin and frizzled hair, then enslaved, founded along the banks of the Nile River, the fundamental laws of science that govern the world, while much of humanity was still in a barbaric stage.'

In 1799, Napoleon's artillery officers discovered the now famous Black basalt trilingual inscription called the Rosetta stone. In 1822, this became the basis of Champollion's decipherment of hieroglyphics, *Medu Netcher*. In 1836, Sir Godfrey Higgins published *Anacalypsis* in 2 vols. In this masterful work he identified the ancient races and military, political, spiritual, and religious luminaries who were Black, from Osiris to Jesus. A powerful work of erudite scholarship, *Anacalypsis*, challenged all comers to contest its revelations.

Black History Everyday – Part Two Photo. Brother Nova Felder and Sister Veronica Nickey at **CEMOTAP's** Forum on Dr. King's influence.

FREDERICK MONDERSON

Black History Everyday - Part Two Photo. **We Shall Not be Moved March**. Faces in the Crowd.

In the age of political, military and economic imperialism, intellectual advantage became an extension of that frame of mind and pursuit. Archaeological excavation in the Nile Valley got a significant boost in the years 1870-1930. Not only was that discipline placed on a systematic and scientific footing, particularly through the sequence dating methods of Sir Flinders Petrie, the "father of Egyptian archaeology. Still, a number of organs of literary expression were inaugurated to chronicle the constantly unfolding spectacular discoveries. The *American Journal of Archaeology* was a prominent publication among numerous others. In 1898 the statue was discovered and the temple excavated in the 1903-04 Archaeological Season, the "Mortuary Temple of Nebhepetra Mentuhotep II was discovered

BLACK HISTORY EVERYDAY
PART TWO

at Deir el-Bahari, Thebes. A statue of the king was found wearing his heb sed attire and red crown symbolic of the Lower Egyptian Kingdom. The statue was removed and to this day resides in the Cairo Museum

A phenomenon occurred which is not dissimilar by today's standards, "All the news printed to fit." All that *American Journal of Archaeology* IX (1905: 98) could say of a physio-ethnological nature was, the "thick lips with edges defaced by sharp ridges, the heavy chin and the muscles emphasized round the corners of the mouth and nose, are derived from the mannerisms of the late Sixth Dynasty." Again, remember Malcolm's admonition: "No matter what the man says, you better look into it!"

For black readers then, in an age of slavery, civil war, and aftermath reconstruction, "Jim Crowism," "tenant farming," "separate but equal," discrimination, and racism, it was difficult for those black readers who could not analyze *American Journal of Archaeology's* description. For them it had no meaning! No major publishing vehicle in the United States carried it until W. Stephenson Smith in *The Art and Architecture of Ancient Egypt* (1959), 56 years later, dared to say Mentuhotep II had "black flesh.' The statue is in the same place in the museum, but for more than half a century Black reader did not know the Theban Mentuhotep II of the XIth Dynasty was a black king. That is, until Dr. Ben-Jochannan began carrying African-Americans to Egypt in vast numbers to "let the monuments teach." That too, is why Dr. Monderson, a student of the august elder, intends to continue the tradition of research, writing and publication as well as carrying our people to Egypt to expose them to the ancient African heritage and legacy. Not simply Mentuhotep's statue in the Cairo Museum but the wonderful temples of Karnak, Luxor, Deir el-Bahari, Abydos, Dendera, Edfu, Esna, Kom Ombo, Philae, and Kalabsha and Beit Wali, and Abu Simbel, invites all, with their wonderful architectural, spiritual and intellectual enlightenment.

"Tutankhamon," as Prof. Clarke liked to say, "was a minor king who got a major funeral." In 1922, Howard Carter discovered his tomb in the Valley of the Kings. Two life-like statues of the boy king stood at the entrance to the burial chamber.

Comparative analysis is a potent tool or weapon in dismantling and destroying the myths of distortion. The French scholar Jean Yoyote in Georges Poesner's *Dictionary of Egyptian Civilization* (1963: 291) speaks of Tutankhamon's treasures: "Everything was there. Nests of sarcophagi, statues of the king, golden jewelry, magical and everyday furniture, golden shrines, and alabaster and faience vases, the whole comprising an unrivalled collection of objects for the study of the arts and ritual ceremonies." Elsewhere (p. 293) he says: "The everyday requirements of a prince were buried with him, including; weapons, chariots, vessels, embroidered garments, chests and other pieces of

BLACK HISTORY EVERYDAY
PART TWO

furniture. The funerary equipment of the glorified dead was always plentiful - canopic jars, ushabtis of every material and figures of gods, to which must be added portable shrines and the blackened wooden statues, which had been used in the funeral rite. Everything was costly and worthy of a king." Again, elsewhere (p. 75) "The Red and Black Land." Red the desert, black, the plain. Where the Nile "rose to flood the land and replenish it with new soil each year." Or, should I say, "Red equals death and Black equals Life!" Interesting, everyone skirts around the meaning and significance of the Black wooden statues buried with the king.

At the 1998, **ASCAC** Conference at City College, New York, in a taped interview, Prof. Obenga informed "Kemet" or "Black Land" referred to the indigenous people and not the land, per se. That is to say, as we equate *Bilal as Sudan* (Land of the Blacks) or *L'Afrique Noire*, **Black Africa**, the contemporary designation that refers more correctly to the people who inhabit the area. Dr. Obenga said the word does not appear with the derivative for land and that it is for the Black people. Even further, while this may not still be, owing to the reorganization of the Museum, "Blackened wooden statues" of the Kings Amenhotep I and Amenhotep II, among others were observed by this writer. Interestingly enough, juxtaposed in the case was a black wooden statue of a panther. The placement of the panther in the case confronts and contradicts such claims those similar

FREDERICK MONDERSON

statues as the two from Tutankhamon's burial chamber only had ceremonial uses.

In 1985 as the nation approached the 500th Anniversary of the celebration of Columbus' discovery of America, this in itself a distortion, Dr. Cheikh Anta Diop wrote a letter to the *Journal of African Civilization*. It discussed the finding of tobacco, a New World strain, in the Mummy of Rameses II. This mummy of the New Kingdom monarch, discovered in the late 19th Century, began to decay. It was rushed to Paris to undergo scientific surgery to arrest the decay. The Senegalese scholar Diop who wrote *The African Origin of Civilization: Myth or Reality*, was qualified enough to be part of the examination team in the "repair chamber." The only Black scholar accorded that privilege. Perhaps had he not been there, the manifestation of the discovery and the tenacity to defend its meaning and significance would probably not been made manifest. Dr. Diop was also mentioned in **UNESCO's** final report at the Cairo 1974 Conference on the 'Peopling of the Nile Valley.' They commended Cheikh Anta Diop and Theophile Obenga as being "the best prepared" of all the participants at the conference.

BLACK HISTORY EVERYDAY
PART TWO

Black History Everyday - Part Two Photo. Faces and signs in the crowd for the 50th Anniversary March on Washington.

Black History Everyday - Part Two Photo. Faces and signs in the crowd for the 50th Anniversary March on Washington.

Of significance, the esteemed multi-disciplinarian deduced that New World tobacco in Rameses' stomach meant he smoked the stuff or consumed some before death. Even more important, however,

FREDERICK MONDERSON

it meant his emissaries visited the New World and returned! This meant Africans were in the New World nearly 3000 years before Columbus. In addition, at the 1992 Temple University Diopian Conference, papers were presented showing the Malian king Abu Bekr and a fleet of ships left for the New World at the start of the fourteenth century nearly 200 years before Columbus. This being so, Africans should be celebrating the 700th year of that adventure. Much of this is not known, though we celebrate 500 years of the exploration, conquest and exploitation and extermination of New World peoples and cultures. Let's not forget, "records in the logs of Magellan's ships" indicate as they were crossing the Atlantic, "Africans in long canoes' were observed returning from the New World. Equally, Dr. Charsee Macintyre argued for the arrival of "little Africans" in the New World as early as 120,000 years ago. Prof. Betancourt questioned those dates though he did suggest "firm dates at 70,000 years" before our era in the New World.

Malcolm X looms large in African people's history. A student at Temple University once submitted a dissertation request to show the "Norse Epics" were those of Blacks. Also, that "Eric the Red" was not the white, full red bearded, individual so often pictured. He was like say, Malcolm as "Detroit Red." The rather articulate and well-known Professor responded, "Well, without a lot more documentation, I can't sell this to the Graduate Board." So, it got the sort of "Let's kill it in Committee" treatment!

BLACK HISTORY EVERYDAY
PART TWO

Finally, and cut this short, Dr. Cheek Anta Diop, also with an opportunity to examine the Cairo Mummies, in his Magnum Opus, *Civilization or Barbarism: An Authentic Anthropology*, informed the mummies had their skins peeled like potatoes to hide their blackness! All this and so much more, distorted, omitted and hidden from Black readers.

"Whose Streets? Our Streets!" Rev. Al Sharpton.

Black History Everyday - Part Two Photo. Charlie Rangel, David Dinkins, President Aristede, Jesse Jackson and Major Owens.

"No Justice! Not Peace!" Rev. Al Sharpton.

FREDERICK MONDERSON

8. SHARPTON, TODAY
BY
DR. FRED MONDERSON

Returning to New York the weekend of August 17, 2014, a Newspaper "Headline" report indicated "Sharpton Slams Christie" for "dancing while Ferguson burns!" Sharpton, himself just returning from Ferguson, Missouri, posed the question "Why have men of substance, seeking to become President have not spoken out on Ferguson." However, as everyone has seen Rev. Sharpton vilified on TV, in Tabloid articles and "Letters to the Editor," one has to wonder what motivated Sharpton's role in the Tawana Brawley Affair, to begin with. The shortsighted and prejudiced view just undervalues the true measure of the man!

In this situation, Al Sharpton did what any self-respecting gentleman would have done. He came upon a young Black woman who claimed she was raped by a bunch of white men, one of whom later committed suicide. Sharpton fought legally but was stained by developments generated by the behemoth of the law as practiced by legal power brokers.

Today we recognize the word gentleman has lost its true meaning. Once upon a time, for example, the term "Southern Gentlemen" conjured up a mythical individual who even took his hat off when a lady passed. When we see the vitriol directed toward

BLACK HISTORY EVERYDAY
PART TWO

President Obama by "Southern Gentlemen" as Mitch McConnell; "Waterloo" Jim DeMint; "You lie" Joe Wilson; "Stupid" Senator Grassley; this notion is indeed mythical compared to Sharpton's commitment and resilience which is real! His "Damn the Critics" attitude, full-speed ahead activism is not inconsistent with Presidential admonitions and steadfast behaviors.

Black History Everyday - Part Two Photo. We Shall Not be Moved March. Faces in the Crowd.

Back in 1941, after A. Philip Randolph spoke at a White House dinner decrying the practice of excluding Blacks from government jobs. He threatened to "March on Washington!" President Franklin D. Roosevelt listened intently to the message, passed out cigars and after a long pause

FREDERICK MONDERSON

insisted, "Mr. Randolph, you want change? Go out there and make me do it!" That's the American way.

The problem with the Brawley affair is that Black women have little value in this society. They are not considered beautiful, irrespective. White women, on the other hand, are considered the epitome of beauty. Witness her lofty position in the images in the Jefferson Building of the Library of Congress where no Black women are shown exhibited, though they are in the security detail. This is a classic example of the white woman as the symbol of beauty. Still, Michelle Obama can hold her own with the best of them.

Remember "Dynasty" days on TV. In one episode, the heroine poisoned the hero at the end, and in the next frame of the TV ad the same woman was shown as a symbol of beauty, pitching a hair product, as she threw her hair back.

Tawana Brawley and Sharpton were vilified for years. In that horrifying experience, the "powers that be" came and smashed the truth. In the "Central Park Jogger Case" they came in with guns blazing and ruined the lives and spirit of five young Black men. Donald Trump called for the death penalty. Years later they were judged innocent of the crime and awarded a settlement, too little, too late! To even this restitution Mr. Trump objected.

BLACK HISTORY EVERYDAY
PART TWO

Again, White over the Black woman dictates, glorify Bonnie with Clyde but vilify Assata Shakur, Joanne Chesimard. The reason President Obama engender enmity in his efforts to govern is because his father chose to "Marry not live with" his mother.

Nevertheless, from Bensonhurst to Brawley and Amadou Diallo to Sean Bell with Garner and Michael Brown in Ferguson along the way, standing and marching to shine the light of truth is a testament to Sharpton's involvement as a civil right leader whose vision and efforts have grown tremendously over the years. Sharpton is unique. Bishop Washington saw uniqueness when he began cultivating the boy preacher at 7 years of age. Rev. Jesse Jackson also tapped that youngster to head the Youth Division of Operation Breadbasket of **PUSH**.

This show of genius, notwithstanding, in their nefarious criticisms, many enquire, "Where is Rev. Sharpton's church?" Jesus did not have a church. However, he did castigate the hypocrites and money-changers in church. Sharpton's church is in the streets and in the many churches he is invited to address due to respect of the man and his work! Like Jesus, Sharpton calls out perpetrators of injustice and oppression and has paid a price, not just in words but in blood when he was stabbed in Bensonhurst. Yet, he forgave his assailant. This assault was not unlike that of Dr. King who told of the young white girl who wrote saying she prayed and thanked god the knife wound was inches away from his heart. Sharpton too

FREDERICK MONDERSON

came within inches of leaving the Civil Rights Movement without a champion of courage, vision, tenacity and resilience, who stands irrespective for what is right, yet he pays a price in vilification.

In the journey that shaped the civil rights icon evident today, Sharpton dared to run for the Senate, Mayor and President, all the while cultivating the greater vision to see and understand the issues from the "bird's eye view." In that Presidential bid, Sharpton, primarily a winner, proved a master of organizational institution building by establishing chapters of the **National Action Network** throughout the country. This is so evident at the organization's "Keeping the Dream" Convention in April of every year to honor Dr. King, where many boast of the **Voice** they now have thanks to Al Sharpton's activism.

Being human, Sharpton certainly has faults but who is without sin! More important, however, his activism shines light on and keeps the issues of discrimination, brutality, joblessness, health care and social welfare "on front burners." Therefore, in lieu of any substantial individual standing up and calling attention to those important issues of Black concerns, Sharpton is the man! When he calls, many come running! In the Diallo protests, many "men of big affairs" lined up to get arrested. In the "Sean Bell shooting" incident he called and some 50,000 came to "Shop for Justice" in Mid-town. Partnering with Martin Luther King III, he spearheaded the 50th

BLACK HISTORY EVERYDAY
PART TWO

anniversary "March on Washington" in 2013. And he continues to speak out on the "Central Park Five" issue, the "Tribute to Michael Jackson," "Prison violence at Rikers Island," the deaths of Trayvon Martin and Eric Garner at whose march he presided, and much, much more.

In the final analysis, many are praying for God to protect and strengthen Sharpton for him to remain standing until "righteousness rolls down like a mighty stream" and "justice is meted out to all men" in equal measured proportions, irrespective.

Black History Everyday - Part Two Photo. Dr. Jack Felder and Sonny Carson addressing an audience of young people.

"No justice, no peace. You don't give us any justice, then there ain't going to be no peace." **Sonny**

FREDERICK MONDERSON

'Abubadika' Carson. Quoted in the *New York Times* [July 6, 1987]

"[*On his first day of school:*] Certainly not then, but years later, I began to perceive of this as the beginning of the most magnificent kind of programming that's ever been devised by any system in the history of mankind. For then it begins. White, white, white, white .... White, white white, all through the years; a succession of the Washingtons, the Lincolns, the Jeffersons, the Shermans, the Lees – and, occasionally a Booker T. Washington and a George Washington Carver.... This, then, was the beginning of my education." **Sonny Carson**. *The Education of Sonny Carson* [1974]

9. SONNY CARSON: BORN VISIONARY BY DR. FRED MONDERSON

For the longest, Sonny Robert Carson has held the New York City Council in disdain. Perhaps rightly so, for he knew, in all probability, in view of the recent scandal of the present Council, who so vehemently and disdainfully rejected his street naming request, and may very well be looking down from that ancestral perch, shaking his head and exclaiming 'I told you so!"

BLACK HISTORY EVERYDAY
PART TWO

Perhaps if he was here these days, Sonny would have marched on and picketed the Council for its flagrant misappropriation of public funds. This is something no group has done so far. However, when it comes to money, Sonny did recognize the value. In fact, he recognized the potency of an economic boycott, and, while taking lots of heat for this activity, he led several boycotts of the targets initiation of some inappropriate action directed against people of color, especially in Brooklyn.

Black History Everyday - Part Two Photo. Faces and signs in the crowd for the 50th Anniversary March on Washington.

FREDERICK MONDERSON

Black History Everyday - Part Two Photo. Faces and signs in the crowd for the 50th Anniversary March on Washington.

Now in view of the unending police misconduct across the country, police brutality, racial profiling, nooses, the Sean Bell verdict and marches to close down main arteries of the City of New York, and now the recent Congressional interests on holding hearings on police behavior, Sonny would say there is only one answer, **ECONOMIC BOYCOTT**.

Remember when, according to Dick Gregory, businessmen threatened to kick in Richard Nixon's door and say "What's wrong with you boy?" Then, until Black folks come together, draw a line in the sand, and offer a moratorium for an economic boycott, disrespect and distain will prevail. Let us, for argument say, for 90 days Blacks refuse to go in these stores, businesses, car dealers, etc., and object to purchase all but essential necessities. Imagine

BLACK HISTORY EVERYDAY
PART TWO

downtown Fulton Street, Flatbush Avenue, Church Avenue, Atlantic Center, Kings Plaza, Queens Boulevard, Fordham Road in the Bronx, all these economic vital points, beginning to see no customers for weeks. Then imagine the idea spreading across the country, then the hundreds of billions of dollars Blacks spend will be held back for a specified time, there will most certainly have to be "change."

Short of taking the struggle to this next level, the oppressors will concede our right to protest and wait out the cooling off period. When Mayor Bloomberg was asked about the recent Sean Bell verdict protest, the TV clip showed all he said was: "This is America and people have a right to protest. In some countries people do not have this right." Of course, he moved from believing the shooting was "excessive" to the belief that judicial verdicts are inviolate. Now, while the masses did not accept the O.J. Simpson verdict; they did accept the Robert Black verdict; and the innumerable verdicts from Rodney King to Sean Bell that exonerated the perpetrators. One thing for certain, Sonny Carson did and would have kept his activism focused on all these issues.

Like most urban youth, Sonny first served time in the US Army in Korea and upon returning home ended up in prison. There he seemed to find himself and set about on a road of social and nationalist activism. First, he advocated for jobs in places where Blacks shopped and then he moved to mom and pop

FREDERICK MONDERSON

ownership of small businesses and with time his name and popularity began to grow.

Sonny Carson, very early played a pivotal role in halting construction of the federal Office Building in downtown Manhattan, when it was discovered this area was an early colonial African Burial Ground. With the Black Watch Movement, he spearheaded the effort that laid the foundation which resulted in the site being declared a national monument and the Chi Wara Memorial erected in Foley Square before both Federal and State Courthouses. This activism began the recognition of the site as having national resulted significance and everything that resulted regarding its landmark status flowed from his efforts. He was opposed, however, to treatment of the bones.

There is nothing like success to breed success and over the years Sonny expanded his activism into education, fueled by a nationalist outlook, reflective of the maladies that gave birth to the civil right movement.

While Langston Hughes, the Harlem poet, could write of seeing "rivers," Sonny rightfully saw death. First Patrice Lumumba, the name of his own son, Malcolm X, and later Martin Luther King, Jr. There were many more in between, then Tupac Shakur and later Biggie Smalls. These two deaths particularly disturbed him. Black violence spawned by the crack epidemic, the emergence of gangster rap brought

BLACK HISTORY EVERYDAY
PART TWO

more death and according to Sonny. "I'm tired of attending funerals," particularly for young people.

Sonny was certainly known, and by that time a principal of the "School of hard knocks," his reputation attracted attention nationally. During the second Bill Clinton administration, the Commerce Secretary Ron Brown was killed in a plane crash, and while the nation mourned for this hero, Sonny Carson received an official and specific "Do not come to the funeral" dis-invitation from the government. Nevertheless, Sonny continued to attend funerals for the good, the bad and the indifferent.

However, there was more to Sonny than funerals. After his "Success" in the Ocean-Hill-Brownsville school boycott that changed New York City Board of Education hiring practices, created de-centralization and opened the door for Black and Latino administrators, he had come of age. Naturally, many people viewed him negatively and have never forgiven him for opening the door to community control and minority administrators and teachers. More importantly, it sent a message to the powers that Blacks were tired, had matured through activism with a more universal consciousness about local, national and international affairs and would be involved thenceforth.

From social and civil activism, education activism and economic activism, Sonny "Abubadika" (AB), moved into organization building. He was a founding

FREDERICK MONDERSON

member of Malcolm-King College's evolution into Medgar Evers College of the City University of New York. Sonny Carson was a founding member of the Bedford-Stuyvesant Restoration Corporation on Fulton Street. Its goal was to revitalize the Bed-Stuy community in North Brooklyn through low-interest loans and economic developing skills aided by job training in various fields.

Sonny Carson founded the Committee to Honor Black Heroes and successfully renamed Malcolm X and Marcus Garvey Boulevards in Brooklyn and the Malcolm X and Toussaint L'Ouverture schools. He laid the groundwork for renaming Fulton Street for Harriet Tubman Avenue. At the height of the crack epidemic, he founded The Black Men's Movement and Black Men Against Crack. He was a founding member of the December 12 Movement.

While he consistently remained an education activist from his days as chairman of the Education Committee of the Urban League, Brooklyn Branch, his other involvements included the already mentioned attending funerals. He also took on unscrupulous landlords on behalf of tenants, leading boycotts of Korean stores because of their treatment of Blacks. He fought against the then Bureau of Child Welfare that caused much disruption of families. Many kids were taken from their homes. Sonny took on the Giuliani administration for its callous treatment of Blacks and in wake of the "Million Movement," he launched a "Million Voter

BLACK HISTORY EVERYDAY
PART TWO

Drive" in New York to unseat the Mayor, whose popularity was saved by the tragedy of September 11, 2001.

Black History Everyday - Part Two Photo. Faces and signs in the crowd for the 50th Anniversary March on Washington.

Black History Everyday – Part Two Photo. Drs. Leonard and Rosalind Jeffries and Sister Fredricka Bey beside Minister Hafiz Mohammed at **CEMOTAP** on Saturday January 25, 2020.

FREDERICK MONDERSON

Black History Everyday - Part Two Photo. Faces and signs in the crowd for the 50th Anniversary March on Washington.

For most of his career, Sonny Carson was concerned, challenged and saddened by the music industry's spawning "Gangsta Rap," which portrayed Black women in a disgusting manner. At one point he challenged the music giant Sony in a face off entitled "Sonny Versus Sony." He also challenged the young lyricists to "tone it down," but encouraged them to continue to create constructive lyrics.

As a life-long vocation and saddened by its debilitating behavior towards Blacks, Sonny challenged the Prison Industrial Complex. For decades he fought the psychological emasculation prisons in America perennially unleashed while subjecting Black manhood to debasement on a daily

BLACK HISTORY EVERYDAY
PART TWO

basis. As such, he received hundreds of calls from across the nation regarding prison conditions and police misconduct. Just as, near the end of his life, he recognized the viability of the vote, he equally fought for the rights of prisoners to be enfranchised after paying their debt to society. Equally, Sonny wanted to establish libraries in prisons so that prisoners could undertake literacy enhancement efforts to aid their understanding prison duties and responsibilities, as well as the workings of the wider world. Sadly, he hoped Mike Tyson, from his position of visibility would have played a role in this effort as part of his "Give back."

Alas, Mike Tyson was a "no show."

Black History Everyday - Part Two Photo. **We Shall Not be Moved March**. Faces in the Crowd.

FREDERICK MONDERSON

The greatest accomplishment of Sonny Carson, considered his "final triumph," was the repatriation of the "Runaway Slave" to Ghana in West Africa to create a site of African-American pilgrimage.

The "Runaway," Samuel Carson, ran away from slavery in South Carolina, served in the US Navy and died during the Mexican War in 1845. He was buried in the Brooklyn Navy Yard. In the mid-1990s, the Navy discovered his ancestor's remains and handed it over to Sonny. Immediately he began advocating for the Black veterans who were buried there. He published in the *Afro Times*, a number of names of Black veterans buried in the Navy Yard hoping their descendants would trace their names and seek to connect with their ancestors.

Black History Everyday - Part Two Photo. Attorney Carl Thomas, George Murden, Chief James "Bar Kim" Parker and other "Old Timers" at Akbar.

BLACK HISTORY EVERYDAY
PART TWO

For the "Runaway" Sonny created the "Bones Committee" that met for nearly two years and finally decided to bury him in Ghana. While the millions of slaves who came to the Americas came through the "Door of No Return," Sonny created a "Door of Return," using his ancestor, Samuel Carson. While this happening got good publicity around the world, it was practically blacked out in the United States. However, amidst all the preparatory events before the "Runaway's" departure, there was a ceremony held in Prospect Park's "Drummers' Grove." These events were photographed and published in the Daily Challenge, July 31-August 2, 1998 as a centerfold piece. Later it was registered as historical art in the Library of Congress, by the photographer and autographed by the writer Fred Monderson on the day of burial August 1, 1998, establishing a spiritual connection between ceremony and burial.

Upon his return to the United States Sonny continued his lifelong work of activism in the many diverse areas that challenged Black and Latino people. He worked to enhance Black/Latino cooperative relationships. Brooklyn was paid one of the most revered "Going Home" ceremonies involving churches, a march from Brooklyn Bridge through the Black community, and forums to honor the home grown "bad boy," Sonny Carson, who evolved into a local hero; having made lasting impressions on his community as he tried to help better its lot. For his unending efforts in aid of community betterment, we

FREDERICK MONDERSON

remember Sonny "AB" Robert Carson, born May 18, the day before Malcolm X.

Black History Everyday - Part Two Photo. Rev. Sharpton on "No Justice, No Peace!"

"The inclusion of slaves in apportioning representation, and the admission of new states represented in Congress on the same basis as the old states, were for the south alternative methods of implementing its expected numerical superiority. Farrand artificially separates these two questions, which were debated together in the crucial week of July 6-13. Nor is he correct in asserting that the

BLACK HISTORY EVERYDAY
PART TWO

adoption of the three-fifths formula for the representation in the House was a foregone conclusion. The formula had previously been accepted only as a formula for taxation, and it was only as a formula for taxation that it appeared in the New Jersey plan. What was at issue in the Convention was whether the three-fifths formula should be extended to representation as well. The two applications were very different: as William Paterson and Luther Martin remarked, taxing slaves discouraged slavery, while giving them political representation rewarded it. Years later Rufus King stated that the three-fifths clause had been regarded as a great concession; at the Convention, once the crisis was passed Charles Pinckney affirmed that the rule of representation in the House had been the 'condition' of compromise on the rule of representation in the Senate." Melvin Drimmer. *Black History: A Reappraisal.* [1969]

"Not until westward expansion reanimated sectional bitterness in the Missouri Compromise debates of 1819-20 did Congress find itself wracked again by the problem of Negro slavery. Americans had learned to fear its divisive power, particularly after the fist and bitterest clash in 1790. Jefferson's "fireball in the night" of 1820 was actually a second alarm. The first conflagration had been brought under control and been quenched, many thought, in 1807." **Winthrop D. Jordan**. *White Over Black: American Attitudes Toward the Negro 1550-1812.* [1971]

FREDERICK MONDERSON

10. THAT MISSOURI COMPROMISE BY DR. FRED MONDERSON

Contrasting the actions of the Chief Executive when Missouri first became an item of significance and how President Obama responded to the current situation says much about how each view of the issues and though things change, how very much they remain the same. James Monroe was president when the Missouri Compromise became an issue of historical, political and moral significance and his impact seemed minimal. On the other hand, after Ferguson exploded, President Obama directly intervened by sending a high-level delegation to investigate and act. Now, as the community in Ferguson, Missouri await the Grand Jury decision on whether to indict officer Darren Wilson for the killing of the unarmed teenager Michael Brown and in anticipation Governor Nixon declared a state of emergency in readiness of unlawful behavior; a young rapper and activist remarked to CNN Anchor Don Lemon, covering developments, "The racism of white supremacy is embedded in the DNA of this state." This belief, therefore, forces a look at some aspects of the state's history particularly from the inception of the **Missouri Compromise of 1820**; a significant milestone in the question of slavery and subsequently inequality of Blacks in that

BLACK HISTORY EVERYDAY
PART TWO

now famous or infamous state of Missouri, the "Show Me State!"

Black History Everyday - Part Two Photo. We Shall Not be Moved March. Faces in the Crowd.

The **Missouri Compromise** was an important development in the legislative history of the New American Republic coming as it did in aftermath of the War of 1812 which ended in 1815 and the beginning of Internal Improvements as the Industrial Revolution began to take hold in America. That year of 1820, with the Compromise of 1787 or "Three-fifths Clause" as a backdrop designed to appease the slave-holding South, efforts to occupy and exploit the vast tracts of land acquired in the Louisiana Purchase, the future of enslaved Blacks in American was bleak at best! The dynamics unleashed in the Cotton Gin

FREDERICK MONDERSON

revolution of 1793 conflicted with the shortcomings stemming from outlawing the Slave Trade in 1808 then the labor demands and wealth aspirations of plantation owners mounted and they demanded much from legislatures and protective forces. In Florida, generally under Spanish rule, the Seminole nation (Native Americans) had long been a place of refuge for runaway Blacks that was a source of irritation for slave-holding elements. So, General Andrew Jackson was dispatched with a force to cross over to Florida to punish Seminoles for their acts of mercy in aiding runaways. This occurred in 1818 and if you add the creation of horrendous "slave farms" producing dreaded coffles of slaves chained and restrained in the most barbaric manner, this signaled Black lives within and outside the United States was not worth much, except as a commodity to a heartless, get rich slave-owner class. After all, the entire "New World" seemed an enormous plantation where professing Christian White men, guided by the Bible, practiced the most inhuman crime against humanity lasting for centuries.

BLACK HISTORY EVERYDAY
PART TWO

Black History Everyday - Part Two Photo. Planks hanging as the unfortunate Africans lynched between 1870-1950 and no one held accountable in the various counties in and outside the South. What an American tragedy.

FREDERICK MONDERSON

Black History Everyday - Part Two Photo. Faces and signs in the crowd for the 50th Anniversary March on Washington.

BLACK HISTORY EVERYDAY
PART TWO

Black History Everyday - Part Two Photo. Faces and signs in the crowd for the 50th Anniversary March on Washington.

Thus, the Missouri Compromise of 1820 was accepted to achieve political balance by admitting into the Union one Slave State, Missouri; and one Free State, Maine. Harold G. Syrell in *American Historical Documents* (New York: Barnes and Noble, (1960) 1965: 177) explained it best in the following statement. "Missouri, part of the Louisiana Purchase, applied for admission to the union as a slave state in 1819. At the time there was an equal number of Slave and Free states, and neither wished the balance to be changed in favor of the other. James Tallmadge, a representative from New York, offered an amendment to the enabling act that would have gradually eliminate slavery in Missouri. The act as amended passed in the House but failed in the Senate. Meanwhile in December, 1819, Maine applied for

FREDERICK MONDERSON

admission as a free state. In the Senate the two admission bills were combined and were finally accepted by the House after the addition of a compromise amendment, introduced by Senator Jesse B. Thomas of Illinois. In November, 1820, when Missouri's Constitution was submitted to Congress, it contained a clause unacceptable to the antislavery groups. Henry Clay, then, formulated a satisfactory compromise proposal, which was adopted on March 2, 1821."

Black History Everyday - Part Two Photo. We Shall Not be Moved March. Faces in the Crowd.

Constance Baker Motley, in an **Introduction** to "The Legal Status of the Negro in the United States" in John P. Davis' *The American Negro Reference Book* (Englewood Cliffs, New Jersey: Prentice Hall, Inc., 1964: 484) discussed the case involving Dred

BLACK HISTORY EVERYDAY PART TWO

Scott and its impact on the status of enslaved Africans in America languishing on the altar of the Missouri Compromise of 1820. Ms. Motley writes: "In 1857 in the momentous Dred Scott case, nine members of the Supreme Court reviewed, at length, the prior and then current legal status of Negroes in the United States. At that time, most Negroes were slaves. Some had been freed by their masters in accordance with the legal procedures established by the law of the slaveholding states; others had likewise purchased their freedom. Dred Scott had been a slave in Missouri. In 1834 he had been taken by his master, an army surgeon, into the free state of Illinois. Subsequently, he was taken to the territory which is now Minnesota. There slavery was prohibited by the Missouri Compromise of 1820. In 1838 Scott was returned to Missouri and later sold to another army surgeon. In 1853 Scott brought suit in a Federal court in Missouri claiming to be a free man. His claim was that he had become free upon being taken into free territory and consequently remained free upon his return to Missouri." It is to be noted, the many years he was languishing as a slave in an institution where untold millions were supplying free labor generating a significant portion of the nation's wealth!

However, as this courageous writer and activist continued, she noted: "The New York citizen who claimed to be his master defended on the ground, among others, that Scott could not bring suit in a Federal court because he was not a citizen of Missouri. Scott had just lost a suit on his claim to freedom in Missouri courts. The New York master asserted the Federal court would have jurisdiction of the suit only if Scott could show diversity jurisdiction, i.e., a suit by a citizen of one state against a citizen of another. Thus, two questions required resolution: first, whether Scott was a citizen of Missouri, and second, whether Scott had been freed by being taken into free territory. The latter question involved a determination whether Congress had the power under the Constitution to prohibit slavery in the territories, thus making Scott a free man in Minnesota. Chief Justice Taney's adverse conclusions on these questions were concurred in by the majority. He held Congress did not have power to prohibit slavery and consequently the Missouri Compromise was unconstitutional. He held Scott was still a slave because the highest court of the state of Missouri had held in Scott's case when it was before it that under the law of that state a master did not lose his property right in his slave by taking him to a free state like Illinois." Which, as stated above, "the legal procedures established by the law of the slave holding states" would have prevented Scott from being free and thus having no rights.

The tipping point in that famous Supreme Court case of *Dred Scott v. Sandford of 1857*, as Chief Justice Taney ruled: "Can a negro [sic] whose ancestors were imported into this country, and sold as slaves, become a member of the political community formed and brought into existence by the Constitution of the United States, and as such become entitled to all

BLACK HISTORY EVERYDAY
PART TWO

rights, privileges, and immunities, guaranteed by that instrument to the citizens? One of which rights is the privilege of suing in a court of the United States in the cases specified in the Constitution….The only matter in issue before the Court therefore, is, whether the descendants of such slaves, when they shall be emancipated, or who are born of parents who had become free before their birth, are citizens of a State, in the sense in which the word 'citizen' is used in the Constitution of the United States.'"

Ms. Motley rightly concluded, "Taney ruled that Negroes were not citizens within the contemplation of the Constitution. He based this on what he claimed to be the Negro's legal status throughout the civilized world at the time of the adoption of the Constitution. This status was a non-citizenship status, and he said, 'so far inferior, that they [the Negroes] had no rights which a white man was bound to respect." Given that the civilized world created and perpetuated a barbaric system of inhumanity of man towards man; yet, being born within the boundaries of the nation ought to have been sufficient. Such a situation later became law under the 14th Amendment to the Constitution, but the Court seemed to be favoring the planter class who benefitted from denying Africans those protections citizenship conferred. Notwithstanding, even when the Civil War Amendments conferred this right, it was often ignored and denied by persons who, in essence, controlled the land. In many respects, the oppressor tends to bend the law, and to ignore and suppress these rights.

FREDERICK MONDERSON

Nevertheless, it goes to show, "This view of the Negro's legal status at the time of the adoption of the Constitution was disputed by the dissenting justices. One dissenting justice found that: 'At the time of the ratification of the **Articles of Confederation** [which preceded the Constitution], all free native-born inhabitants of the states of New Hampshire, Massachusetts, New York, New Jersey, and North Carolina, though descended from African slaves, were not only citizens of those States, but such of them as had the other necessary qualifications possessed the franchise of electors on equal terms with other citizens."

Given what is stated, does the Roger Taney, planter class mentality still pervade in its many guises?

Black History Everyday - Part Two Photo. Faces and signs in the crowd for the 50th Anniversary March on Washington.

BLACK HISTORY EVERYDAY
PART TWO

Black History Everyday - Part Two Photo. Faces and signs in the crowd for the 50th Anniversary March on Washington.

Black History Everyday - Part Two Photo. Faces and signs in the crowd for the 50th Anniversary March on Washington.

FREDERICK MONDERSON

Black History Everyday - Part Two Photo. **We Shall Not be Moved March**. Faces in the Crowd.

Black History Everyday - Part Two Photo. **We Shall Not be Moved March**. Faces in the Crowd.

BLACK HISTORY EVERYDAY
PART TWO

Black History Everyday - Part Two Photo. We Shall Not be Moved March. Faces in the Crowd.

Black History Everyday – Part Two Photo. Sharpton and Crump's March on Liberty Square, Washington, DC. The people came out for this important March.

FREDERICK MONDERSON

Black History Everyday - Part Two Photo. The Equal Justice Initiative (EJI) community Remembrance Project invites community members to visit lynching sites and gather soil to honor the lives of those killed and terrorized by racial violence and injustice. This soil represents collection from over two dozen racial terror lynchings.

BLACK HISTORY EVERYDAY
PART TWO

"We boast of the freedom enjoyed by our people above all other peoples. But it is difficult to reconcile that boast with a state of the law which, practically, puts the brand of servitude and degradation upon a large class of our fellow citizens." **Justice Harlan, dissenting** in *Plessy v. Ferguson* [1896].

"We want our freedom now; *we want it* all; *we want it* here. **Martin Luther King**.

"*I want very much to talk with you. About Africa. You see, Mr. Asagai, I am looking for my identity.* **Lorraine Hansberry**. *A Raisin in the Sun.*

11. THE SUPREME COURT AND ITS JUSTICES
BY
DR. FRED MONDERSON

Presidential power to appoint a Chief Justice of the United States Supreme Court allows him sometimes to trump the opposition, particularly if his numbers are down, as in the case of President George W. Bush. Importantly, some Presidents have had no impact on the Court, others get to appoint an Associate Justice and the lucky ones get to appoint the Chief Justice. Of course, the "not fortunate ones" do get to appoint judges to "inferior courts." Interestingly, in the Post

FREDERICK MONDERSON

World War II era, Republican Eisenhower, Nixon, Ford, Reagan and both father and son Bush Presidents have impacted on and will impact on the Court.

Black History Everyday - Part Two Photo. **We Shall Not be Moved March**. Faces in the Crowd.

With President George W. Bush's leadership questioned on Iraq and Afghanistan and even his slow response to the catastrophe of Hurricane Katrina, many people began writing the final chapter of the sun setting on his presidency! His nominee John Thomas, to replace Justice Sandra Day O'Connor was in for a fight. Lo and behold, and sadly, Chief Justice William Rehnquist died and the President turned around and re-nominated John Thomas for Supreme Court Chief Justice. An outsider, straight up the ladder, to be Chief Justice is indeed rare; yet, it's just the way things can turn

BLACK HISTORY EVERYDAY
PART TWO

around sometimes. To explain these dynamics, an attempt to trace the essentials of this extraordinary institution and its leading men allows this writer's readers a condensed glimpse at a process that affects their lives in more ways than one.

The **Constitution of the United States** divided the federal government into 3 Branches, the **Legislative**, **Executive** and **Judicial**. The **Legislative Branch** creates the laws, the **Executive Branch** executes the laws and the **Judicial Branch** interprets the laws. Under George Washington, The **Judiciary Act of 1789** created the Supreme Court with a Chief Justice and 5 Associate Justices. Over the years the numbers have grown to 8 Associate justices and there have been attempts to change this now set number of 9 justices on the Supreme Court. The Judiciary Act was also an entity empowered to create inferior or lower courts. This judicial power gave the Supreme Court and other federal courts the authority to hear certain kinds of cases. Thus, these courts have the power to rule in cases involving the Constitution, national laws, treaties, and states' conflicts. As such then, Supreme Court rulings have the power to shape government public policies on issues of great national and international concern from the beginning of the Republic to today.

FREDERICK MONDERSON

According to the **Constitution, Article 3, Section 2, Subsection 1**, the Supreme Court has General Authority and this judicial power "shall extend to all cases, in law and equity, arising under this Constitution, the laws of the United States, and treaties made, or which shall be made, under this authority; to all cases affecting ambassadors, to public ministers and consuls; to all cases of admiralty and maritime jurisdiction; to controversies to which the United States shall be a party; to controversies between two or more states; between citizens of different states; between citizens of the same state claiming lands under grants of different states."

Subsection 2 states: "In all cases affecting ambassadors, the public ministers and consuls, and those in which a state shall be party, the Supreme Court shall have original jurisdiction. In all the other cases mentioned, the Supreme Court shall have appellate jurisdiction, both as to law and fact, with such exceptions, and under such regulations, as the Congress shall make."

Keep in mind, the Constitution actually created only one court, the Supreme Court. It gave Congress the ability to establish lower or "inferior courts." More than two centuries later, under constitutional and judicial changes, the Federal courts system has evolved into an institution that consists of three tiers. "At the lowest level are 94 U.S. District Courts. These are the courts where federal trials take place. The second level in the courts system includes 12

BLACK HISTORY EVERYDAY
PART TWO

U.S. Courts of Appeal. These courts hear cases 'on appeal.' At the third level is the highest court of appeal, the Supreme Court."

The Supreme Court in its capacity has heard cases from aid to church supported schools, affirmative action, campaign financing, civil rights, the Constitution, Executive Orders, impeachment, internment of Japanese Americans, interstate commerce, jurisdiction of justices, legislative veto, military actions, Mohammed Ali's refusal to serve in the military, poll tax, racial discrimination, racial quotas, reapportionment, right to be informed on charges, search and seizure, taxes, treaties, voting, work place and rules plus a whole lot more.

Even more important, however, in the Checks and Balances dynamic created by the Constitution, the Supreme Court can exercise checks on both the President and Congress. Because Judges are appointed for life and are free from executive control, they can sometimes, through judicial activism, become "wild cards" on the bench and as such can declare Executive Acts unconstitutional and rule in unpredictable manners in the interest of the wellbeing of the state even though this is not always the case.

FREDERICK MONDERSON

Black History Everyday - Part Two Photo. Attendees at Rev. Sharpton's Legislative Breakfast in January 2016.

Black History Everyday - Part Two Photo. Faces and signs in the crowd for the 50th Anniversary March on Washington.

BLACK HISTORY EVERYDAY PART TWO

Black History Everyday - Part Two Photo. Faces and signs in the crowd for the 50th Anniversary March on Washington.

Regarding Congress, these judges can, through the process of **Judicial Review**, declare acts of Congress, unconstitutional. This power to declare acts of Congress unconstitutional comes from the famous case of *Marbury V. Madison* in 1803, when Chief Justice John Marshall asserted the power of the judiciary and declared an act of Congress unconstitutional. In establishing the **Judicial Review** process, that is, **the power of the Supreme Court to review any act of Congress**, Marshall determined, it is the "unmistaken power of the Supreme Court to state what the law really is." Of course, nowhere in the Constitution does it say the Supreme Court is granted the power of **Judicial Review**. Different types of powers are granted under the Constitution. There are **delegated and implied powers**, and even **concurrent powers**. A delegated power is clearly stated, as in the case when the Constitution says Congress or the Executive has the power to "regulate interstate commerce," "coin money," "appoint judges" or to "execute the law." The implied power means that given certain circumstances, the respective party can use a discretionary power. In the case of the Supreme Court, the founding fathers implied **Judicial Review** so as to keep an eye on the Congress and the President. As they say, this is where John Marshall asserted this Discretionary Power. Concurrent Power, in addition, is when both federal and state governments have the power to act simultaneously as in the case of "taxation" or "military" preparedness.

Irving Gordon in *American Studies* (1975: 222) says of the *Marbury v. Madison* decision: "Marshall reasoned that (1) **The Constitution is supreme law of the land**; (2) **The Supreme Court is the final interpreter of the Constitution**, and therefore (3) **The Supreme Court may declare unconstitutional and inoperative any law contrary to the Constitution**. Acting

BLACK HISTORY EVERYDAY
PART TWO

boldly and confidently, **Marshall thus established the precedent of judicial review.**"

Black History Everyday - Part Two Photo. We Shall Not be Moved March. Faces in the Crowd.

Even further, in subsequent years: "During Marshall tenure (1801-1835), the Supreme Court did not invalidate another federal law but did declare several state laws unconstitutional. To 1975, the Supreme Court has held some 80 federal laws (out of 40,000 laws passed) and some 1000 state and local laws unconstitutional. Among democratic nations this power of the Supreme Court remains unique."

John Marshall was the fourth Chief Justice of the Supreme Court. *Marbury v. Madison* (1803) caused

FREDERICK MONDERSON

him to make a most significant impact on American constitutional law. According to Carl Brent Swisher's *Historic Decisions of the Supreme Court*, federalists and Jeffersonian Republicans vied for power and this forced the courts to act. "Jeffersonians were opposed to interference by a Federalist Judiciary. Yet, here Marbury, whom President John Adams had appointed a justice of the peace, was asking the Supreme Court to issue a **writ of mandamus** to compel Secretary of State Madison to give Marbury the commission entitling him to hold that office. The **Judiciary Act of 1789** authorized the Supreme Court to issue **writs of mandamus** to remedy wrongs of this kind, but the Constitution did not clearly authorize Congress to pass such an act." He said it was not the right of the court to issue a mandamus but it was the right of the court to review all acts passed by Congress.

There have been a number of cases both at the federal and state level declaring federal and state laws and acts unconstitutional. The first such case was *Dred Scott v. Sandford* in 1857 with Chief Justice Roger Taney presiding. Scott, a slave in Missouri, taken into the free territory of Minnesota, was returned to Missouri. He sued for his freedom having set foot on free soil created by the **Missouri Compromise of 1820** that declared such territory free. Taney ruled, in a very biased manner, as the majority opinion that Scott was not a citizen and could not bring suit in a US court. Gordon (1979: 222) says

BLACK HISTORY EVERYDAY
PART TWO

further: "Assuming an activist stance, Taney stated further conclusions that (a) **slaves are property**, (b) **Congress may not deprive any person of the right to take property into federal territories**, and consequently, (c) the **Missouri Compromise, which prohibited slavery in part of the Louisiana Territory, was unconstitutional**."

There were other cases regarding the issue of constitutionality as *Schecter Poultry Corporation v. United States* (1935); *United States v. Butler* (1936); *Youngston Sheet and Tube Company v. Sawyer* (1952), each having an impact on the constitution and American history and public policy.

At the state level, the significant cases were *Dartmouth College v. Woodward* (1819); *McCulloch v. Maryland* (1819) *Gibbons v. Ogden* (1824); *Wabash, St. Louis and Pacific Railway Company v. Illinois* (1886); *Lochner v. New York State* (1905). These too are historic and the first discussed in American history and government classes.

Each Chief Justice has imprinted his mark on the Supreme Court beginning with the **Marshall Court** (1801-1835); the **Taney Court** (1835-1864); the **Salmon Chase Court** during

FREDERICK MONDERSON

Reconstruction (1965-1878); **Hughes Court** (1930-1940); **Warren Court** (1953-1969); **Burger Court** (1969-1986); and **Rehnquist Court** (1986-2005). Many people have praised the recently departed Rehnquist for his intellect despite his narrow interpretation of the Constitution. Whereas his immediate predecessors Warren and Burger have used a broad interpretation. "Strict constructionists" of the court reasoned, if it's not in the Constitution it gets no hearing, while "loose constructionists" take a more liberal stance and say, "well, let's open the door a little."

Andrew Jackson appointed Roger Taney Chief Justice in 1835 and in the climate of antebellum slavery he represented the evil face of a system that degraded and destroyed Black men, women and children in a horrendous experience whose influence still pervades in the social fabric of this society. This racism can be perceived in response in aftermath of hurricane Katrina as evident in the "Black belt" states of Louisiana, Mississippi, Alabama, Georgia, etc.

An interesting point is appended here for clarification on an important ruling in Supreme Court history. President Abraham Lincoln appointed Salmon P. Chase of Ohio to replace Roger Taney. Page Smith in *The Constitution: A Documentary and Narrative History* (1980: 440) had this to say: "In the first session of the Court after the new chief justice took his seat, John S. Rock of Massachusetts was admitted

BLACK HISTORY EVERYDAY
PART TWO

to practice before the Court. *The New York Times* newspaper published an account of the event: "The black man was admitted. Jet black, with hair of an extra twist-let me have the pleasure of saying, by purpose and premeditation, of an aggravating 'kink'- unqualifiedly, obtrusively, defiantly 'Nigger'- with no palliation of complexion, no let-down in lip, no compromise in nose, no abatement whatever in any facial, cranial, osteological particular from the despised standard of humanity brutally set up in our politics and in our Judiciary by the Dred Scott decision-this inky-hued African stood, in the monarchial power of recognized American Manhood and American Citizenship, within the bar of the Court which had solemnly pronounced that black men have no rights which white men were bound to respect... By Jupiter, the site was grand! 'Twas dramatic too." [The Court, incidentally, had never said that "black men have no rights which white men were bound to respect."]

Nevertheless, Frederick Douglass, in response to this ruling, in *Black History* (1974: 96) Norman Hodges declared: "The Supreme Court is not the only power in the world.... Judge Taney cannot bail out the ocean, annihilate the firm old earth or pluck the silvery star of liberty from our Northern sky."

FREDERICK MONDERSON

Black History Everyday - Part Two Photo. Faces and signs in the crowd for the 50th Anniversary March on Washington.

Black History Everyday - Part Two Photo. Faces and signs in the crowd for the 50th Anniversary March on Washington.

BLACK HISTORY EVERYDAY
PART TWO

In the era of **Reconstruction** (1865-1877) the Court favored the South in most of its rulings. Hodges (1974: 138) says: "The Supreme Court, too, played a significant role in the oppression of Black citizens. The federal court system, in its decisions, tended to reflect the political mood and temper of the times. The Supreme Court handed down a series of decisions that gravely compromised the power of the federal government to protect Black rights in the South. As early as 1878, the Court struck down a Louisiana ban on segregation in interstate transport because it was a "burden" on privately operated interstate commerce. In 1882, it ruled against sections of the **Enforcement Act of 1871** which stipulated punishment for persons acting in violation of the Fourteenth and Fifteenth Amendments. The Court continued its attack on Black rights in 1883, when it declared the landmark **Civil Right Act of 1875** unconstitutional. This Act had given Blacks access to the "full and equal employment of privately-operated public facilities, such as inns, theaters, railroads, etc. The Court held that the Fourteenth Amendment prohibited state discrimination, rather than individual discrimination. Thus, it deprived millions of citizens of the needed protection of federal enforcement of their constitutional rights. This decision particularly was used as precedent by the South to justify 'Jim Crow' laws, that were later enacted."

FREDERICK MONDERSON

**Black History Everyday - Part Two Photo.
Mutula Shakur** is welcome here at **CEMOTAP.**

In wake of this, a number of terrorist groups such as the Knights of the White Camelia, the Ku Klux Klan, and the White League emerged to terrorize Blacks in effort to reestablish white supremacy in the south. Hodges (1974: 127) says: "Hooded night riders erected burning crosses in Black areas at night and terrorized the Black populace with beatings, tarring and feathering, mutilations, threats, torture, and lynchings. Members of the Klan rode in conspicuous caravans at election time to intimidate the Blacks, and the brazen White League members sat at the polling places, in full view, with loaded guns on their laps in order to prevent the freedmen from casting their ballots. The Klan and its companion organizations

BLACK HISTORY EVERYDAY
PART TWO

stirred up hatred against Blacks and fermented riots against them at the slightest provocation or pretext." Now one can understand why individuals as Stokeley Carmichael (Kwame Ture), in the 1960s, were so serious when they went South to register Blacks to vote!

All developments after **Reconstruction** led to the famous *Plessy v. Ferguson* (1896) case challenging a Louisiana law that required "Separate but equal" accommodations on the train. According to Hodges (1974: 145) who wrote: "The Court upheld the state law and gave constitutional approval to the "separate but equal" doctrine. The Court denied that 'the enforced separation of the two races stamps the colored race with a body of inferiority…if this be so, it is not by reason of anything found in the act, but solely because the colored race chooses to put that construction upon it."

The dissenting Justice John Marshall Harlan of Kentucky, wrote the minority opinion sating: "We boast of the freedom enjoyed by our people above all other peoples. But is it difficult to reconcile that boast with a state of the law which, practically, puts the brand of servitude and degradation upon a large class of our fellow citizens, our equals before the law. The thin disguise of 'equal' accommodations … will not mislead anyone, or atone for the wrong this day done… Our Constitution is color blind, and neither knows nor tolerates classes among citizens."

FREDERICK MONDERSON

The **NAACP** was founded in 1909 and within half a dozen years were able to win a victory, In *Black History*, Hodges (1974: 172) recounts: "The Supreme Court, in 1915, struck down the notorious 'grandfather clause' as unconstitutional. In 1917, the Court nullified a Kentucky law that provided for "Jim Crow" communities in Louisville. And on the question of justice for Blacks, the Supreme Court ordered a new trial for a Black man convicted of murder by a jury from which his Black peers had been excluded."

In the past century, Charles Evans Hughes was appointed Chief Justice by President Herbert Hoover in 1930 and served during the New Deal era, often clashing with President F.D. Roosevelt. When the President threatened to "pack the court" with more judges to facilitate his agenda in this critical time, Hughes became liberal and helped pass two important pieces of legislation by a narrow margin of 5 to 4. These **New Deal** laws were: **The National Labor Relations Act** to guarantee collective bargaining and the **Social Security Act**, that have had such far-reaching implications for American public policy. Some say Roosevelt lost the battle but won the war!

Nevertheless, during Roosevelt's tenure the Court became more liberal. "In 1932, in the first of two celebrated **Scottsboro** decisions, the Court ruled (*Powell v. Alabama*) that the defendants had been

BLACK HISTORY EVERYDAY PART TWO

denied their right to counsel, and that such denial was a violation of their Fourteenth Amendment rights. In a second **Scottsboro** opinion in 1935, the Court held that Blacks had been excluded from Alabama juries over an extended period of time, and that this fact proved the existence of discrimination in violation of the accused's Fourteenth Amendment rights. In these historic decisions the Supreme Court seemed to advance away from the racist tendencies that had perverted the dispensation of justice by some of its members in the past."

President Dwight Eisenhower appointed Earl Warren Chief Justice in 1953. He presided over the famous *Brown v. Board of Education of Topeka Kansas* in 1954 and in the 1960s began exerting influence, according to John J. Newman and John M. Schmalback's *United States History* (1998: 602) "on the criminal justice system, the political system of the states, and the definition of individual rights." Gordon (1984: 231) offered commentary on the Liberal and activist course of the Warren court in three major areas: "(1) in the Brown Case, the Warren Court unanimously held racial segregation in schools unconstitutional, thereby contributing to the movement for black civil rights; (2) In the Baker Case, the Warren Court held legislative apportionment to be a judicial matter, thereby furthering democracy through more equitable election districts .... (3) In several cases affecting persons accused of crime, the Warren Court insisted

FREDERICK MONDERSON

upon protection of their rights to a lawyer and against self-incrimination."

Black History Everyday - Part Two Photo. The audience at **National Action Network's** "Power and Policy Forum" on Dr. King's Holiday, Monday January 20, 2020.

Black History Everyday - Part Two Photo. Faces and signs in the crowd for the 50th Anniversary March on Washington.

BLACK HISTORY EVERYDAY
PART TWO

Warren Burger was appointed Chief Justice by President Richard Nixon in 1969 to reflect his campaign pledge to appoint judges who would "interpret the law-not make the law" and "interpret the Constitution strictly and fairly and objectively." While opposing judicial activism, according to Gordon (1984: 233-34), "The Burger Court upheld busing to remedy *de jure* school segregation; however, in the absence of deliberate discrimination, it struck down inter-district school busing; it granted broad discretion to trial judges to close criminal pretrial hearing to the press and public but later reaffirmed the right of the press and public to attend criminal trials; it supported a voluntary affirmative action program in employment; it held that national defense took precedence over equal rights for women and approved draft registration only by males; it struck down a Texas law denying free public education to children of illegal aliens; it struck down the practice of Congress of overruling specific executive actions by the so-called legislative veto. The Court declared this practice a violation of separation of powers."

FREDERICK MONDERSON

Black History Everyday - Part Two Photo. We Shall Not be Moved March. Faces in the Crowd.

The last, William Rehnquist was an important modern Chief Justice whose conservatism turned back the liberal leaning of the Warren and Burger tenures. *The New York Times* **Obituary** of September 4, 2005, offered the following commentary: "With a steady hand, a focus and commitment that never wavered, and the muscular use of the power of judicial review, he managed to translate many of his long-held views into binding national precedent." *The Times* said further, praising his lengthy tenure: "But his ultimate success was also a testament to his own tenacity and skill. He combined an unfaltering sense of mission with high intelligence, patience, the strategic prowess of a serious poker player, which he was, and the attention to detail of an art-lover and serious amateur painter,

BLACK HISTORY EVERYDAY
PART TWO

which he also was. He had held many of his views since early adulthood, and he took the long view: with seeming nonchalance, he would plant a phrase in an opinion in the expectation that it would take root, blossom, and prove even more useful in some future case. Time proved him right, not always, but often enough."

Black History Everyday - Part Two Photo. We Shall Not be Moved March. Faces in the Crowd.

Major decisions of the Rehnquist Court, according to the New York *Daily News* of September 4, 2005 included: "*Texas v. Johnson* (1989) - The court ruled that flag-burning was protected speech under the First Amendment; *Planned Parenthood v. Casey* (1992) - The court, widely expected to overturn *Roe v. Wade* decision, reaffirmed the right to an abortion instead, but opened the door to new restrictions; *Lee v. Weisman* (1992) - The court ruled that sanctioned prayer at public school graduations violates the Constitution; *United States v. Lopez* (1995) - The court, led by Rehnquist, struck down laws that prohibited bringing a gun near a school; *Bush v. Gore* (2000) - In its most controversial opinion, the court decided 5-4 along political lines to end a recount of presidential election votes in the state of Florida, ending Al Gore's challenge to George W. Bush; *Stenberg v. Carhart* (2000) - The court struck down a Nebraska ban on "partial birth" abortion and said all abortion restrictions must contain an exception for the health of the mother; *Dickerson v. U.S.* (2000) - The court, led by Rehnquist ruled that taxpayer-funded school vouchers could be used for religious schools; *Gonzalez v. Gaich* (2005) - The court ruled that federal laws against medical marijuana trumped state laws allowing its use; *Roper v. Simmons* (2005) - The court outlawed the death penalty for prisoners who committed their crimes while under 18."

Those of us who remembered the Congressional hearings when Clarence Thomas was appointed as an Associate Justice were both proud and disappointed. He was replacing the venerable Thurgood Marshall as a Black man on the court. However, for a Black man, Clarence Thomas, represented a surprisingly conservative wing of the court and he proved true to expectations on both sides of the divide. Nonetheless, he was at the time touted as being the youngest justice, will outlive many of the older ones

BLACK HISTORY EVERYDAY
PART TWO

and he will one day become Chief Justice. Years later he would confess at the **Black Bar Association** meeting of never realizing Blacks would dislike his interpretation of the true meaning of the Constitution, against affirmative action, etc. Some thought he wanted to come home and be accepted by Black America. Nevertheless, "well played" and he "played well" according conservative standards but was denied the elusive prize of becoming Chief Justice when they chose the "other Thomas;" John that is, not Clarence!

Black History Everyday - Part Two Photo. "**I can't breathe**," Eric Garner's last cry, so says a wheelchair protester in **Sharpton and Crump's March on Washington**.

FREDERICK MONDERSON

Black History Everyday - Part Two Photo. "The face that led the Walk!"

Black History Everyday - Part Two Photo. Faces and signs in the crowd for the 50th Anniversary March on Washington.

BLACK HISTORY EVERYDAY
PART TWO

Black History Everyday - Part Two Photo. Faces and signs in the crowd for the 50th Anniversary March on Washington.

Black History Everyday - Part Two Photo. Faces and signs in the crowd for the 50th Anniversary March on Washington.

FREDERICK MONDERSON

Black History Everyday - Part Two Photo. **We Shall Not be Moved March**. Faces in the Crowd.

Black History Everyday - Part Two Photo. **We Shall Not be Moved March**. Faces in the Crowd.

BLACK HISTORY EVERYDAY
PART TWO

Black History Everyday - Part Two Photo. Faces and signs in the crowd for the 50th Anniversary March on Washington.

Black History Everyday - Part Two Photo. Faces and signs in the crowd for the 50th Anniversary March on Washington.

FREDERICK MONDERSON

"The blues is not simply a music to titillate; it is a hard-fought way of life, and as such should unsettle and unnerve whites about the legacy of white supremacy. **Cornel West**. *Democracy Matters*. [2004]

"One of the most inflammatory confrontations in the coming race war has been building up for years, and on many battlefields. Americans are brandishing hand grenades over 'affirmative action.' And some who throughout their lives practiced or tolerated the most egregious racism and discrimination are now waging conflict over their assertion that the victims of three hundred years of white racism are now the underserved beneficiaries of 'reverse racism.'"

12. THE WHITE HOUSE CONTRADICTION
BY
DR. FRED MONDERSON

I was in Washington, D.C. on Sunday, August 17, 2014 about 5:00 pm walking on 15th Street and made the turn at the Treasury Department building to enter the rear "White House Street Plaza." Alongside Lafayette Park, Capitol Police vehicles approached the corner barriers with lights flashing and sirens blaring. Approaching the classic White House viewing location; I saw a Secret Service agent and his dog whiz by. Nearby in the street a Baptist preacher

BLACK HISTORY EVERYDAY
PART TWO

was wailing about "the King of Kings;" the "144,000;" "Preparing for death and heaven and hell;" "Corruption in the American system of government;" and much more could be seen.

As we got closer to the fence for the customary photographs, there stood a compelling contradiction! A white male, naked except for a pair of very short-shorts with tattooed writings on his chest and back, was facing the fence and White House. In apparent glee, he stood there jerking his middle finger unendingly. He did seem to have companions nearby. As onlookers gazed in disbelief the fellow continued his weird behavior. This, then, was the contradiction plain and simple! Why? But first!

The law enforcement interest was generated by the appearance and continued behavior of this individual as the Secret Service and Capitol Police observed his shameless behavior. They sent in the "dogs" to detect at least, whether he was on or had drugs in his possession. This was probably the only way to remove this citizen since in expressing his First Amendment Rights of Free Speech, there was no explosive threat. The police could only stand helpless but vigilantly observing this vivid example of "white trash" jubilantly thrusting his middle finger skyward thereby sending an obscene message to the White House and its occupants.

As to why! This is a shameless desecration of the nation's most sacred space. This lower-class behavior is a continuum of the climate of disrespect engendered against President Obama and his family! Now, as to the preacher working up a frenzy, this is not unusual. This is "church" in the street! The other protesters, one about nuclear proliferation had been long-standing beside the Lafayette Park with its floral decoration and Jackson and his canon on guard behind. Another gentleman sat in the street playing a recording of former President Jimmy Carter explaining the pros and cons of the Arab-Israeli conflict. Both protests, however, were peaceful and civilized, unlike the other lewd demonstration.

Hypothetically speaking, foreign visitors, of whom there were many, observing this "freak show," were amazed that such behavior could be directed towards the White House and its occupants. However, the problem manifesting there on that day was not about "wales acting as minions" but "a roach thinking he is an eagle." What we have witnessed in recent years is a climate of disrespect for President Obama created by government officials, senators, governors, important people and the press. These supposedly responsible leaders have shamelessly created a climate of hatred for President Obama and his family that we, the people, must never forget. Dr. Leonard James often taught, "The higher monkey climbs. The more monkey exposes himself." Nevertheless, and often, we are reminded, a given officer or uniform philosophically represents the value of a given social institution. So, for example, when we respect the policeman, we respect the man, the uniform and the

BLACK HISTORY EVERYDAY PART TWO

philosophical principle of law and order which they all symbolize and stand for.

Black History Everyday - Part Two Photo. We Shall Not be Moved March. Faces in the Crowd.

Mr. Obama did not inherit his political position. He happened to be the son of an African father who married a white American female from Kansas; both of whom were of modest means. Nevertheless, the hatred for Mr. Obama really stems from the hatred against his father for marrying a white female! Visit the Jefferson Building of the Library of Congress. Notice how images depict the white female as pristine, the epitome of female beauty! That this African choose to marry, not live unmarried, to the beautiful lady meant nothing to these individuals who by their practice of hatred for others really betray

FREDERICK MONDERSON

their true pathological selves. Such hatred is also most malignant for persons in interracial marriage; especially if the male partner is Black.

On Mr. Obama's part, through hard work, competence, resilience, fortitude, organizational skills and tenacity, he won the Presidency of the United States. In the history of this nation and the millions who have lived and died on these shores, only 43 men previously accomplished this feat. Less than half did it twice and one, four times, because of prevailing circumstances as a result of World War II.

Black History Everyday - Part Two Photo. Faces and signs in the crowd for the 50th Anniversary March on Washington.

Most people believe that the Presidency of the United States is a hallowed institution that also makes the individual inhabiting the position and sacred space, special. Thus, like the Officer and the uniform, both the man and the office must be respected. As such,

BLACK HISTORY EVERYDAY
PART TWO

any behavior that impugns the man sullies the institution. Therefore, the crass attitudes and behaviors of the mud-slingers at Obama; those who throw stones to break the window; speak volumes not of noble souls' magnanimous actions but men of vile temperaments and questionable character.

In Meridian Park in Washington, DC, a statue sits as a memorial to President John Buchannan with an inscription that reads: "He walked on the mountain tops of the law." Such a tribute says much for this gentleman, certainly attesting to a noble spirit. Today evidence of elegance of mind and nobility of spirit are missing in that "City on the Hill" – Washington, DC.

For centuries there has been a certain kind of behavior which was called psychosexual pathology. Today its "intellectual, cultural and ethnic heritage envy," that has become pathological. This behavior involves attacking a work ethic that is creative and successfully superior which generates the venomous hatred we see directed toward Mr. Obama as President heading the most powerful nation on earth. The disgusting behavior of the citizen referenced above was motivated by the behaviors of the many winners of the "Little Man" award who created that climate of contempt.

First and foremost, Mitch McConnell (R. Kentucky): One has to wonder how the people of "The Great State" of Kentucky could countenance the petty behavior. John Boehner, the Speaker of the U.S. House of Representatives who disrespected Mr. Obama; Then we have "Waterloo" Jim De Mint, formerly (R. South Carolina); Donald Trump, seeking a birth certificate and college transcript, as if he did not himself own one; "You Lie" Wilson (R. South Carolina); "Gangster Government," "God told me to run," Michele Bachmann; "a fraud" Senator Ted Cruz; "Poison the Well" Rick Santorum; "Lipstick on a pig" Sarah Palin; "Healthcare is Slavery" Benjamin Carson; and last but not least, John McCain, privy to this and more, yet his open attempts to demean Obama did not preclude him from trying to become President of the United States!

Some have accused Senator McCain of milking his "Hero" name for nearly half a century. Yet, comparatively out of nowhere "Po Boy" Obama was elected twice mostly through masterly organizing his assets and relentlessly pursuing his objective.

We cannot forget malicious psycho/spiritual lepers and powerful commentators like Charles Krauthammer, Michael Goodwin, and other sick minions, particularly Rush Limbaugh and Sean Hannity, all of whom possess and use malevolent vocabularies devoid of any respectful terminology when it comes to their commentary on Mr. Obama. Certainly, constructive criticisms are always welcome from honest critics. But destructive malicious commentary and blatant denial of any of Mr. Obama's accomplishments buttressed by lies are

BLACK HISTORY EVERYDAY PART TWO

behaviors unworthy of responsible men in such high positions.

Somehow, they all manifest a Ron Paul reflection on George W. Bush moment, for when asked, "Can you name one good thing President Obama has done?" That "liberal" paragon of virtue, Ron Paul, thought looong and haaard and honestly confessed, "I can't think of anything good Mr. Obama has done!" Jesse Jackson once insisted, "Stay out of the bushes!" Mr. Paul did not and stole a phrase and mentality from George Bush though Mr. Paul turned that phrase on its head, but with the same meaning!

Now, if these respectable individuals could so disparage Mr. Obama, they certainly provide incentive and justification for bottom of the barrel types to vent as this fellow did in front of the White House. Strange that this individual felt justified in his highly disrespectful conduct. Obviously, given Mr. Obama has been subject to more threats, vilification and derision than any other President, a very dangerous climate and in which sinister behaviors including doing bodily harm to the nation's leader by some hate-filled lunatic is a real possibility. Nonetheless, the superior intellect and noble spirit which Mr. Obama embodies impels his critics to expose their deep fear and hatred of the Black man who occupies the White House!

FREDERICK MONDERSON

Black History Everyday - Part Two Photo. Faces and signs in the crowd for the 50th Anniversary March on Washington.

Black History Everyday - Part Two Photo. Faces and signs in the crowd for the 50th Anniversary March on Washington.

BLACK HISTORY EVERYDAY PART TWO

"I am infamous because I cannot be frightened nor coaxes into supporting the Democracy, I am infamous because from the very day the constitutional convention met in this city, I have championed the cause of the down-trodden colored people. From that day to this I have not failed, whenever the opportunity presented itself, to cast my vote and raise my voice in behalf of the class I represent. I have stood firm at my post of duty." Pinckney Benton Stewart Pinchback. *Speech to the United States Senate*]1872]

Black History Everyday - Part Two Photo. We Shall Not be Moved March. Faces in the Crowd.

"A Negro who does not vote is ungrateful to those who have already died in the fight for freedom …. Any person who does not vote is failing to serve the cause of freedom – his own freedom, his people's freedom, and his country's freedom." Constance Baker Motley. *Keynote address to annual convention of the Southern Christian Leadership Conference.* [1965]

FREDERICK MONDERSON

Black History Everyday - Part Two Photo. Faces and **Black Lives Matter** sign at Sharpton and Crump's "March on Washington."

13. VOTING RIGHTS AND REDISTRICTING
BY
DR. FRED MONDERSON

Attorney General Eric Holder gave an interesting speech on Tuesday December 13, 2011 at the **Lyndon B. Johnson Library** in which he took on the issue of redistricting that has been causing some concern, particularly across the South, as the nation gears up for the 2012 national elections; perhaps the "most important national elections of our lifetime." President Johnson, who signed the 1965 Voting Rights Act would have been proud of Mr. Holder whose Justice Department promises to move aggressively in reviewing, according to *The New York Times* Wednesday December 14, 2011 in which Charlie Savage's article "Holder Signals Tough

BLACK HISTORY EVERYDAY PART TWO

Review of State Laws on Voting Rights" explained: "Voting laws that civil rights advocates say will dampen minority participation in next year's election. Pulling no punches and promising to use the full weight of his department to ensure that new electoral laws are not discriminatory, the Attorney General held protecting ballot access for all eligible voters 'must be viewed not only as a legal issue but as a moral imperative.'" Thereupon he called on all Americans to urge their "political parties to resist the temptation to suppress certain votes in the hope of attaining electoral success and, instead achieve success by appealing to more voters." This issue is so significant, for some time, groups across the country have been sounding the alarm expressed through the media and in protest marches. However, the belief is the government had been "eyeballing the situation" and has chosen the appropriate time to act.

Whether it's the **NAACP** and the **NAACP Legal Defense Fund** in its report entitled "Defending Democracy: Confronting Modern Barriers to Voting Rights in America" or The **NAACP's** President and CEO Benjamin Jealous' "Stand for Freedom" these long-standing defenders of Civil Rights understand the situation most for they have chronicled trends enacted by Republican controlled statehouses particularly after the "Tea Party" successes in the 2010 national and state elections.

FREDERICK MONDERSON

Especially after the last election, for some time now, attention has been focusing on voting rights as it has been and will be affected through redistricting which occurs every ten years after the census count. The argument is valid that the dominant political party in state legislatures has a tendency to redraw the lines in a manner that benefits that party's incumbent members and the new candidates they intend to field. This method of manipulating the political boundaries has been called "Gerrymandering" after an original theorist called Jerry. Apparently, such an individual had been assigned to draw up a particular voting district and he skewed the configuration to such an extent, one observer remarked the new district lines looked very much like a salamander. The author then responded, "This is not a salamander, it is a gerrymander!" The name stuck and so, any attempt to carve an unusual district voting lines that include certain groups or exclude or hinder voting rights of others, is considered "Gerrymandering."

Plato and Greenberg in *The American Political Dictionary* (1989: 129-30) describes "Gerrymandering" as "drawing of legislative district boundary lines to obtain partisan or factional advantage," explained the significance of this practice in that: "Most redistricting laws enacted by state legislatures show evidence of varying degrees of boundary manipulation for partisan advantage. Historically, gerrymandering resulted in gross overrepresentation of rural areas in the House of Representatives and in most state legislatures. In

BLACK HISTORY EVERYDAY
PART TWO

1964, the Supreme Court ruled on this issue (*Davis v. Bandemer*, 478 U.S. 109) redistricting should be drawn on a basis of substantial equality of population. Nevertheless, the boundaries of districts that are substantially equal in population may still be drawn to secure partisan advantage, and gerrymandering persists. Thus, a minority of a state's voters may elect a majority of that state's congressional delegation and a majority in both houses of the state legislature. A legislative majority can often maintain its power position by influencing elections through control over district boundaries. Critics of Gerrymandering claim that it violates the 'one person, one vote' rule laid down by the Supreme Court in a number of apportionment decisions because gerrymandering can add to or subtract from the electoral power of voters. In 1986, the Supreme Court ruled on this issue (*Davis v. Bandemer*, 478 U.S. 109) when it held that partisan political gerrymandering is subject to constitutional challenge even if the one person, one vote rule is met. Such a challenge may stand, said the Court, if the drawing lines results in continual frustration of the majority will or the effective denial of influence to a majority."

However, while this "pre-carving" may not be considered illegal, it certainly is unethical and immoral in that it seeks to diffuse, limit or diminish the voting strength of one or more groups to aid or advance the cause of another to give that group an edge at upcoming elections. This time around the focus of victimization has been on African-

FREDERICK MONDERSON

Americans and Latinos whose population numbers have increased disproportionately in several states in the South. This is because they tend to vote Democratic. These voters were also the keys to President Obama's re-election in 2012. As such, Mr. Holder's interest in the new laws is justified particularly and especially since several Democratic governors have vetoed state laws that attempt to establish such unfair principles.

Black History Everyday - Part Two Photo. **We Shall Not be Moved March**. Faces in the Crowd.

"Gerrymandering" is not the only way in which the voting strength and *ipso facto* voting power of different, albeit minority, groups are targeted as part of a general strategy of disfranchisement. In various regions of the country people convicted of a felony are deprived of their voting rights. Some have argued

BLACK HISTORY EVERYDAY PART TWO

in several southern states the criminal justice system is used as a mechanism to disfranchise minorities who disproportionately comprise prison populations. In some states, felons are prevented from voting for life; in others this prohibition is extended for a number of years after completing their sentence. In this, the argument has been made that misdemeanor criminal behaviors are oftentimes elevated to felony status and as such these individuals are removed from the voting rolls. Advocates for these dispossessed persons in response have argued once a person has paid the debt to society then all of his/her natural and civil as well as political rights should be reinstated!

Another method used to purge the voting rolls is to insist people who have not voted in recent elections be deemed ineligible. However, while this may create a gray area, nefarious individuals with a party agenda often take the initiative and remove persons in unscrupulous moves. This form of behavior is a throwback to the past Civil War era when southern voting and polling individuals went to great lengths to deny and invalidate the intent of the 13th, 14th, and 15th Amendments to the Constitution that followed the conflict. To recall, southern polling officials required of "Freedmen" that they take literacy tests, show proof of property qualification, provide evidence of paid poll taxes and these individuals even invented a "grandfather clause" which held, if one's grandfather had previously voted, then regardless of one's literacy, intellectual or other qualifying factors, they were still entitled to vote. Naturally, Blacks *en*

FREDERICK MONDERSON

masse, who had been enslaved and denied the ballot previously were automatically disqualified under the "Grandfather Clause" rule. Thereafter, for more than four decades the "Grandfather clause" held sway and helped some and hurt other voters until it was declared unconstitutional by the Supreme Court in 1915. Matching these "legal machinations" of voting denial, threats and intimidation in face of a national government turning a deaf ear, Black voting rights had been effectively nullified and a manipulated "White Primary" further alienated those hardy enough to attempt to exercise the franchise.

In one example, former Secretary of State Condoleezza Rice tells how her family became Republican voters. Apparently when her father tried to register as a Democrat in the South, he was asked to determine "how many beans were in a jar;" an impossible task. Instead, a Republican Registrar easily registered him as a Republican and the family has remained so ever since. Perhaps this is why there is such an uproar because Eric Holder, unlike many previous national and state Attorney Generals, particularly in the South, has chosen to use the full weight of the national government against such skullduggery!

BLACK HISTORY EVERYDAY PART TWO

Black History Everyday - Part Two Photo. Another face who "Walked the Walk!"

Black History Everyday - Part Two Photo. Faces and signs in the crowd for the 50th Anniversary March on Washington.

FREDERICK MONDERSON

Black History Everyday - Part Two Photo. Faces and signs in the crowd for the 50th Anniversary March on Washington.

In "Classic Jim Crow era" after the Civil War, there is evidence of "white men with guns at polling stations" and this was purposely designed to intimidate newly minted Black voters. In such behaviors, the "secret nature of the ballot" was betrayed and an individual's voting preference was reported to his employer the next day, almost certainly to get him fired from a hard-won job. In addition, signs indicating polling sites were often turned around sending voters in the opposite direction only to be often waylaid by highwaymen as all part of the "conspiracy to nullify Black" and other minority votes. For the longest, these sinister deeds did not exhaust efforts to block legitimate Black ballot expression. What is interesting, as late as the 2008 national election Republicans engaged in similar dishonest practices such as insisting, on "Day

BLACK HISTORY EVERYDAY
PART TWO

One Republicans vote" and on "Day Two Democrats vote." This strategy was designed to confuse persons not really astute about the voting process. Flyers with misinformation were distributed in Black areas. People were informed if they had outstanding warrants or parking tickets the police would be there to arrest them if they turned up to vote. People's jobs were threatened if they tried to vote and a whole lot more such strategies were used to dissuade would-be voters who tended to vote Democratic. In addition to the above, other legal disqualification methods may be mentioned including "mental incompetents, election law violator and vagrants" and hardly ever have these impediments been reversed.

In addition to these restrictions, what Dr. Benjamin F. Chavis, Jr., in "Stand Up for Voting Rights" in *Afro Times* December 17, 2011, p. 4, has called "repressive and counter-productive" measures include: "Restrictions to Early Voting: The early voting period has been reduced in a number of states. This will mostly affect Black voters, as research shows African-Americans have been much more likely to take advantage of early voting. They accounted for 22% of early voters during the 2008 general election in Florida."

FREDERICK MONDERSON

Black History Everyday - Part Two Photo. **We Shall Not be Moved March**. Faces in the Crowd.

In addition, there are Residency Requirements where, "Some states have increased the amount of time a citizen must live in a state to be entitled to vote. This particularly affects African-Americans and Hispanics, as they are most likely to move from state-to-state, and are therefore less likely to have lived in there for the required length of time." Seems the biggest item has been as Chavis states: Requiring citizens to have Photo-ID, with documentary proof of their citizenship. Some states will not accept student ID, even if issued by the state, whilst those elderly voters who were born during the time of legalized racial segregation and who were therefore not issued with birth certificates, will also have difficulties at election time."

BLACK HISTORY EVERYDAY
PART TWO

While the 13th Amendment freed the slaves, the 14th gave citizenship to persons born in the United States and the 15th Amendment, adopted in 1870, forbade any state from denying persons the right to vote because of race, color, or previous condition of servitude. Jack C. Plano and Milton Greenberg in *The American Political Dictionary* (1962) (1989: 71) summed up the significance of the Fifteenth Amendment in the following: "Although the Fifteenth Amendment does not give anyone an absolute right to vote, it does prohibit any discrimination because of race or color. Not until recent years have Blacks made significant advances in realizing the goals established by the amendment. In 1960, for example, the Supreme Court ruled that the racial gerrymandering of Tuskegee, Alabama, so as to exclude all Black voters from city elections violated the Fifteenth Amendment (*Gomillion v. Lightfoot*, 364 U.S. 339). The **Civil Rights Acts** of 1957, 1960, 1964 and the **Voting Rights Acts** of 1965, 1970, and 1975 were passed by Congress and the Twenty-Fourth Amendment prohibiting poll taxes was adopted to aid Blacks in overcoming the various devices used by some southern states to frustrate the purposes of the Fifteenth Amendment." It may well be that history has repeated itself as "Gerrymandering" is paramount in the rush to redistrict in the several states and as such Attorney General Eric Holder's intervention is not only timely but necessary.

FREDERICK MONDERSON

We recognize it is time in preparation for the 2012 elections; for the process of redrawing political boundaries based on the newest census data affecting states that gain or lose population numbers. This helps in allocating how recourses are dispensed and representation in local school board, city council, county commission and state legislatures determined. Plato and Greenberg (1989: 143) have argued: "Redistricting decisions typically are made by partisan majorities in the legislatures, and the partisan nature of the undertaking is often reflected in the final results, called gerrymandering. In the past, large cities were underrepresented and rural areas tended to be grossly overrepresented because of state legislative refusals to redistrict on a population basis."

Black History Everyday – Part Two Photo. Senator Kirstin Gillibrand at Sharpton's "Power and Policy Forum" on Dr. King's Holiday, 2020.

BLACK HISTORY EVERYDAY
PART TWO

"Ain't gonna let nobody turn me around. I'm gonna keep on a-walking, keep on a-talkin' Marchin' up to freedom land! *Ain't Gonna Let Nobody Turn Me Around. Negro Spirituals.*

"The right to vote is the right upon which all of our rights are leveraged and without which none can be protected." **Benjamin Todd Jealous**. *Keynote address at the convention of the National Association for the Advancement of Colored People, Los Angeles* [July 25, 2011]

14. "WE BE MARCHING" BY DR. FRED MONDERSON

INTRODUCTION

African people have marched and marched and marched for a whole lot of reasons. In recent years, however, we have marched for unity, to demonstrate solidarity, to call attention to iniquitous behavior and to address and right wrongs within the social fabric parameters of American society, and, by extension, the world.

While we must thank Minister Louis Farrakhan for the clear and farsightedness of organizing the phenomenal "Million Marching," alas, the bright intention of that inspiring point of light seems to have dimmed. Like all great ideas, follow-through is important and while the underpinnings may very well be progressing slowly, the outward manifestations are that the movement has slowed, but it was again rekindled in the 2015 **"Justice or Else," Million-Man March** celebrating the 20th Anniversary of the "initial March." This **20th Anniversary** revealed a profound philosophic concept of repeating anniversaries of Millions of African-American men and women coming to the nation's capital emphasizing the power of unity and "speaking truth to power." Again, for this powerful idea we must thank Minister Louis Farrakhan and his Nation of Islam followers. Much more significant, disciples of the marching philosophy have and must continue despite questionable perceptions because this is the American way and it's always one way to call attention to injustice and bigotry and all ills of a racial nature.

Black History Everyday - Part Two Photo. Faces and signs in the crowd for the 50th Anniversary March on Washington.

BLACK HISTORY EVERYDAY
PART TWO

Black History Everyday - Part Two Photo. Faces and signs in the crowd for the 50th Anniversary March on Washington.

Notwithstanding, science has shown early man emerged in East Africa and migrated or marched south, north west and finally east. These efforts were for exploration, to secure food and shelter and progressively peopling the globe. In the process, early manmade discoveries, experimented and manufactured a wide repertoire of tools and established conventions and practice later called culture. He developed language, used fire, established sites for resting, cooking, making tools, cutting up animals, ceremonial sites and even burial sites or graves. And, still he marched.

Early man continued his trek heading east until he reached the tip of Asia and finally crossed the Bering

FREDERICK MONDERSON

Straits reaching what became the Americas. He kept marching all over the twin continents and by this time, some scholars believe, early man had marched to people the world.

One thing was certain, while injustice per se, was not conceived, the "justice" in early man's forays was to fulfill the Biblical admonition, "multiply and populate the earth." The success of this adventure is measured in the domestication of plants and animals, the development of technology for hunting, farming, fishing, navigating waterways, fighting, for domestic use and personal and cultural adornment. The said technology helped develop the practice of building for domestic, civic, religious, military, mortuary and festive purposes. All these structures needed decoration and thus perfected the art of painting, sculpture and equally the fine arts of making jewelry for personal purposes and other uses. Therefore, it is easily evident, the "first marchers," who left Africa, achieved the "justice" they unknowingly set out to achieve for they bequeathed to humanity the utility of the march and all the benefits, as indicated, and attendant thereto.

BLACK HISTORY EVERYDAY
PART TWO

Black History Everyday - Part Two Photo. We Shall Not be Moved March. Faces in the Crowd.

b. Ancient Man Marched down the Nile River

The rudiments of ancient Egyptian civilization were long in the making as the dynamics so characteristic of the culture emerged and laid the foundations that sustained pharaonic existence. However, as these unfolded, trade patterns and dynamics developed, internecine conflict emerged, generated by the success of the emerging wealth. While authorities differ, around 3100 B.C.E. the Theban Narmer or Menes mobilized a military force and marched or sailed north to conquer and unify his country. By all conventions he probably descended the Nile River by boat. Nevertheless, from then on, marching or movement of groups became a principal means of a military machine that was active not simply in unifying but also in pacifying, consolidating, maintaining and defending the state from internal and external enemies. We see this in the efforts to create and sustain the Middle Kingdom by Thebans, after the travails of the First Intermediate Period following the Old Kingdom collapse.

c. Imperial Egypt marched to conquer

In response to Hyksos invaders who marched into Egypt, conquered, spread destruction and instability, then founded the 15th and 16th Dynasties. The 17th Theban Dynasty, according to Flinders Petrie in "Egyptian Religion," in Hasting's *Encyclopedia of Religion and Ethics*, "coming from Nubia held Thebes as its capital," then mobilized its military apparatus to deal with this foreign impudence. As these Thebans marched forward down the Nile conquering, incorporating and driving the invaders further northward, they finally expelled the despoilers.

The 18th Dynasty was an extension of the 17th Dynasty and they continued to march to an imperial tune. Not only did Kamose and Ahmose then Thutmose I expel then pursue the invaders, but Thutmose III marched into South-western Asia for 18 annual campaigns pursuing imperial exploits. The famed **Battle of Megiddo** was the first and most

BLACK HISTORY EVERYDAY
PART TWO

memorable of his military marches. In these campaigns he established Egyptian suzerainty over an enormous area of South-west Asia. Subsequently, the threat of the Egyptian army on the "March" was sufficient to quell ambitions, aspirations of vassal rulers of that region even lands to the south of Egypt.

Nevertheless, aspirants of rebellious intent are ever present and opportunistic and, thus, the script had to be re-written by Amenhotep III, Horemhab, Rameses I, Seti I and with grater fanfare by Rameses II at the **Battle of Kadesh**, during the 19th Dynasty. The same challenges faced Ramesses III of the 20th Dynasty as he recounted on the walls of his Mortuary Temple at Medinet Habu his "marches" to contend with the "Invaders from the sea."

From the 20th Dynasty into the 24th Dynasty internecine fighting among aspirants to the throne of Egypt, forced Piankhi the Ethiopian, in the tradition of the "ancestors" to march northward, set things straight and found the 25th Dynasty. With all the attendant challenges, this dynasty ruled Egypt for a century and was followed by one more, the 26th, the last native Dynasty. After this, Egyptian power and control collapsed and it was almost 25 centuries later before native Egyptians would rule their country again. In the meantime, all manner of armies marched into Egypt wreaking destruction, sometimes building and repairing and finally settling down as conquerors. The Assyrians, the Persians, Greeks, Romans, Christians, and finally Arabs all marched into Egypt and left evidence of their being there. Therefore, in this period, only foreign rulers marched in and on behalf of Egypt.

d. Inner Africa to the Rescue

Many an argument has been made that as the invaders began to attack Egypt after the 25th Dynasty retreat to Ethiopia, the fundamentals of the culture "marched back up the Nile" and sought refuge in inner Africa. After all, the "bosom of Mother Africa" is what gave birth to the Nile Valley cultural flowering experience of which Egypt and Ethiopia were her two most prominent children in the ancient world. After ruling the entire Nile Valley, from the headwaters to the Mediterranean, the Ethiopians retreated or were forced to retreat to their capital at Napata. They returned with much Egyptian culture and professional administrators, who were gainfully employed at Napata. Within two centuries of this move, the Ethiopians relocated their capital from Napata to Meroe and ushered in a new lifestyle with the exploitation of iron as evidence from the "slagheaps of Meroe." With this new and more durable military weapon, agricultural implement and domestic instrument, many scholars believe the Ethiopian marched across the Sudan to settle in West Africa. Significantly, there are oral traditions and cultural technology to support this contention.

Nevertheless, as the ingenuity of human aspirations would dictate, the Medieval West African Empires of

BLACK HISTORY EVERYDAY
PART TWO

Ghana, Mali and Songhay emerged and provided civilizational stability in the age of Middle African history. The hall marks of their success were the availability of gold, effective administration and security of an extensive trade pattern that brought merchants from great distances, wherein sound government administration of justice and bureaucracy predominated, agricultural exploitation of the Niger River Valley as a source of water through irrigation, an extensive and well-worked fishing industry, a commercial route that brought success to vendors and merchants from neighboring locations. Even more important, a large army marched throughout the Western Sudanic savanna region to maintain security and stability for government to function protect the trans-Saharan trade and enforcing the law as the various kings tried to effectuate them with reforms and policies in the peoples' best interest.

Black History Everyday - Part Two Photo. We Shall Not be Moved March. Faces in the Crowd.

FREDERICK MONDERSON

III.　West African Experiences

Marching through the western Sudan, the armies of Ghana, Mali and Songhay were able to preserve the integrity of the state and the lucrative Trans-Saharan trade. By providing security for, first the "silent trade" and then the Trans-Saharan Trade at International, National and Local levels of markets, the governments and nationals of these states prospered. Technology, arts and crafts, agriculture and literacy flourished. Islam made great inroads, first by destroying Ghana, and helping Mali then destroying Songhay. Nevertheless, Islamic scholars helped in adding to the architectural landscape, aiding in government administration and they also wrote extensively on the history and culture of the region.

Fortunately, the literary tradition they found and intermingled with has enabled modern research to unearth a wealth of Sudanic science and intellectual activity. The work of Islamic travelers, merchants and scholars recorded a rich cultural history of the Western Sudan. We now know the administration of justice was foremost. Intellectual activity flourished at Djenne and Timbuktu Universities where African scholars lectured to foreign and local students. The also wrote historical, scientific and philosophic treatises. Much of this has survived.

BLACK HISTORY EVERYDAY
PART TWO

The "book trade" as part of Sudanic commerce was especially important. Scholars and wealthy families prided themselves in possessing extensive libraries of local and imported manuscripts. The famous scholar Ahmed Baba possessed a library of 5,000 volumes which was extremely extensive for this early time as a personal possession. The periodicals **Tarik al-Fattah** and **Tarik al-Sudan** contained rich extracts of the history, culture, mores and folklores of the peoples, activities, states and monarchs.

When, around 1591, Al Mansour of Morocco, marched across the Sahara with an army equipped with firearms and attacked Songhay, much as his predecessors, the Almoravids did to Ghana c. 1076, the death knell was sounded for the last of the Western Sudanic Empires. Agriculture was disrupted as farmers were diverted to fight the invaders. The Trans-Saharan trade was interrupted, the revenue foundations it provided for government and military administration was lost and thereby destroyed the work of the state. Learning, literacy and intellectual activity was stamped out. Many scholars were exiled to Morocco. Some libraries were destroyed. Ahmed Baba's library was made to accompany him as a captive prize. Any good Islam may have done in West Africa was overshadowed by the vile actions of Al Mansour and his marauders.

FREDERICK MONDERSON

Black History Everyday - Part Two Photo. Faces and signs in the crowd for the 50th Anniversary March on Washington.

Black History Everyday - Part Two Photo. Faces and signs in the crowd for the 50th Anniversary March on Washington.

BLACK HISTORY EVERYDAY PART TWO

Thus, with the Western Sudanic Armies defeated and crushed by the superior firearms of the invaders, their governments destroyed, agriculture halted the Trans-Saharan "Golden Trade of the Moors" dried-up, intellectual activity no longer encouraged and so, the "Golden age" of West Africa came to an end. All economic activity shifted to the West African coast where a new enterprise was beginning with the arrival of European merchants. Alas, a new and horrific chapter in the march of African people was about to be written.

A. Slavers marched their captives to the sea

As the extensive and lucrative nature of New World possessions became more manifest, a new frontier for forced labor was opened. Apparently, the missionary Bishop Bartholomew de Las Casas came to the New World in wake of the Conquistadors destruction of the native population. Seeing the death, devastation and despair, he appealed to the Pope in Rome to act to save the Native Americans; yet he was mindful of the need for laborers to transform the rich and lucrative tracts of land now given to the conquerors. Thus, the cry became "Let's bring in the Africans who were non-Christian, unfamiliar with the local terrain, and could not blend in, were great agricultural workers and could work for long hours in the hot sun." In response to Bartholomew de Las Casas' request the Pope did issue an edict authorizing the transportation of Africans to provide the needed labor for the Haciendas and plantation system then developing in the Americas.

Black History Everyday - Part Two Photo. Lining-up to get a seat at Sharpton's "Power and Policy Forum on Dr. King's holiday, 2020.

Thereafter, from as early as 1441, then 1503 to 1888 the great nations of Europe and even America, once the coastal areas were depopulated to fill Slave Trade needs, ventured inland and marched captured Africans to the coast. Taken across the Atlantic and disposed to do plantations work, they build new societies for their captors in the Americas without pay, and under the most brutally horrible and inhuman conditions.

BLACK HISTORY EVERYDAY
PART TWO

While each nation, viz., England, France, Spain, the Netherlands, Germany (Brandenburg), Portugal, America, et al., were involved at different levels and duration, every-body benefited from Slave Trade and Slavery. That is, all but the Africans! And so, for centuries, African people languished under the yoke of "naked Imperialism" perpetuated by hostile and uncaring practicing Christian nations. With the new reality came justificatory denial of the Africans' humanity and even the right to learn and be educated. Through Judicial fiat the African was reduced to the sub-human level of chattel. When his humanity was finally recognized and the right to learning finally acquired, it was a mis-education that narrated him out of the order and process of human achievement under the false notion that God and cultural and scientific achievements were European or of European making and extraction. The African was taught the falsity, "Africa and Africans were outside the realms of history." The mindset that fabricated racist human inequality argued, "God is white. He made man in his own image who is white. This White Man is thus superior in the natural order and therefore is so in the social. The African who is Black is inferior in the natural order and thus must be inferior in the social order." However, having denied the African humanity before his own conscious awakening, European man was only concerned with profit, privilege and power and the African humanity be damned. Out of ignorance or malice, these people ignore the fact, the first gods were black!

FREDERICK MONDERSON

History is replete with anomalies and the one apropos to the Americas occurred in 1492. Following the awakening of Europe from the "Dark Ages," "Renaissance" and "Reformation," two Atlantic states, Portugal and Spain emerged as the first two sea-faring nations. As such, they came to spearhead Atlantic travel for adventure and commercial gain.

In fact, the Portuguese had been gradually encroaching along the West African coast from around 1440 A.D. or C.E. In 1441, Portuguese sea-farers captured a parcel of West Africans and took them to Lisbon, Portugal. And, thus began the European Slave Trade in Africans or the Atlantic Slave Trade; thievery misnomered trade; often falsely called the **African Slave Trade**. It is interesting how use of words can create images and ideas in the minds of people that one group wishes to portray to dominate another group.

Nevertheless, following Columbus' discovery in 1492, Rome divided "the world" between Portugal and Spain in the **Treaty of Tordesillas** of that year. Portugal got all of Africa, and to the east, while Spain received everything "overseas," that is, all of the "New World." Portugal protested this, and as a good Christian nation, and "Defender of the faith," the division was corrected by moving the **Line of Demarcation 300 Leagues to the West**. As a result, Portugal received a foothold on the South American mainland, Brazil, while Spain retained the

BLACK HISTORY EVERYDAY PART TWO

rest. In this arrangement, later enshrined in the **Hacienda Treaty** of 1714 at the **Treaty of Utrecht**, Spain was prohibited form capturing Africans in Africa and "marching" them across the seas. This activity, a heinous crime in itself with religious Christian sanction was committed not simply against Africans but humanity in general.

No less significant, as the Slave Trade got underway millions of souls were lost to Africa. With today's hindsight and in view of Western, European and American "dis-information" techniques we cannot trust conservative figures even from the best-intentioned writers, that Africa lost 15 million people in the Atlantic Salve Trade. After all, these are the writers of the same hue that subscribe to the farcical claim "Africa is not a part of world history;" "There is no history of Africa, only a history of Europeans in Africa;" "the Ancient Egyptians were Europeans;" "The Nilotic monuments demonstrate Negroes (Africans) were nothing but slaves in Egypt from time immemorial," and so on.

The disparity in recording is gross. The quintessential African-American scholar W.E.B. DuBois was pretty accurate in his comprehensive researches and analyses that show, "Africa lost 100 million" men, women and children in the horrific "crime against the human spirit." DuBois listed all the nations involved in rape, murder, cheating, kidnappings, unethical behaviors, etc., misnomered "Trade" where no equal

FREDERICK MONDERSON

exchanges were practiced. He listed the duration of the trade; ships named and not named; lists of enslaved persons exported, persons killed in resisting their captors; the numbers who died and littered the pathways in marches to the coast; those who died in coastal holding centers of castles awaiting overseas shipment; and the dying and dead thrown overboard, all in a more accurate accounting. One could also take into consideration the possibility since we're dealing with unethical people, the existence of two sets of books, under-counting, ghost ships, people dying in the holding centers, and the private African dealers tricked once aboard to sell their captives and who were perhaps never counted. Hence, we arrive at figures grossly devoid of undercounted.

Black History Everyday - Part Two Photo. Faces and signs in the crowd for the 50th Anniversary March on Washington.

BLACK HISTORY EVERYDAY
PART TWO

Black History Everyday – Part Two Photo. Sharpton and Crump's March on Liberty Square, Washington, DC. People!

Black History Everyday - Part Two Photo. Faces and signs in the crowd for the 50th Anniversary March on Washington.

With the counting over, the Africans were forced from their native land, and were "marched" across the Atlantic in ships as they faced the tempestuous nature of the seas, the vicissitudes of coffin-like

FREDERICK MONDERSON

confinement, bad food, poor medical treatment, improper disposal facilities, putrid air, cruelty of the seamen, all having a devastating psychological impact on the African physical, spiritual and psychic persona. The was part of the "Middle Passage" where the African spirit and humanity was debased, dislocated, de-centered, disconnected and left in disrepair.

Softened-up in the Trans-Atlantic voyage, upon arrival, as Bob Marley says "fighting for survival," "fighting on arrival," they were paraded, oftentimes naked, before lecherous, yet "Good natured" persons who "examined" them "publicly" before purchase. This further completed the psychological emasculation that, coupled with legal sanction, the "Negro" was now reduced to "a beast." We must carefully evaluate the mindsets of the innumerable "Engineers" who perpetuated this early physical and emotional psychological form of "genetic engineering." So much so, the millions of years of physical evolution was now completely reversed and there stood the African, naked on the shores of America, defenseless, debased, property of men without compassion in a newly transformed Christian land. After this, he was marched off to till and transform the plantation lands, fearful of the overseer's whip, cruelty of the master and fear and intimidation of the oftentimes, self-appointed, policeman and slave catchers. All working "to make them stand in fear."

BLACK HISTORY EVERYDAY
PART TWO

Black History Everyday - Part Two Photo. We Shall Not be Moved March. Faces in the Crowd.

Now here's the African, captured, marched to the sea, transported through the "door of no return," exposed to the natural and unnatural cruelty of the Atlantic voyage, dispersed in America, victimized through legal sanction, families torn apart, separated, the marched off to the fields; thus, the African now faced his future reality of hopelessness. Captured, he was transported from his natural surroundings, stripped of his name, his culture, his history, his manhood; the African now began his long march of survival in a long-lasting and brutal institution of slavery. then human and later civil and social as well as educational rights. Only the Lord knows how he made it through. Perhaps it was the resilience of the indomitable African spirit in collaboration of the watchful eye and metaphysical and spiritual help of the ancestors who would not allow them to succumb and strengthened their spines to withstand the unspeakable cruelty.

It would be sometime before some would consider the malady as events and time took their toll over the centuries and the Slave Trade was finally outlawed, first by the Britain in 1807, and then America in 1808. Yet, the "Internal Slave Trade" unfolded in this country. From the depths of the South, viz., Mississippi, Alabama, Tennessee, Georgia, slave farms were raised and Black men and women were "grown" and consigned to unimaginable depths of despair to procreate and enhance the wealth of the white masters measured in the number of enslaved Africans one owned. Terence Stampp in the *Peculiar Institution* called it, "to make them stand in fear!" In this disgusting dynamic, slave coffles could be seen shackled, marching to market, not to purchase but to be sold! Interesting, and grossly contradictory, while "White slavery" was illegal, "Black slavery" was legal!

In the long march forward, generations after generation, after generation, after generation, the whip, the sub-human living conditions withered the urge to run away, more often than not falling victim to slave catchers, "putting on ole Massa," and finally being in spirit with **Crispus Attucks**, the first authentic American hero, as he marched into martyrdom to free a nation that refused to recognize his right to freedom, even his humanity. Then a line

BLACK HISTORY EVERYDAY
PART TWO

in the **Declaration of Independence** offered a glimmer of hope before it was "white out" to be replaced by the more "generous" offer of a **Three-Fifth Compromise**. Still we marched in the Revolutionary War, Salem P and company, to support the **Articles of Confederation**, and, victorious, the **Constitution of the United States**. There being no change, the African again marched and fought in the **War of 1812** and were at the **Battle of New Orleans** in 1815. There is record of at least one Black Marine buried in the segregated Brooklyn Navy Yard as early as 1801.

A stubborn lot, Blacks were; for, while some of them ran away to Florida and were sheltered by the natives, the rest kept marching and fighting right through Andrew Jackson 1818 incursions to punish the Seminoles for their acts of mercy! But alas, Gabriel Prosser (1900) and Denmark Vesey (1822) said "**Let's fight for us**!" David Walker said, wait a minute, let's "**Appeal**" this thing, while Nat Turner equally affirmed, as Patrick Henry did, "**Give me liberty or give me death**" as he dispatched many before his time. Sure, Patrick Henry coined the phrase in the halls of American liberty. He, however, was already free but did not die, while Nat Turner was never free and died, paying the ultimate price. Still, Blacks continued to march and die for American liberty, equality and justice, refreshing the "**Tree of**

FREDERICK MONDERSON

Liberty" with the very essence and finality of their being.

The "**Runaway Slave**" Samuel Carson marched and died in the Mexican war of 1844. Some believe it was all in vain for nearly a dozen years later, Chief Justice Taney clarified things in the **Dred Scott Decision of 1857** which declared "Slaves were not citizens and could not bring suit in American courts." Even further, the good Chief Justice added, "A black man has no right which a white man was bound to respect!" Some believe, 150 years later, this belief is unchanged! Still, Black marched in the "War Between the States" or **Civil War**, and were victimized by both sides. Yet, the North was more amenable, more liberal, and more supportive.

The **Radical Republicans** articulated an agenda that effectuated the 13th, 14th and 15th Amendments, **Civil Rights Acts**, **Land Grants to Black Colleges** but fell short on the 40 acres and a mule promise of Abraham Lincoln. Still, these legislative gains became effete in face of the Ku Klux Klan (KKK), Knights of the White Camelia, White Citizen's Council activities of lynchings, intimidation, the conundrums of share-cropping, Jim Crow and implication of *Plessy V. Ferguson* (1896) falsity of "separate but equal" which was really "separate and unequal." Hence, the Supreme Court had to overturn this long-standing judicial ruling in *Brown v. Board of Education of*

BLACK HISTORY EVERYDAY PART TWO

Topeka, Kansas some 58 years later in 1954. Even then it was a struggle to gen *Brown* implemented.

Despite the hourly challenges, daily battles and yearly wars for self-preservation, human-dignity, survival, while some Black marched to escape the South, some marched-up San Juan Hill to save Teddy Roosevelt in the Spanish-American War, but got no credit. In wake of the "Tar and featherings," the lynchings, rampant racial discrimination, Booker T. Washington founded Tuskegee Institute in 1881, with its wonderful legacy of Black self-help and self-advancement. Marcus Garvey founded the **Universal Negro Improvement Association** (**UNIA**, 1917) that enjoyed tremendous successes in the late teens and early 1920s. Other leaders formed the **National Association for the Advancement of Colored People** (**NAACP**, 1909) and the **National Urban League** (1910).

Despite the social and other forms of humanitarian need for the work of these organizations, Blacks were recruited and marched overseas to fight and "**Save the World for Democracy**" they never experienced at home! W.E.B. DuBois, through the Crisis newspaper did remind all, "**We went abroad fighting and we return home fighting**." This simple yet profound statement

FREDERICK MONDERSON

sends a powerful message to purveyors of race wars, millions of Black Veterans are trained and will resist, especially under the banner of "**Mighty Michelle Brigades!**"

To reiterate, back then at the start of World War I, when the implications of African colonization, resulting imperialism, militarism, nationalism and murder of Arch-Duke Ferdinand in Sarajevo that created World War I, Black-Americans were marched overseas "To save the world for Democracy." Later, as DuBois put it, "We left fighting, we fought and now we return fighting" to challenge "Jim Crow" and all forms of odious American practices. Meanwhile, Marcus Garvey marched through Harlem in majestic splendor as he rallied the faithful and proud Africans worldwide under the **Universal Negro Improvement Association** banner and the Red, Black and Green flag.

BLACK HISTORY EVERYDAY
PART TWO

Black History Everyday - Part Two Photo. We Shall Not be Moved March. Faces in the Crowd.

b. European incursions marched Africans as beasts of burden

Eric Williams in his book *Capitalism and Slavery* (1944) argued, "The abolition of the slave Trade and ultimately Slavery was an economic necessity rather than a humanitarian venture." To support his view, he chronicled the lucrative gains from the Slave Trade accrued to Britain, one of the principals in the forced removal of Africans to support plantation agriculture and derivative industries in the New World products developed in their home country.

FREDERICK MONDERSON

Black History Everyday - Part Two Photo. Faces and signs in the crowd for the 50th Anniversary March on Washington.

Black History Everyday - Part Two Photo. Faces and signs in the crowd for the 50th Anniversary March on Washington.

Williams argued the "Triangular Trade" transformed Britain and equally Europe economically, technologically, militarily, commercially, politically, socially and even intellectually. He showed how

BLACK HISTORY EVERYDAY
PART TWO

banking, insurance, textile industry, boat-building and ancillary trades, expansion of Wharfage, excise taxes, metal works, sugar refineries and distillation and a whole lot more gained immensely from the Slave Trade. Seaport facilities and towns such as Liverpool, Bristol and London expanded tremendously as merchants built grand and extensive mansions from profits of the trade.

Nevertheless, despite naysayers, abolitionists Clarkson, Granville Sharpe, Wilberforce, Buxton, Et. al., waged their humanitarian campaign as a "friends of the enslaved African." Clarkson especially noted the trade was taking a toll on British seamen whose mortality rate was also high. Many of these same seamen were shanghaied into slave trade service. When one considers how the seamen were treated, then consider what happened to the cargo. Sadly, however, the seamen, impressed into Slave trade service, had no compassion on their less fortunate "brethren."

Some defenders of the trade argued and petitioned Parliament regarding the indispensable nature of the economic aspects of the trade on their lives. They also agreed the trade was a "Nursery" for British seamen to be ready for war at sea. Clarkson, however, was able to show investigative Committees of Parliament, many seamen aboard the Slavers were shanghaied and forcefully recruited, them punished for runaway or jumping ships or refusing to serve. When Parliament finally saw fit to outlaw the Slave

FREDERICK MONDERSON

Trade in 1807, she deployed a squadron of the Royal Navy to Sierra Leone colony in West Africa with the specific mission of patrolling the waters off the West African Coast. There they then set out to board Slavers, rescue enslaved cargoes and repatriate them to the West African colony. Unfortunately, when a Slaving vessel spotted a naval vessel in the distance, they would march their slaves on deck and then toss them overboard. By the time the Navy got there, they could boast: "See, we have no slaves."

The lucky ones were rescued. They were resettled in Sierra Leone, the abolitionist colony, established in 1787 after the **1772 Somerset Case** ruling by Chief Justice Mansfield that held "English soil is too sacred to allow slavery." Thereafter, all English enslaved Africans in England were rounded up, along with a few undesirable white females and marched off to Sierra Leone. Therefore, the four elements of the Sierra Leone population consisted of English freed slaves, enslaved person rescued on the high seas, the native population and the Blacks who served with the British in the losing Revolutionary War effort against America. These were first marched to Canada at war's end and later repatriated to create the most diverse population in West Africa. It also raises another question as to why the British did not want them in Canada as sparsely populated that area was at the time.

Meanwhile as these efforts unfolded, a new onslaught faced Africa. Gone were the days of "Naked

BLACK HISTORY EVERYDAY PART TWO

Imperialism." The new strategy became "Enlightened Imperialism." That is, we'll help the Africans, at a price! Thereafter the continent began to be opened by explorers, adventurers, settlers, merchants, and missionaries, among others.

Black History Everyday - Part Two Photo. We Shall Not be Moved March. Faces in the Crowd.

The Boers in South Africa since 1652 began to march inland after the British secured the Cape of Good Hope in 1814. By the mid-1820s, Shaka the Zulu Chieftain had begun his march to build a Zulu nation. Untouched by western military strategy, he was able to innovate a number of techniques including the Assegai, a short stabbing sword that required his soldiers to engage in close combat. He pioneered a standing army in Africa, created barracks to house them and also innovated age-grade regiments rather than encourage tribal loyalties. His expansion threatened the Boers' inland trek, so they conspired with his brother, Mpande, to literally stab or spear Shaka in the back in 1828. They promised him the kingship of the Zulu nation if he was successful. Within 8 years, by 1836, the Boers successfully captured the Zulu land and tamed the Zulu spirit.

In North Africa, Mohammed Ali, a Turkish general, sought to separate Egypt from the Turkish Empire, and consolidate his power there. He, however, had to deal with the Mamelukes, the traditional rulers of Egypt, under the suzerainty of the Turkish Sultan. Once assigned to Egypt, after a successful year of agriculture, he sponsored a state banquet and invited the Who's Who in Mameluke Society.

The Protocol was no weapons were permitted in the main banquet hall. As events unfolded, and everyone was lavishly well-fed and drunk, Mohammed Ali moved his assassins in who slaughtered the Mamelukes and he now established complete control of Egypt. The first thing Mohammed Ali did upon seizing control was to promote the native Egyptians to the highest echelons of the military. Next he gave them a role in their government. He made land reforms. Bright young people were sent abroad to western educational institutions to study medicine, science, technology, business in is effort to transform his nation. Much of this he was able to do, including

BLACK HISTORY EVERYDAY
PART TWO

establishing a hereditary dynasty to follow him, without borrowing money from western nations.

In East Africa, the Ethiopian dynastic line traceable back to the union between Solomon and the Queen of Sheba, Ra Mangasha, Johannes IV, Menelik and lastly Haile Selassie maintained all efforts to keep their nation free of colonialism at the end of the 19th and into the 20th Century.

A special detour needs be added here because of continuing historical distortion of a recurring theme. Dr. ben-Jochannan commented on this in his works.

A.E.P. Weigall, an English Egyptologist, wrote colorfully about Egypt after the discovery of Tutankhamon's tomb in 1922 and had great influence in Europe and America. In his book *Flights into Antiquity* (1920) he had presented a photograph of the **Queen of Sheba** which shows her as white, a European by all standards. Back in 1999, this writer commented on an article produced in *The Weekly World*. It featured an article entitled "Scientist discovers the home of the Queen of Sheba." The story goes on to say: "British archaeologists have discovered the home of the Queen of Sheba, located in the Southern Nigerian forest region." Again, the photograph presented is that of a white woman! The question is: "What does this tell us?" A number of truths are evident to the erudite and critical scholar.

FREDERICK MONDERSON

First, for eons the Queen of Sheba was thought to be Ethiopian. Ethiopian "holy men" today claim they possess the **Ark of the Covenant** in Ethiopia and that it was brought back by the Queen of Sheba after her visit to King Solomon. Are we to believe the Ethiopian kingdom extended from West Africa across the entire continent from West to East? Lines of communication must have been very clear and open for her to hear about Solomon in Israel, then decide to visit him. Therefore, she had to March across the continent, then march up to Israel to visit the King. On the way back, why then did she leave the **Ark of Covenant** in Ethiopia and schlep back to Southern Nigeria. Equally, Nigeria 1,000 years before Christ, the seat of a kingdom, must have certainly been a robust economic and social entity. This was at a time when even Greece was in its egg.

Second, what is a white woman doing ruling a kingdom in the heart of Africa? This smells of the Edgar Rice Burroughs creations of "Tarzan" and the like of the "Phantom," mythical Englishmen with extraordinary powers to outwit Africans that Hollywood carried to the most absurd lengths.

BLACK HISTORY EVERYDAY
PART TWO

Black History Everyday - Part Two Photo. Faces and signs in the crowd for the 50th Anniversary March on Washington.

Third, we know she was not white because Sheba has been quoted as saying: "I am black, but comely." In fact, what she actually said was: "I am black and comely." The Queen was not apologizing for her blackness, but praising it. After all, she ruled over a kingdom of Black men and women. Are we to imply that all those people, in a powerful kingdom in Africa, before Greece and Rome, certainly Western Europe, were ashamed of their Blackness when according to their belief system, their god created them in his own likeness?

FREDERICK MONDERSON

We know she was a beauty. We also know Solomon had many wives but she upset the applecart. Perhaps she brought out the best in him. This legendary wise man for that one time was a hit. We hear no more about the wives of Solomon, only about the Black Beauty from Ethiopia. Ivan Van Sertima has argued, rightly so, the Queen of Sheba's Kingdom was vastly greater than Solomon and his interest was beyond her beauty but considerations of political and economic alliances. Now imagine this big woman apologizing to a little man! So, he won a "piece," underscoring the power of the African woman and woman in general for their ability to intrigue the male, and send him a message in so many ways.

Black History Everyday - Part Two Photo. We Shall Not be Moved March. Faces in the Crowd.

Four, we know the Ethiopians are Black; still, writers continue trying "to wash this Ethiopian white." The

BLACK HISTORY EVERYDAY
PART TWO

stereotype of the Queen saying "I'm black but comely" is constantly trotted or marched out when dubious scholarship is presented or a racial type is reinforced. The Queen said, "I am black and comely."

Elsewhere in West Africa, the Nok Culture was sophisticated well before the Christian era. So much was going on throughout the continent, to quote Teshlone Keto: "Hegel should have said he did not know African history.'

Just prior to Mohammed Ali's rise to power, in the aftermath of the French Revolution and subsequent War in Europe, the British Admiral Lord Nelson pursued Napoleon to Egypt and fought the "Battle the Nile," which in fact, was not fought on the Nile. Nevertheless, in Napoleon's sojourn in Egypt, besides his military, he took linguists, artists, architects, and other scientists or savants. They made systematic studies of all the existing temples and published a monumental work, now a classic, *The Description of Egypt*. Officers in Napoleon's artillery regiment discovered, at a place called Rosetta, a tri-lingual inscribed stone, later called the Rosetta stone. Within just over two decades linguists led by Champollion deciphered the hieroglyphic script, laying the foundation for the later discipline of Egyptology. It should be pointed out, later in the 19th Century, Flinders Petrie, the English archaeologist and Egyptologist described the discipline of Egyptology as knowledge of its history, geography and linguistics or language.

FREDERICK MONDERSON

By mid-19th century, all manner of people began converging on Africa from the north, south, east and west. While in the north interest in Egyptian antiquities attracted many types, who created what Brian Fagan later described as **The Rape of the Nile**, in West Africa it was March for Timbuctoo and to discover the source of the Niger. What is significant, however, all over, missionaries, merchants, explorers, adventurers, scientists, agriculturalists, imperialists, colonialists, butterfly-enthusiasts, writers, settlers, all Europeans, all converged on Africa. All made Africans march as beasts of burden to tote their possessions, materials and comfort while in the heart of Africa. Those who lived or worked in Africa, generally regarded the natives as unequal or inferior in their own land. The Boers of South Africa are typical but not the only ones with this mindset.

c. Leopold of the Belgium marched and decimated millions for balata and rubber in the Congo.

As the various interests converged, explored and made discoveries in Africa, they created what later became "spheres of influence" for their governments. In this undertaking, merchants devised trade patterns and markets; missionaries sought to replace the Slave Trade with agricultural produce; scientists; botanists, mineralogists, agriculturalists, all did scientific explorations to determine Africa's economic

BLACK HISTORY EVERYDAY
PART TWO

potential. Through a number of strategies Africans were dragged into the now expanding global cash and money markets and economy.

As the **Industrial Revolution** unfolded in Europe, Africa's economic potential in developing world commerce made her an important prize. The "spheres of interests" gradually merged into *de facto* pre-colonial holdings. Notwithstanding, conflict began to develop between European nationals over, what belonged to whom. As a result, the German Chancellor Bismarck called the **Berlin Congress** from 1884-1885, to, in effect, **Partition Africa on Paper**, along the general lines established in the "Spheres of Interest" configuration. By the end of the Congress, Africa was partitioned between basically the same slave trading nations. The problem arose when these nations sought to implement **Partition on Land**, for the Africans were willing, ready and able to fight.

Not trade but murder, kidnapping, rape, robbery, and injustice, organized and sustained systematic mayhem against a people for the duration of centuries. Na'im Akbar refused to equate the Holocaust with the Slave Trade. He argued, "Persons lived through the Holocaust but no one lived through the institutions of Slave Trade and Slavery." The beginnings of colonialism through implementation of partition were in many ways similar to the experiences of the Slave Trade. Naturally, after the

FREDERICK MONDERSON

Berlin Congress, the European powers had to convince the Africans that they, Europeans owned African lands, and much of this was done through the barrel of a gun.

Easily, the best person who could explain this conundrum would be Dick Gregory. He would probably put it over this way.

Imagine "me and my old lady" sitting on the sofa watching Television in our living room. A stranger walks up, opens the door, sits on the couch and nudges us to move over. Next he takes the remote and changes the channel. When I say "What the heck you're doing" he says, "I'm the new owner. Yes! We met last year and I took possession of your property." All I could say is, "You're kidding, right? "No, I'm not," he replied.

Imagine, Salve Trade and Slavery, "Naked Imperialism," expropriation of land, wars of pacification, colonialism, "Enlightened Imperialism," the travails and dynamics of direct and indirect rule. These are the seed germs that breed racism, discrimination, unequal treatment Africans worldwide are today victims of perpetuated centuries of physical and psychological abuse.

While the French got big chunks of Africa in North, West, and Central regions of the continent, Britain received equally large shares in West, South, Central, East and North Africa. The Portuguese got Angola,

BLACK HISTORY EVERYDAY PART TWO

Mozambique and Guinea-Bissau; Germany got South-West Africa (Namibia), Cameroons, Togo and Tanganyika (Tanzania and Zanzibar); Italy got Libya and Somalia; Belgium, the Congo; etc. The best example of colonial exploitation occurred in the Congo under King Leopold's administration. Belgian hunger for rubber exemplified the problem of African raw resources as a principal cause of World War I.

Black History Everyday - Part Two Photo. **We Shall Not be Moved March.** Faces in the Crowd.

d. Africans Marched to Protest Colonization in Africa

The principal causes of World War I include nationalism, militarism, Imperialism as part of the **"Scramble"** for Africa to secure raw materials for industry in Europe, and ultimately the murder of the

FREDERICK MONDERSON

Austrian Arch-Duke Ferdinand in Sarajevo. As the war waged, the French Premier Clemenceau sent the French Parliament Deputy Blaise Diagne to French West Africa to recruit more than 100,000 soldiers in their cause. The British did the same in Africa and the Caribbean.

There was a direct relationship between World War I and World War II. The players were essentially the same on the same sides. Africans were again marched into this second conflict. However, the minds of Black Men in the Black World began to change the global perception and mentality of Black Men. Thanks to the work of W.E.B. DuBois and his Pan-African cadre of boldly thinking Africans the world was forced to come to grips with the African will to resist.

Black History Everyday - Part Two Photo. Faces and signs in the crowd for the 50th Anniversary March on Washington.

BLACK HISTORY EVERYDAY
PART TWO

Black History Everyday - Part Two Photo. Faces and signs in the crowd for the 50th Anniversary March on Washington.

The first significant such even occurred when W.E.B. DuBois called for the **First Pan-African Congress** in 1900, a movement that began to pay attention and articulate concerns of African people, particularly those in Africa. His efforts were matched by Booker T. Washington, an early Pan-Africanist who was creating "**The Tuskegee Model**" of self-reliance and independence, while seriously raising concerns about conditions in Africa and America relating to treatment of Black Men and Women and ownership of their land. Another significant event was the emergence of Marcus Garvey and the **Universal Negro Improvement Association** and **African Communities League** which will be discussed later. The next most important such development is Dubois' call for a second, yet again First **Pan-African Congress** in 1919. The major problem this faced was where would the venue be? The British, Americans initially the French and several European Powers balked at the notion of Black men meeting to discuss Black issues on their territory.

The "Father of Pan-Africanism" DuBois played his hole-card, Diagne, the French Deputy who recruited untold numbers of Africans for Clemenceau. Finally, the French Premier relented and told DuBois to go ahead but keep the gathering in a low-key manner. DuBois figured since the world would gather in Paris in 1919 to discuss the terms of the **Versailles Peace Treaty** ending World War I, this was the appropriate venue to raise the issue of African real-estate.

The knowledge gained here and the other Pan-African Congresses between the two wars; the emergence of unionization as a political force in Africa; the experience gained in both wars proving the white man's blood was red not blue; and points of Black intellectual lights shining from various areas particularly those influenced by Marcus Garvey, brought the **Fifth Pan-African Congress** to Manchester where Africans resolved to work and march for independence. The great African minds of the 20th Century were there and resolved they would return home, and march, agitate and advocate

BLACK HISTORY EVERYDAY
PART TWO

unionization, decolonization, self-government and independence. Their successes were evident when, by the 1960's, nearly two dozen African states became independent after Ghana on March 6, 1957.

An interesting conundrum is recounted here. In 1976 as a student at Oxford University, Exeter College, this writer was privy to a discussion wherein an Oxford Don pointedly said: "If in 1900 we (the British) had realized how wealthy Africa truly is, we would have put in place provisions that it would never revert to the Africans." Nevertheless, though much of Africa was granted independence, the European powers put in place what Kwame Nkrumah called Neo-Colonialism where they were still able to wield considerable influence over African economies and the viability of these states.

In the United States I.

Because of the nature of the United States of America, the condition and mentality of the Black man there was different to all other Blacks worldwide. More things happened to the Black man in America than anywhere else where African people were located. There was more brutality meted out to the Black man in America, he fought in more American wars than all others, he had more opportunities than other African peoples and today he wields more influence and economic, academic, political and intellectual power than most people on the globe. However, all the gains he made can be

FREDERICK MONDERSON

compared to a regiment fighting and having to slug it out for every inch of territory gained. Except, notwithstanding, the regiment would one day "Stand down," this has not been so with the Black man in America where he has faced challenges every minute, fought battles every day and wars every year," so to speak.

Black History Everyday - Part Two Photo. We Shall Not be Moved March. Faces in the Crowd.

A. Marcus Garvey marched in the streets of Harlem

The Black phenomenon in America during the first quarter of the 20th Century was Marcus Garvey, the Jamaican born Black man; who founded the UNIA, that at one time boasted a membership of

BLACK HISTORY EVERYDAY
PART TWO

400,000,000 Africans world-wide. Garvey arrived in New York in 1916 to meet Booker T. Washington who died a year earlier. He was impressed with Washington's philosophy of acquiring technical skills to hold industrial jobs and the founding of his school Tuskegee Institute as part of the "Tuskegee Model" of economic self-reliance for independence. However, the death of his idol did not dissuade Garvey and he settled in Harlem. In no time, he established the **UNIA** and **African Communities League** and was holding conventions, rivaling the political movements of the time. His newspaper was called *The Negro World*.

In his *Magnum Opus, The Philosophy and Opinions of Marcus Garvey*, he tells he dismayed at the condition of the Blackman at the start of the 20th Century, so he set about to remedy it. Accordingly, he wrote: "I looked around for our men of big affairs and could find none." So, he created titles to reflect the emerging consciousness of Black upliftment. Garvey styled himself **Provisional President General of Africa**. He created titles as "Duke of the Nile" and "Count of the Congo." Recognizing the impending struggle to free "Mother Africa" from the grips of colonialists and imperialists, he created the regiments of soldiers and the **Black Cross Nurses** as their Combat Medics. He designed all uniforms. He founded the **Black Star Line** to conduct trade within the Black World. Then in 1922

FREDERICK MONDERSON

he created the **Red, Black and Green** flag which is represented as the blood of the Black Man to free the green land of "mother Africa."

After this Garvey held his conventions with magnificent parades displaying the most splendid colors, uniformity, discipline, all in a respectable and orderly manner that reflected the dignity of the Black man. Considering where he had come from; from the depths of despair in the horribly inhuman institution of Slavery, Garvey had Black men and women flying high without touching a drop of anything. Perhaps that mood is comparable to the feeling felt by the millions of Black men and women who descended on Washington, DC, October 16, 1995, which will be discussed later.

Garvey's people marched with pride and dignity in great expectation of the future upliftment of the race. Little did he or they realize success breeds contempt and ill-will. Perhaps they did. The "powers that be" were threatened! A printer by trade, he published his own newspaper, *The Negro World*. In addition, his speeches and writing cover the full gambit of human relations. As such, he was teacher, preacher, philosopher, leader, businessman, organizer and much more. Since Garvey claimed to represent more than 400,000,000 Black men and women, he was "the most dangerous man in America." There is no question Garvey made mistakes but these were miniscule compared to his good intentions and the pride he instilled and still instills and inspires. A full-

BLACK HISTORY EVERYDAY
PART TWO

blooded Jamaican Black, he distrusted mulattos based on experiences in his native Jamaica. He never understood color within the context of American history, culture and social process. This was one of his mistakes.

That distrust caused him to be at odds with W.E.B. DuBois, an ardent advocate for Black progress. Garvey's enemies exploited this distrust and plotted with other coloreds to bring him down, accusing Garvey of fraud. The **Black Star Line** was a great idea with many flaws. It was a great alligator that gnawed at the economic viability of the organization Garvey administered. Another of Garvey's faults is he trusted without verifying, and the captain of the **Black Star Line** bilked him. However, because of what the line meant in terms of potential trade and Black prestige, he poured in more and more funds to keep it afloat. This contributed to charges of fiscal mismanagement. Soon Garvey was arrested, charged with fraud for using the mails to solicit funds, tried, convicted, imprisoned, later pardoned and then deported. There is no question there was a political witch-hunt designed to derail the movement he founded and set in motion.

After Garvey was convicted and being led, handcuffed, to **Atlanta Federal Prison** he made one last prophetic statement that was full of true intent and sweet irony. He said: "You have caged the lion but the cups are running free out there. Look for

FREDERICK MONDERSON

me in the whirlwind." How right he was for the cubs have grown and their cubs have had cubs, never to forget the experiences and intent of Marcus Garvey. Even more important, the pride and significance of the Red, Black and Green is alive and well and enjoys more meaning and significance today, than for quite some time.

Black History Everyday - Part Two Photo. We Shall Not be Moved March. Faces in the Crowd.

All this notwithstanding, Garvey marched us into history with an ardent and fervent activist intent and demeanor that until we are truly free, there's no stopping us. That is why we view August 17, (1887) Garvey's birthday, as a day of national consciousness for truly, ours is **One God, One Aim, One Destiny**.

BLACK HISTORY EVERYDAY PART TWO

b. Blacks marched for jobs in the New Deal and to fight fascism and later communism

Perhaps the tailwind of Garvey's downfall hooked America and the Western World contributing to the calamity of the **Great Depression**. In fact, while World War I damaged Europe, America was unscathed and her industry mobilized to feed the needs of the war. The take off at war's end was rapid and America especially enjoyed unprecedented prosperity especially in material possessions. Houses, cars, intangibles, mostly on credit, fueled a bubble that ultimately collapsed by 1929. The **Federal Reserve System** created in 1913 had not evolved to today's standards of tracking the economy, making adjustments along the way and thus the consequences of the exorbitant and rapid growth of the economy resulted in the catastrophe of stock market crash and the resultant depression.

FREDERICK MONDERSON

Black History Everyday - Part Two Photo. Still another face who "Walked the Walk" at the Equal Justice Initiative Memorial in Montgomery, Alabama.

Black History Everyday - Part Two Photo. Faces and signs in the crowd for the 50th Anniversary March on Washington.

BLACK HISTORY EVERYDAY
PART TWO

Black History Everyday - Part Two Photo. Faces and signs in the crowd for the 50th Anniversary March on Washington.

Well, if white America sneezed and then caught a cold, imagine perhaps a virulent case of the flu struck Black America! Six decades out of slavery, Southern "nullification" of the fundamentals of the 13th, 14th, and 15th Amendments and Reconstruction, physical assault of Charles Sumner on the House floor, through disfranchisement, via poll taxes, literacy tests, land taxes, grandfather clause, Jim Crowism, tenant farming economic peonage, the consequences of *Plessy V. Ferguson's* "Separate but Equal" ruling of the Supreme Court, lynchings, tar and feathers, Ku Klux Klan, Knights of the White Carnelia, White Citizen's Council, riots, discrimination, intimidation, the works, but like Maya Angelou said "**Still I Rise**," the Black experience in America has been one unforgettable experience!

FREDERICK MONDERSON

In retrospect, perhaps it was the motivating pride, dignity and self-respect that the great minds of the early 20th Century in the persons of Booker T. Washington, W.E.B. DuBois and Marcus Garvey that spawned and galvanized the **Harlem Renaissance** is what pulled us through! Then again, perhaps we could also add the experiences gained from our boys being marched off to fight and "save the world for democracy."

Fact is, whether others disagree or not, having served in the military and fought under the colors, Blacks gained insights into fighting for themselves. Claude McKay reminded, in his **If We Must Die** poem we may be "pressed to the wall, dying, but fighting back." Later DuBois would confess Garvey's Program was sound!

All this, notwithstanding, the intellectual consciousness gained from total Black experiences forced them to view political realities differently. While some have argued Lincoln was ambivalent towards Blacks, his part led by **Radical Republicans** championed their cause and thus for six-decades Blacks voted Republican. That is, despite the compromising betrayal that brought Rutherford B. Hayes to the Presidency after Ulysses S. Grant, this ended **Reconstruction** as well as denying Blacks the "40 acres and a mule" that President Lincoln promised which was never delivered. Seriously, considering all that happened

BLACK HISTORY EVERYDAY
PART TWO

from the end of the Civil War to the Depression, yet Blacks still stayed loyal to a Republican Party that no longer championed their interests.

While Teddy Roosevelt's **Fair Deal** argued in 1910: "When I say I believe in a fair deal, I don't mean give every man the best hand, All I mean is ... that there shall be no crookedness in the dealings" perhaps, in his view, Blacks were not in the game or at the **Table**. However, when his counterpart and cousin, Franklin Delano Roosevelt promised in 1932 a **New Deal** with a chicken in every pot, thanks to his wife Eleanor, some consideration was given to Blacks. As such, Blacks then marched in great numbers into the Democratic camp and primarily remained Democrats to this day.

Black History Everyday - Part Two Photo. We Shall Not be Moved March. Faces in the Crowd.

FREDERICK MONDERSON

Yet, for the next two more decades, the march through the American social order was a bit easier, however, still challenging. It is reasonable to argue; Black marching shoes were more firmly fastened at the boot-straps owing to the Democratic F.D.R. Administration being more sympathetic to their concerns. This can be argued as because of the new found and significant constituency in their voting strength. FDR's wife Eleanor made the First Lady position more meaningful. She helped organize a "Kitchen Cabinet" of Blacks.

We must not, however, underestimate the impact of A. Philip Randolph's activism, particularly in insisting on a March on Washington in 1941.

While the **New Deal** addressed the plight of the nation's whites, Blacks received a small share of the largesse. They marched and received some jobs, were able to work and own farms, purchase houses. In the **New Deal** cultural growth arising out of the **Harlem Renaissance**, Black artists painted murals and Black Americans provided the musical beat to which the nation marched, "swing" and danced. As the impending danger of World War II approached, Blacks signed up to serve in the military even though they were restricted to segregated units.

The Pan-Africanist world view made them more acutely aware and sympathetic to the injustice of Italian aggression in Ethiopia. Nevertheless,

BLACK HISTORY EVERYDAY
PART TWO

segregated units did very well in World War II and the Black Activist Sonny Carson has told the story of how his uncle was among one of the first soldiers to liberate one of the Holocaust Death Camps where so many Jews perished. Equally too, the **Tuskegee Airmen** gained fame as aerial aces whether as solo fighters or fighter escorts. They seem to have taken a page from the book of the **Underground Railroad** Conductor Harriet Ross Tubman who boasted "I never lost a passenger."

There were a whole lot more like them. Harry Belafonte the actor and singer has told how, at the end of World War II, he became an activist. We are often told Audie Murphy was the most decorated World War II veteran. This is not so, argued Belafonte. It was a Black veteran like himself. Returning home from service in Europe, in his military uniform, the Black veteran chose to ride the front of the bus in the segregated South in 1945-46. The driver called the cops to remove him. They marched or dragged him off the bus, as he screamed, "I'm a veteran, just home from Europe, fighting to save the world for Democracy." The racist southern cops beat him to death, right there on Main Street, shouting "This is not Europe, this is America." Here then, came of age one of Garvey's "Cubs" who, like his "siblings" spawned their own, echoing an old African philosophical admonition, "Let the circle be unbroken" or more appropriately, "Let the struggle continue" as we march forward.

FREDERICK MONDERSON

From that battlefield emerged the Pre-Civil Rights era that equally began a close identification with Africa and its assertion to challenge colonialism.

F.D.R. is the only President elected more than twice, in fact, four times, owing to World War II. He died in the first year of his fourth term and was succeeded by his Vice-President Harry Truman. Truman did two significant things when coming to the Presidency. The first was his 1948 desegregating the military. Several things led to this realistic development. To the Black combat veteran, the invincibility of the white man was a myth. A straight shot could take him out and many Black veterans were returning home with lots of combat experience. With the emergence of the Soviet Union and its allies pursuing the expansionist philosophy of communism, the struggle came to retain a world-wide state of belligerence. Thus, the American military had to operate within the outward appearance of equality.

BLACK HISTORY EVERYDAY
PART TWO

Black History Everyday - Part Two Photo. Faces and signs in the crowd for the 50th Anniversary March on Washington.

Black History Everyday - Part Two Photo. Faces and signs in the crowd for the 50th Anniversary March on Washington.

The second significant act of President Truman was to issue the **Truman Doctrine** which stated essentially, "We will do anything and go anywhere to combat communism." This policy, therefore, guided and drove the anti-communist challenge for the next

FREDERICK MONDERSON

half century and Blacks had become a permanent and significant component of the military machine that would challenge communism.

Meanwhile, in the aftermath of *Plessy V. Ferguson* (1896) and its "Separate but Equal" philosophy, in reality, "Separate and Unequal," Black legal eagles and their white allies, perennially challenged the legal system being able first to overthrow the **Grandfather Clause** in 1915. For the next 38 years a number of small legal victories emboldened Black legal eagles in preparation for the historic *Brown V. Board of Topeka, Kansas* in 1954. Of significance was Thurgood Marshall's legal victory in *Smith v. Allwright* outlawing the White Primary!

Black History Everyday - Part Two Photo. We Shall Not be Moved March. Faces in the Crowd.

The **1963 March on Washington** in which Dr. Martin Luther King, Jr., issued the now historic "I have a dream" speech recently celebrated its 50th Anniversary in 2013. Many persons of all colors of

BLACK HISTORY EVERYDAY
PART TWO

the American Rainbow were there. Following the coroner's determination that Eric Garner was murdered, Rev. Al Sharpton and Attorney Benjamin Crump led a March on Washington at Freedom/Freedom Square facing the office of the District of Columbia local government office in protest. This followed in wake of the **Million Man March**; the **Million Woman March** in Philadelphia; the **Million Youth March** in both Harlem and Brooklyn; then the **Million Family March** in Washington. Then there was the **Million Mom March** to protest gun violence. The **Million Man March 20th Anniversary** "Justice or Else" has set the stage for Rev. Al Sharpton's Martin Luther King's Weekend protest march (January 14, 2017) on Eve of Donald Trump's Inauguration on January 20, 2017.

FREDERICK MONDERSON

Black History Everyday - Part Two Photo. Hands raised in "Don't shoot, I'm Black" salute at **Sharpton and Crump's March on Washington**.

"And I will do everything that I can as long as I am President of the United States to remind the American people that we are one nation under God, and we may call that God different names but we remain one nation." **Barack Obama**

BLACK HISTORY EVERYDAY
PART TWO

"Acts of sacrifice and decency without regard to what's in it for you create ripple effects. Ones that lift up families and communities that spread opportunity and boost our economy." **Barack Obama**, *Arizona State Commencement Speech*, 2009

15. OBAMA: WORSE PRESIDENT? PHOOEY! BY DR. FRED MONDERSON

In a Quinnipiac University poll, President Obama was named the worse President since World War II! Naturally, skeptics need to query the nature and type of questions asked to arrive at the stated conclusions. Equally, the conscious level of those polled must be taken into consideration. Accordingly, "30% of persons" questioned felt Mr. Obama was the worse President! Apparently, this poll is conducted perennially and the last time it was conducted, in 2006, was two years into President George Walker Bush's second term. At that time, he was voted the worse in this category! Without question, there was "much on his plate." However, many believe what Republicans, especially, are saying about President Obama is what they say about Black people period! Considering his situation, be that as it may, we must remember, ever Mr. Obama must remember, Malcolm X said, "You're not catching hell because you're an American. You're catching hell because you're Black!" After all, Vice-President Biden was right in saying, "They're trying to put you back into slavery!" Fact is; assessing contemporary developments; dye-in-the-wool racists cannot comprehend the magnificence of Mr. Obama. He is well educated, very intelligent, compassionate, a humanitarian, far-sighted, historically conscious and cool under fire while possessing an unbelievable work ethic. So, with him on the 20th floor, 1st floor occupants cannot conceive such brilliance in a Black man!

The parallel is simple as T.D. Jakes tells it. A giraffe was feeding at the tree top, enjoying the cool breeze, fresh greenery and staring into the promise of the clear blue skies yonder. Along came a tortoise, hailing the ruminant and enquiring, "How're you doing?" The giraffe looked down and answered, "Great, the view is wonderfully spectacular, the shrubs are delicious and the air is refreshing. And You?" The turtle responded, "Looks like a terrific mess. All I see is garbage and the smell is awful." "You need to come up a notch and enjoy all these benefits!" Fact is; both gave honest answers. However, while Obama grazes in refreshing tree top sunlight, his detractors are muddled in turtledom!

Nevertheless, before we consider the questions, it is interesting to note some factors regarding the state of the nation under Mr. Bush's watch which Mr. Obama inherited and masterfully addressed as President!

BLACK HISTORY EVERYDAY
PART TWO

First of all, 2006 was five years since the "second attack" on the World Trade Center on 9/11/2001, resulting in the "shock and awe" response visited on the Taliban in Afghanistan! The Taliban harbored Osama bin Laden, leader of Al Qaeda, who "Declared war on America," and credited with the attack. The year 2006 was also 3 years into the invasion of Iraq that ultimately toppled Sadam Hussein, resulting in nearly 5,000 American military deaths and thousands more injured. This does not include Coalition forces and Iraqi casualties, military and collateral, and the trillions of dollars spent in a war Americans considered useless, wasteful and ill-considered.

The significant players in the Bush Administration included Vice President Dick Chaney, Donald Rumsfeld as Secretary of Defense, Condoleezza Rice as National Security Adviser and ultimately, replacing General Colin Powell as Secretary of State. Based on the information supplied him, Mr. Powell testified to the Security Council of the United Nations that Sadam Hussein possessed weapons of mass destruction (WMD) with a launch capacity that was very rapid. He was even tied to purchasing uranium from Niger in West Africa to make his weaponry more effective. However, while both wars ensued, a number of interesting variables began to surface and in total proving much of this intelligence was considered faulty, if not purposefully deceitful.

FREDERICK MONDERSON

Black History Everyday - Part Two Photo. We Shall Not be Moved March. Faces in the Crowd.

Black History Everyday – Part Two Photo. People shouting "No Justice, No Peace!"

Significantly, as it turned out, Mr. Chalaby, an Iraqi national who wrote a book on Ancient Egypt was an "American friendly," who fed them inside information about Sadam's armaments. As it turned out, "Chalaby had this thing against Sadam," and targeted the Americans at him using purposely faulty intelligence. However, when the "stuff hit the fan," Chalaby fled to Iran, at that time an enemy of Iraq.

BLACK HISTORY EVERYDAY PART TWO

Black History Everyday – Part Two Photo. Still more people shouting "No Justice, No Peace!"

Black History Everyday - Part Two Photo. Faces and signs in the crowd for the 50th Anniversary March on Washington.

FREDERICK MONDERSON

Black History Everyday - Part Two Photo. Faces and signs in the crowd for the 50th Anniversary March on Washington.

Apparently and second, evidence indicates, Sadam Hussein had tried to assassinate Mr. Bush's father, President Number 41, in Kuwait; so, Mr. Bush, President Number 43, was rather eager to get back at Sadam! The crafted web of deceit revealed even more details. Vice-President Dick Chaney was shown to be connected to Halliburton, a contractor company doing business in Iraq with great financial success. Even more important, it was persuasively argued, Iraqi oil would pay for the expense of the war, though this too proved misleading! Equally significant, however, as the occupation unfolded, General Shinseki informed Congress it would require some 500,000 troops to garrison Iraq but he was ridiculed and so, the conflicts revved up in face of Iraqi insurgency and the same happened in Afghanistan,

BLACK HISTORY EVERYDAY
PART TWO

though the deaths were not as numerous but still significant.

In as much as the American leadership initially raised the question of Sadam's intentions, the international community remained skeptical and so, Mr. Bush "chose to go it alone." In response, the international community took a dim view of America, thanks to the impetuosity of Mr. Bush, the warlord! This reality stained America's foreign relations image for the rest of Mr. Bush's term! One American woman was overheard saying in the Cairo Museum in 2005, "It has gotten so we don't want to say we're Americans because all Bush wants is war!"

At home, the economy was in serious disarray. There were bank failures; Wall Street numbers dropped precipitously and the DOW fell to near 6500; high unemployment became the order of the day; the automobile industry was in crisis; the nation's infrastructure had begun to crumble; an energy crisis unfolded; foreclosures were up, new housing starts were down; teachers and first responders' jobs were on the chopping block; and with unemployment up and taxes down, state and local governments faced challenging realities. Now, in this bleak moment in America's history, Senator Barack Hussein Obama, from the great state of Illinois, declared his candidacy for the Presidency and the rest is history, literally and figuratively!

FREDERICK MONDERSON

After a grueling and well-regulated successful campaign and possessing a beautiful wife, two lovely daughters and a wonderful mother-in-law, like a bright-eyed and bushy-tail knight whose hair was still black, Mr. Obama stepped into the fray to rescue his nation! Just as Jim Santorum would confess after his failure in 2012, "lots of things get said in a campaign;" Mr. Obama felt "the many lights" of this great nation would forget the campaign rhetoric, come together, put their shoulders to the wheel, help to "remove the car from the ditch," and move the nation forward. However, this was not to be! Nonetheless, Mr. Obama set about to tackle the myriad foreign and domestic challenges facing the nation, many believed, was in a near failed-state status! Still, rather than condemn his adversaries, Mr. Obama politely but confidently confessed, "Politics is a contact sport" and considered these persons "Good ole boys just acting out!" Unfortunately, this was not the case!

Still, facing the future with a positive attitude, one of the first and significant acts of a new president is to venture abroad, let friends and enemies get a taste of the new executive and lay out a view of the path he intends. This Mr. Obama did wonderfully well. Even more significantly, he astutely "deployed his better half," "Mighty Michelle," who not only wooed the world but provided the cover for him to win allies, put enemies on notice and addressed the fundamentals of the two wars. He then dispatched a new envoy to the Middle East and pivoted towards

BLACK HISTORY EVERYDAY
PART TWO

strengthening a foothold in Asia for defense and economic realities manifesting in this new century. All this was very well executed.

Next on the domestic front, the president sought to review and strengthen the nation's financial and fiscal policies and practices with a view toward overhauling the monetary system; tackling foreclosure problems and other housing issues; rescuing the auto industry; bailing out the banks; placing a moratorium on impending firing of teachers and first responders such as police officers and firemen; establishing protections for women under the **Lilly Ledbetter Act**; proposing a more equitable arrangement for student loan debt and easing credit card rates; tackling climate change and global warming; creating incentives for more efficient energy systems and creating initiatives for education excellence. Meanwhile his wife Michelle and Vice-President Joe Biden's wife Jill became active advocates for veteran families faced with the challenges of the two wars.

FREDERICK MONDERSON

Black History Everyday - Part Two Photo. We Shall Not be Moved March. Faces in the Crowd.

Unbeknownst to all but a few, the sinisters were at work! While it did not become public until *The New York Times* reported such October 6, 2013, a treasonous group had met and planned a concerted, many pronged campaign designed to sabotage the tenure of the first Black President! Perhaps as the point man, and intoxicated by the glare of the cameras, Senator Mitch McConnell laid it bare, as if speaking for his team, "I intend to make Barack Obama a one-term president!" True to his boast and in subsequent negotiations as Senate Minority leader, after an important meeting, the Senator gave his now famous or infamous "Thumbs-up" code symbol signaling to his "people" "I got that Nigger!" However, it's common knowledge, racist hue

BLACK HISTORY EVERYDAY
PART TWO

mentality held, "A Nigger occupies the White House."

It is hard to believe, high up as he is, Speaker Boehner, did not know of the treasonous Republican meeting even if he did not participate. The "conspiracy" existed certainly from 2008 to 2012, so Boehner's denial is considered farcical! Still, he did disrespect Mr. Obama by not returning his phone calls amidst important negotiations. Even more significant, this "representative of the people" held the nation and Mr. Obama hostage in the Debt Ceiling Debate and later symbolically boasted "We got 98% of what we wanted!" This is incredible, for to get 98% of any pie means all others got crumbs!

Today, Mr. Obama's record speaks for itself. He ended and wound down the war in Iraq and Afghanistan. He gets credit for killing and disposing of Osama bin Laden and severely curtailed the aspirations of Somali Pirates. He represented the United States very well at the funeral for Nelson Mandela in South Africa. The economy has rebounded well! Some 10 million new jobs have been added in the private sector during Mr. Obama's tenure. Rising from 6500 when he took office in 2008, to 17,000 today, the DOW has experienced a vibrancy unimagined even in "good times," in fact, its historical. The week of July 4, 2014, 300,000 jobs were added. Some even joked, "Knowing Mr. Obama would celebrate Independence Day, Republicans called up Hurricane Arthur to rain on Mr. Obama's parade!" Notwithstanding, on a more serious note, Obama paid concerted attention to climate change, a clean air environment and infrastructure repair jobs. Emphasis was also placed on all aspects of transportation, even considering the creation of a high-speed rail system with trains to improve cross-country commute.

Incentives have been offered for innovations in clean energy, better and longer lasting batteries and cars are moving towards cleaner emissions and better gas mileage. Even Black farmers have been paid regarding their long-standing suit against the government!

In education, Mr. Obama created "Race to the Top" to improve performance; issued incentives for parents to return to college; and he bolstered Community Colleges to lay a foundation for technical education in preparing for the future. Still more seriously important, Mr. Obama conceived of an answer to address the nearly 50 million Americans without health care. He campaigned on this issue in two elections, legislated the Affordable Care Act that withstood a Supreme Court challenge amidst acrimonious negative propaganda publicity, and despite technical problems in the health care system roll-out, more than 10 million Americans have signed-up for the insurance protections. With some luck and superb administrative vigilance terrorist attacks on the homeland have been prevented. In fact, a popular T-shirt has a Logo that reads: "Homeland

BLACK HISTORY EVERYDAY
PART TWO

Security: Fighting Terrorism since 1492!" As such, some have considered this nation, the birthplace of terrorism for Ku Klux Klan and Knights of the White Camelia, etc., behaviors towards African-Americans during the 19th and 20th Centuries were certainly classic cases of terrorism.

Black History Everyday - Part Two Photo. Faces and signs in the crowd for the 50th Anniversary March on Washington.

Black History Everyday - Part Two Photo. Faces and signs in the crowd for the 50th Anniversary March on Washington.

FREDERICK MONDERSON

The list enumerated above and much more Mr. Obama achieved despite a Republican "Party of No" actively committed to block-every legislative initiative he proposed. Consider the **Affordable Care Act** was voted against 43 times in the House of Representatives controlled by Republicans and not 1 Obama initiated jobs bill got through. Coupled with this subjective campaign *The Times* article named some 20 right-wing groups that were formed and well-financed, also the training of untold numbers of young people to "provide information about Obamacare," which in fact is nothing but efforts to defame Mr. Obama and his work. So much so, Senate Majority Leader Harry Reid decried the exorbitant spending by saying, "They're trying to buy America but it's not for sale!" Sorrowfully, the President confessed, "All they do is talk about me and block my every effort."

BLACK HISTORY EVERYDAY
PART TWO

Black History Everyday - Part Two Photo. We Shall Not be Moved March. Faces in the Crowd.

The mentality of persons such as the "McConnells" and "Boehners" and their backers hold, Mr. Obama is "A Nigger out of place!" Hence, they must and will do everything in their power to defame him and poison the minds of Americans so a negative perception will linger. Important too, Democrats do not stand up for Mr. Obama! Malcolm X called them "Dixiecrats!"

Most important, enquiring minds wonder whether the Poll asked did Mr. Obama's race play a role in the negative result. After the "Birther Charade," and the many threats, the fact is in both the 2008 and 2012 election Mr. Obama won by a margin of 53-47 percent of the vote. He lost all the "Lynching States" of the South and thus the 30% number is down from the 47% who would never vote for the man.

FREDERICK MONDERSON

Nevertheless, when it comes to the use of Executive Action on part of the President, Mr. Obama was elected to lead the nation. If legislative elements block his every action, he must act on behalf of the people and therefore, Executive Action gets his agenda moving. While the Poll seemed to indicate Mr. Reagan, Bill Clinton and Richard Nixon scored better than Mr. Obama one has to wonder whether only blind persons were asked to examine Mr. Obama's achievements in this poll. History has shown Bill Clinton worked the "Monica Lewinsky matter" in the White House while Hillary was in the next room; Richard Nixon resigned in disgrace after imploring "I am not a crook!" As for Ronal Reagan, for long he was an actor on radio, screen and television shaping his persona in a world of Hollywood many believe is really "make believe." Still, President Reagan, while he deployed "Star Wars" and blew wind at the Russians, their empire was actually tottering, nevertheless. However, he changed his hairstyle and lied about the Contras! More importantly, however, Mr. Reagan was the master of Executive Action, employing it more times than any other president. Therefore, to significantly question Mr. Obama's use of Executive Action in contrast with Mr. Reagan is actually laughable!

The fact is; Mr. Obama is a humanitarian who put people ahead of politics, has been faithful to his wife and kids and intellectually stands as a Gulliver to his Lilliputian challengers. Nevertheless, all things being equal, objectivity trumps subjectivity, which

BLACK HISTORY EVERYDAY
PART TWO

makes the Poll results questionable at best defaming and destructive at worst. Equally, it is strange how Republicans supply ideas to the terrorists who hate America. These people watch the American news on television. And, Mr. Obama tarries on for what else is new!

Finally, in a recent press conference on an impending uptick of American involvement in Iraq, the Chairman of the Joint Chiefs, General Dempsey, spoke with a fearlessness and conviction that expresses sheer confidence in his Commander-in-Chief. Such steadfast composure as the general demonstrated in his leader fails the methodology, assessment and intent of the Quinnipiac Poll!

Black History Everyday - Part Two Photo. We Shall Not be Moved March. Faces in the Crowd.

FREDERICK MONDERSON

"The American Negro must remake his past in order to make his future. Though it is orthodox to think of America as the one country where it is unnecessary to have a past, what is a luxury for the nation as a whole becomes a prime social necessity for the Negro. For him, a group tradition must supply compensation for persecution, and pride of race the antidote for prejudice. History must restore what slavery took away, for it is the social damage of slavery that the present generations must repair and offset." **Arturo Alfonso Schomburg**. *The Negro Digs Up His Past. Graphic Survey* [March 1925]

"My subjects inherit the ignorance and prejudice that belongs to slavery. At this moment they have made but little progress in knowledge. Where could they acquire it, for, in gaining their liberty, they have seen nothing but camps and war?" **Henri Christophe**. *Undated Letter to Thomas Clarkson.*

16. BEN CARSON, SERIOUSLY? BY DR. FRED MONDERSON

Recently, a Washington lawmaker described the Affordable Care Act maliciously dubbed "Obamacare," as "the most dangerous law in American history." This week, at a social conservative gathering, the famed and now retired

BLACK HISTORY EVERYDAY
PART TWO

neurosurgeon from Johns Hopkins Hospital Center and member of the Heritage Foundation, Dr. Ben Carson, described "Obamacare as worse than slavery." Tragic! In a visit to a South American Republic this writer overhead a taxi driver railing at another motorist, "I know you bought your license, but at least learn to drive!"

Dr. Carson is clearly a highly skillful and successful surgeon. However, his comments regarding the Affordable Health Care initiative set forth by President Obama reflects either an abysmal ignorance of African-American history and race relations or a severe psycho-cultural pathology which impels him to seek his "thirty pieces of silver" in the form of approbation from powerful white supremacists who fear and hate President Obama.

Black History Everyday - Part Two Photo. Faces and signs in the crowd for the 50th Anniversary March on Washington.

FREDERICK MONDERSON

Black History Everyday - Part Two Photo. Faces and signs in the crowd for the 50th Anniversary March on Washington.

Inasmuch as lawmakers are enormously wealthy, the lawmaker in question may have bought, or inherited, his seat while still being ignorant of American history. Dr. Carson, on the other hand, may have been too busy conducting brain surgery to have truly studied American slavery, as well as its psycho-cultural aftermath, to make such a reckless, perverse comparison. Let us not forget that Malcolm X reminded us, "The slave master used overseers and several methods of divide and rule to control the slaves" including the "Willie Lynch" syndrome! In an earlier version of today's developments, the Republicans used Michael Steele to attempt the defeat of President Obama. He was a dismal failure and was subsequently fired. Allen West emerged but soon proved a meaningless buffoon. Whether Ben

BLACK HISTORY EVERYDAY
PART TWO

Carson is a "Judas Iscariot" or not only time will tell! Nevertheless, in the record of the oppressor; the lawmakers especially, have historic ties to odious legislation that terrorized and victimized significant segments of the American population. Dr. Carson's involvement, one of perhaps very few Blacks afforded a platform at the ultra-conservative Family Research Council's meetings and probably at several other such gatherings, raises questions as to his motivation, purpose, audience and intent, as well as his knowledge of history, certainly of Black history! It is thus appropriate that a mini-history lesson be used to enlighten individuals such as Dr. Carson and other like-minded individuals about the "most dangerous laws passed in American history!"

Perhaps in his narrow-mindedness, what the Congressman meant refers to are times when the law as applied to all Americans it is dangerous but when applied to African Americans it is not! So. nevertheless, in Dr. Carson's case, he certainly knows medicine but does not fully realize that a Black Republican, people of his hue, a la Michael Steele, J.C. Watts, Allen West, "who all sat by the door," ultimately found the inner portals closed. Thank goodness. he has his profession on which to fall back. In the minds of many Black people especially in that rant against Obamacare, Dr. Carson has certainly fallen from grace and many young students who were inspired by his "gifted hands," must now wonder whether psyche and spirit have been impaired!

FREDERICK MONDERSON

The intent of this essay is to show, some of the most odious laws, sketched below, which proved to be infinitely more oppressive and dangerous as applied to African Americans in this country, more than the Health Care law, **Affordable Care Act** (ACA). This meaningful and comprehensive health care law is designed to address the needs of millions of Americans who have no medical coverage and can only rely on the immediacy of Emergency Room care. Two things can thus be considered in this case. The article in *The New York Times* of October 6, 2013, referenced the hundreds of millions of dollars this Anti-Obamacare movement is collecting and disbursing to disparage Mr. Obama and destroy the protections of the ACA so many have come to realize it is in their best interests and health care.

Black History Everyday - Part Two Photo. **We Shall Not be Moved March**. Faces in the Crowd.

BLACK HISTORY EVERYDAY
PART TWO

Given that speakers are paid a fee for their presentation, it is fair to ask whether Dr. Carson is but one recipient of this money-mill. Second, the article mentions the thousands of persons being trained to extend the task of "informing the public about Obamacare." Granted, some policy laws as huge as Obamacare may have some faults in their initial roll-out. These "pseudo-patriots" such as Dr. Carson, however, are not interested in repairability but in destruction. Which great idea has not had setbacks before being perfected? Surely, we can name Medicare, Social Security, the conquest of space, even formation of the Union of the United States which is still trying, after nearly two and a half centuries, to perfect itself! Most importantly, it is not inconceivable that there may be much misinformation in the anti-Obamacare strategy, but the Affordable Care Act was a principal issue in the Obama Campaign Platform. It was passed by Congress, upheld by the Supreme Court and is the law of the land. Even more important, it is hardly likely to be repealed despite some 42 attempts by House Republicans to repeal this historic piece of federal legislation!

In school, youngsters are reminded that even the brightest students dropout; and that even the most brilliant people sometimes say dumb things! Dr. Carson certainly knows medicine but his understanding of the forces and realities of history is a failure. Perhaps, in his present mental state, if this was an operation his patient would probably come out seriously impaired. When Vice President Dan Quayle mis-spelled potato as p-o-t-a-t-o-e he disappointed a great many. Likewise, when Dr. Carson stood with the Conservative Family Research Council and pronounced that President Obama's Affordable Care Act, maliciously called Obamacare, was the "worse law since slavery," not only did he disappoint untold numbers of adult Blacks, but his status as an icon to many young Blacks took a severe hit! As for this writer, as an American, I feel I must share my thoughts on this misguided statement. Particularly, because similar ones have been expressed among people who have either conspired with or have been funded by surreptitious individuals who plotted to disrupt, subvert and/or obstruct the orderly function of the United States government under the legal administration of President Barack Obama, twice elected by a majority of the American people. These persons are thus guilty of treason!

Let me then first point out some milestones in American History, whether legislative or under cover of legal sanction, that have been the hall-marks of the notion of "the Ugly American." In this vein, it would be helpful to separate Pre - and Post-1863 Emancipation Proclamation issues to establish the context in which Dr. Carson, especially, is not only ignorant, but perverse, malicious and spiteful. This is sadly predictable, considering his alignment with a conservative heritage mindset that reeks of terrorist activities against Blacks in America. It is an

BLACK HISTORY EVERYDAY
PART TWO

established fact that after President Obama's 2008 victory, Senator Mitch McConnell publicly boasted, "I intend to make Barack Obama a one-term President." Morgan Freeman, the Academy Award winner, appearing on CNN's Piers Morgan, asserted that the Senator's statement was "racist!" Freeman's comments also would be apt to Dr. Carson's statement.

Black History Everyday - Part Two Photo. Faces and signs in the crowd for the 50th Anniversary March on Washington.

Black History Everyday – Part Two Photo. "Stop killing Black Youth!"

FREDERICK MONDERSON

Black History Everyday - Part Two Photo. Faces and signs in the crowd for the 50th Anniversary March on Washington.

Now, history has shown that to secure Southern support for acceptance of the initial United States Constitution, the founding fathers established the 3/5th Clause or the **Compromise of 1787**, in which enslaved Africans were counted as "three fifths" of a White person or to have 5 Blacks counted as 3 Whites. Let us also remind Dr. Carson that many a "founding patriot" sent slaves to fight for America's freedom in the Revolutionary War; that one free Black, **Crispus Attucks** was the first to fall in the fight for America's freedom. This means that among America's first patriots was a Black Man, a bona fide hero!

BLACK HISTORY EVERYDAY
PART TWO

The **Compromise of 1820** was also called the Missouri Compromise. It stipulated, among other things, that Maine would be admitted to the Union as a Free State, and Missouri as a slave state. The remainder of the **Louisiana Purchase** (1803) would not become a slave state.

Following the **Compromise of 1820**, in 1832, the **South Carolina Nullification Act** forced President Andrew Jackson to dispatch federal troops to check the rebellious action. Nearly 250 years later, Jesse Jackson pointed out that, South Carolina; home state of former Senator Jim DeMint, who now heads the Heritage Foundation; on whose website Dr. Carson's photo is prominently displayed; and who wanted to create President Obama's "Waterloo;" that this southern state supported 36 state prisons and 1 state college. It is not surprising in such a former "rebellious slave state," that Blacks are the principal occupants of its state prisons and hardly represented at its state college or colleges! There is a message in the man's attire.

FREDERICK MONDERSON

Black History Everyday - Part Two Photo. We Shall Not be Moved March. Faces in the Crowd.

Among its many mandates, the **Compromise of 1850** not only sought to establish north/south, free state/slave state regional balance, but established the **Fugitive Slave Laws** in which, oftentimes both free and enslaved Blacks were returned to southern servitude. Sometimes they were returned from the north to Black slave owners who were often active participants in a system of inhumanity that brutalized and debased the bodies and souls of untold numbers of other African people held in bondage through judicial and administrative fiat.

Black Codes were the legal mechanisms by which enslaved Blacks were dehumanized, controlled and psychologically and often physically

BLACK HISTORY EVERYDAY
PART TWO

emasculated in a system of exploitation that generated great wealth through the plantation culture for principally southerners in the "lynching states." Perhaps, not surprisingly despite this, in the 2012 election, the Republican candidate Mitt Romney won all the southern states with a history of lynching. So much for the "New South!"

In 1857, Chief Justice Roger Taney issued the Dred Scott Decision, a ruling that Dred Scott, an enslaved African American seeking his freedom, was not a citizen and could not bring suit in a United States Court. Even more, this apologist for slavery further ruled, that based on American history, "The Black man has no rights which a White man must respect!" Dr. Carson ought to be aware that even after his outlandish speech in disparagement of President Obama's most important legislative accomplishment by a Black man held in the highest esteem by untold millions of African and other people worldwide; there would be at least one conservative heckler in that group who would have shouted "The Nigger has spoken!" Perhaps it would be, "The Nigger Doctor has spoken!" Then again, while his camp has previously thought the President of the United States, Barack Hussein Obama is a "Nigger," perhaps in his misguided mind, Dr. Carson may also think, though he has probably moved from the door, that he is not a "Nigger." But somewhere along the line he will be reminded, especially if his strategy as a tool of presidential debasement, does not work!

FREDERICK MONDERSON

Abraham Lincoln was very intelligent; a great man and President who realized, "a house divided against itself cannot stand;" and as such, he put his heart, his administration and his life into the Emancipation Proclamation. This bold and courageous act paved the way for the Civil War Amendments - 13th, legally ended slavery; 14th, gave citizenship to individuals born or naturalized in the United States; and the 15th, which empowered Black men with the legal status to exercise the franchise. However, under cover of law, these legislative milestones were often assaulted and desecrated by southern conservatives who were the "powers that be." They were part of one of the most terrifying period in American history which the historian Professor Rayford Logan called "the Nadir," because of the perennial perpetuation of horrific acts of terror against Blacks.

That conservative movement, to win political control of the "prostrate south" during and after Reconstruction, formed "white redeemers" such as the Ku Klux Klan, White Citizens Council, Knights of the White Camelia, etc., and began to systematically terrorize Blacks using fear, lynchings, tar and featherings, and other intimidating actions, and consigning many Black individuals to an inequitable "share cropper system" of economic peonage. In conjunction, Southern conservative lawmakers enacted the "Grandfather Clause," which ruled that "If one's grandfather had voted previously then one could vote." This strategy was used to instill

BLACK HISTORY EVERYDAY
PART TWO

fear and exclude Blacks from the polls since their enslaved grandfathers could not have voted before the 15th Amendment of February 1870. The "Grandfather Clause" was repealed in 1915 because of its inequity and as a pillar of "Jim Crow." A legal requirement that Blacks pay a "Poll Tax" to vote was instituted and Blacks were required to take a "Literacy Test" which some with doctor's degrees could not pass because of the educational and racial machinations involved. All these shenanigans employed contributed to a *de facto* and *de jure* "Jim Crow" state of affairs across the south especially in which ex-slaves were relegated to second class citizenship and were perennially victims of terrorism at will. Meanwhile, the "White Primary" became the order of the day, precluding Blacks from running for elected office and enabling Whites to control the political process! All of this occurred while the federal government pandered to the whims of arch conservatives, irrespective of the party to which they belonged.

Many of those events and circumstances culminated in the 1896 Supreme Court ruling of *Plessey v. Ferguson* that established a "Separate but Equal" rule, which was, in actuality, "Separate and Unequal." This significant ruling particularly affected the education of young children and especially enabled state enforced residential segregation. Thus, more than a year ago in 2011, a CBS 60-Minutes program, investigating a Civil Rights case of murder in which the principal perpetrator was still alive, yet no one was talking but the victim's family; yet still, it was revealed "more than 100 unresolved Civil Rights murders" existed on the FBI books. The report also pointed out, in order to run for and hold political office, individuals had to belong to or espouse the policies of the "lynching states" terrorist ideology. Thus, in that environment and under cover of state law and politics, racially motivated mob violence, lynchings and murder were never seriously challenged in territory under conservatives' control.

Under these unjust laws, Black Americans were denied the fundamental rights of the United States Constitution. Among others, these included Exclusion from Jury Duty, Denial of Freedom of Speech, Voting Rights, and the Right to Assemble. They were also excluded from union jobs until, on the eve of World War II in 1941, A. Philip Randolph, a Black activist labor leader threatened to "March on Washington!" In response, President Roosevelt took some action and the Congress of Industrial Organizations, sister arm of the American Federation of Labor, began enrolling and facilitating the hiring of black workers. At the end of World War II and having succeeded President Roosevelt, President Harry Truman desegregated the armed forces because Blacks had served gloriously to defend this nation as they had in every war in which American has ever been engaged. Even more importantly, the racist behavior of America had begun to be affected by the "winds of change" sweeping the post-war

BLACK HISTORY EVERYDAY
PART TWO

world as newly African nations flexed their independence muscle on the world state at the United Nations.

Black History Everyday - Part Two Photo. Faces and signs in the crowd for the 50th Anniversary March on Washington.

Black History Everyday - Part Two Photo. Faces and signs in the crowd for the 50th Anniversary March on Washington.

FREDERICK MONDERSON

In 1954, Thurgood Marshall, long in the vineyards of challenging laws oppressive to Blacks, was able to successfully argue *Brown V. Board of Education of Topeka, Kansas* that, in fact, overturned *Plessey v. Ferguson*. This significant legal victory forever changed America although racism and discrimination changed its **modus operandi** but still essentially remained the same, if not becoming worse. Lest we forget, however, the movement for change was led by a number of individuals who took a stand against the "Bull Connors of the South," the Klan and the ensuing hatred and racial insanity they represented. This profound movement was led by leadership stalwarts as Reverend Shillingsworth, Martin Luther King, Rev. Abernathy, Harry Belafonte, Rosa Parks, Kwame Toure (Stokeley Carmichael), Fannie Lou Hamer, John Lewis, Malcolm X, Reverend Lowery, Jesse Jackson, Andrew young, and Viola Liuzzo, Andrew Goodman, Michael Schwerner and so many more who stood up to preserve the American Dream. Today these courageous leaders and martyrs would be tremendously surprised, if not sickened, by Dr. Carson's stunning remarks since, in American politics, it has always been, "Where you stand is where you sit and where you sit is where you stand!" Congressman Charlie Rangel explained that the Anti-Obamacare Movement was predicated and driven by hatred for President Obama, a Black male and, therefore, one would have to wonder how Dr. Carson, also a Black male himself could align himself with persons filled with such conservative and racial

BLACK HISTORY EVERYDAY
PART TWO

venom particularly entertained for people who looked like Dr. Carson!

Black History Everyday - Part Two Photo. We Shall Not be Moved March. Faces in the Crowd.

Gerrymandering was essentially a Republican creation though Democrats have also practiced it. Yet, in recent time it encouraged and ably assisted voter suppression as practiced by Republicans. Presidents Kennedy and Johnson's "Great Society" which supported the 1964 Civil Rights laws and the 1965 Voting Rights law required a provision which insisted that the voting law must be extended every 25-years in order for them to remain viable and effective. In an interesting development, despite Dr. Ben Carson "sitting at the king's table, eating his meat," and having climbed to the pinnacle of his profession to make that outlandish proclamation; if the Voting Rights Law expires, Dr. Carson and his children and grandchildren will not be able to vote! However, and even more important, it is evident that the group with whom Dr. Carson is comfortably aligned, the Republicans were accused of innumerable and unimaginable skullduggery on election day at the last two Presidential elections and all under cover of law. Despite their treasonous planning to subvert the government, no one was arrested. Yet, they lost once and will lose again because their record stands serenely blemished!

Let us not forget, Sarah Palin who, to make political points in her losing 2008 effort to run for Vice-President, accused President Obama of "palling around with terrorists." Today, in 2013 she is like a spent comet lost in the great void of the cosmos; even teaming with or "Palling around with Ted Nugent," profound dis-respecter of President Obama. Notwithstanding, the record forcefully shows, after the 2008 presidential election, a group of rich and powerful individuals got together and planned to subvert Mr. Obama's Presidency. This formed the fundamental strategy of the Republican Party going forward. It equally earned them the "Party of No" badge of shame! Some people have rightfully called this behavior treason because these persons plotted to subvert the legislatively constituted United States government under the leadership of President Barack Hussein Obama.

BLACK HISTORY EVERYDAY
PART TWO

What happens in the dark ultimately comes to light and though only visionaries could see such early treasonous machinations; *The New York Times* of Sunday, October 6, 2013, front page and p. 18, article entitled "A Crisis Months in the Making" exposed the repeated strategy after the 2012 election and named names involved in such machinations leading up to the 2012 election in which the strategy failed. It does not take intellectual genius to realize that the same 2008 actors were very much involved and are now exposed in this article. Ed Meese, a named principal conspirator, was United States Attorney General under President Ronald Reagan. In as much as his name surfaced in this article, it established continuity of nefarious, some say racist, treasonous, Republican activity for 2008, possibly continuing for decades down to today. Since many of these old and new conservative activists, articulated a "take no prisoners legislative strategy" and who planned and executed behaviors intended to subvert the will of the American people expressed by the second election of the President of the United States, they should, in fact, have been arrested for their treasonous behavior. The elders have often said, "Show me your company and I will tell who you are!" It is clear that Dr. Carson is quite at home with individuals implicated in treasonous words and deeds. Perhaps this deluded individual feels that his Republican pals will hold moderate tones in his presence as they berate other African Americans!

FREDERICK MONDERSON

Dr. Carson ought to awake from his misguided slumber and recognize the world has become aware and several millions of Africans worldwide are outraged and feel strong revulsion for Dr. Carson, because of his disgusting distortion and omission of the historical record by his shameful, subjective assault upon a public policy set forth by President Obama which is intended to make the human rights of people lacking medical care more affordable and hence more accessible to millions of Americans who had been denied that right.

This self-negation of Dr. Carson, a physician and a person of African descent is unfortunately not necessary. It was prevalent during slavery, for the slave owner would instill the illusion among the house slaves that they were more valued than the field hands. This practice induced and created a class within a caste that fostered resentment among the enslaved. Predictably, it encouraged betrayal of each other in order to find favor from the slave owners. Are people like Dr. Carson as exemplified in 2013 and even today on eve of the 2020 election likewise? Such person openly pander for the "thirty pieces of silver" available to them in the form of approbation by the powerful and callous of heart in the USA?

BLACK HISTORY EVERYDAY
PART TWO

Black History Everyday - Part Two Photo. Faces and signs in the crowd for the 50th Anniversary March on Washington.

Black History Everyday - Part Two Photo. Faces and signs in the crowd for the 50th Anniversary March on Washington.

FREDERICK MONDERSON

Black History Everyday - Part Two Photo. All on stage at Sharpton and Crump's March on Washington.

Black History Everyday - Part Two Photo. We Shall Not be Moved March. Faces in the Crowd.

BLACK HISTORY EVERYDAY
PART TWO

Black History Everyday - Part Two Photo. Faces and signs in the crowd for the 50th Anniversary March on Washington.

FREDERICK MONDERSON

Black History Everyday - Part Two Photo. Brother Fred Monderson and Brother Walter Brown at the 50th Anniversary convention in Montgomery, Alabama.

BLACK HISTORY EVERYDAY
PART TWO

Black History Everyday - Part Two Photo. Luis stands contemplating the scenes at Sharpton and Crump's March on Washington.

FREDERICK MONDERSON

Black History Everyday - Part Two Photo. We Shall Not be Moved March. Faces in the Crowd.

BLACK HISTORY EVERYDAY
PART TWO

17. THE SLAVE TRADE TO THE AMERICAS - CONTINUED
BY
DR. FRED MONDERSON

Figures about the Slave Trade vary. However, credence must be given to the research of the Harvard University and German trained African American scholar W. E. B. Du Bois. In his book, *The Suppression of the African Slave Trade to America 1638-1880,* Du Bois provided a figure of 100 million souls lost to Africa in this experience.

This erudite and eventual nationalist and general scholar, Du Bois counted those killed on land resisting the kidnapping raids of traders in slavery. He added those who died and littered the countryside in the march to the coast. He included those who died on the shores of Africa and those whose bones littered the Atlantic Ocean, as well as those who died in the Americas. His figures include the dead, dying and untold others like those on the **Slaver Zong**, and this, only for the Atlantic and Western trade.

FREDERICK MONDERSON

Black History Everyday – Part Two Photo. Brother Walter Brown in Augusta, Georgia, James Brown's Hometown.

Black History Everyday - Part Two Photo. Faces and signs in the crowd for the 50th Anniversary March on Washington.

BLACK HISTORY EVERYDAY
PART TWO

Black History Everyday - Part Two Photo. Faces and signs in the crowd for the 50th Anniversary March on Washington.

Black History Everyday - Part Two Photo. Faces and signs in the crowd for the 50th Anniversary March on Washington.

FREDERICK MONDERSON

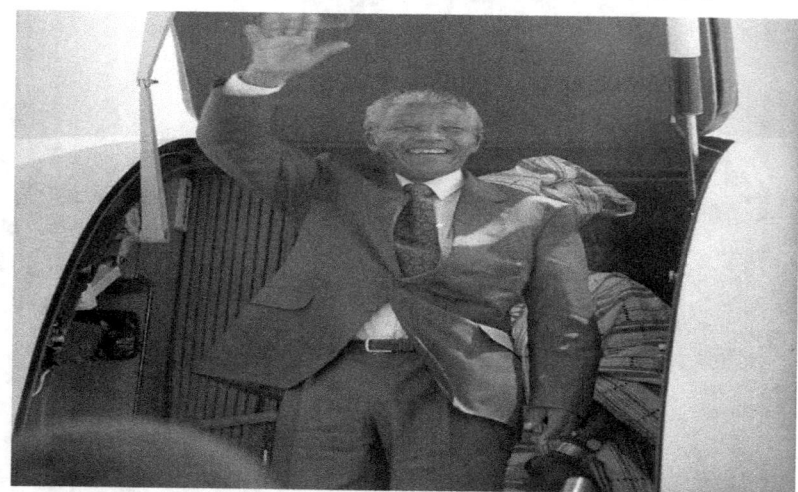

Black History Everyday - Part Two Photo. Image of South African "Freedom Fighter" Nelson Mandela upon arrival in New York after his release from 27-years of imprisonment by the Apartheid government.

Black History Everyday - Part Two Photo. Rev. Al Sharpton beside Sonny Carson, campaigning for Stan Kinnard in Brownsville, Brooklyn.

BLACK HISTORY EVERYDAY
PART TWO

However, this profit motive notwithstanding, things have an uncanny way of working themselves out, for there were individuals whose conscience and high moral standards dictated that they resist and challenge this plague perpetuated by their countrymen. One such instance can be cited of James Fox, an abolitionist quoted as saying during the English Parliament's attempt to regulate the Slave Trade, that: "There can be no regulation of robbery and murder."

Black History Everyday - Part Two Photo. Faces and signs in the crowd for the 50th Anniversary March on Washington.

FREDERICK MONDERSON

Black History Everyday - Part Two Photo. Faces and signs in the crowd for the 50th Anniversary March on Washington.

Black History Everyday - Part Two Photo. Faces and signs in the crowd for the 50th Anniversary March on Washington.

BLACK HISTORY EVERYDAY
PART TWO

Black History Everyday - Part Two Photo. Faces and signs in the crowd for the 50th Anniversary March on Washington.

In this **Zong** remarkable and horrible incident 132 captive Africans were thrown overboard to save the water supply of the vessel. This particular incident of inhumanity is recounted from a contemporary of the incident, Mr. Bandinet, later referred in **Evidence of the House of Lords Committee** (1849: 21 22):

"March 9, 1783, Gustavas Vasa called on me with an account of 132 Negroes being thrown alive into the sea; from on board an English slave ship."

FREDERICK MONDERSON

Black History Everyday - Part Two Photo. Faces and signs in the crowd for the 50th Anniversary March on Washington.

Black History Everyday - Part Two Photo. Faces and signs in the crowd for the 50th Anniversary March on Washington.

The circumstances in this case could not fail to excite a great interest. The master of a slave ship trading from Africa to Jamaica and having 440 slaves on board had thought fit, on a pretext, that he might be distressed on his voyage for water, to lessen the

BLACK HISTORY EVERYDAY
PART TWO

consumption of it in the vessel, by throwing overboard 132 of the most-sickly among the slaves. On his return to England the owners of the ship claimed from the insurers the full value of those drowned slaves, on the ground that there was an absolute necessity for throwing them into the sea, in order to save the remaining crew and the ship itself.... Case tried in the Court of King's Bench before Lord Chief Justice Mansfield .... The ship **Zong**, Luke Collingwood, Master, sailed from the Island of St. Thomas on the coast of Africa, September 6, 1781, with 440 slaves and 14 whites on board for Jamaica ... mistaking Jamaica for Hispaniola ran her for Leeward. Sickness and mortality had by this time taken place on board the crowded vessel, ... Between leaving the coast of Africa (September 6), and the 29 November, sixty slaves and seven white people had died; ... The master of the ship called together the officers of the ship ... stated ... if the sick slaves died a natural death the loss would fall on the owners of the ship; but if they were thrown alive into the sea, on any sufficient pretext of necessity for the safety of the ship, it would be the loss of the underwriters, allowing at the same time, that it would be less cruel to throw sick wretches into the sea than to suffer them to linger out a few days, under the disorder with which they were afflicted .... He then chose out from the cargo 132 slaves, and brought them on deck ... ordered the crews by turn to throw them into the sea. A parcel of them were accordingly thrown overboard. The number so drowned had been fifty-four. Ordered

FREDERICK MONDERSON

another parcel to be thrown overboard ... amounted to forty-two ....

On the third day the remaining thirty-six were brought on deck, and as these now resisted the cruel purpose of their masters the arms of twenty-six were fettered with irons and the savage crew proceeded with the diabolical work casting them down to join their comrades of the former days. Outraged misery could endure no longer; the last ten victims sprang disdainfully from the grasp of their tyrants, defied their power, and leaping into the sea, felt a momentary triumph in the embrace of death."

Later an inquiry determined that the slaver could have made port with the available water. Therefore, the incident of the **Zong** could have been avoided, though the insurance carrier paid the claim under a clause "perils at sea."

In his addition, to create the greater picture, Du Bois included those Africans who died rebelliously on-board ship. These revolutionary Africans too defied the slavers by jumping overboard rather than live as enslaved people in America. Many fought successfully on board, as in the case of **L'Amistad**. However, most rebellions failed and those courageous enough to resist were either killed and thrown overboard or jumped. Notwithstanding, it can be argued, the "Slave Trade," "Middle Passage,"

BLACK HISTORY EVERYDAY
PART TWO

"Triangular Trade," and ultimately "Slavery" have been detrimental to the African and human spirit.

Black History Everyday - Part Two Photo. Sister Viola Plummer in action and makes a point in protest.

FREDERICK MONDERSON

In *Chains and Images of Psychological Slavery*, Akbar (1989: 1) supplies an important commentary that conceptualizes this experience rather well. "Slavery is the modern genesis experience for Africans in the Western World. Contained in this genesis is much about the continued social, economic, political, and cultural reality of African Americans. There is contained in this tragic drama the nucleus of a mind wrought with the agonies of oppression of the most inhuman form, and simultaneously the image of man's greatest triumph over conditions of the flesh."

Black History Everyday - Part Two Photo. Brother Fred Monderson in James Brown's hometown, Augusta, Ga, for the 50th Anniversary Reunion.

BLACK HISTORY EVERYDAY
PART TWO

Even further, Akbar (1989: 1 2) offers a rather interesting and insightful comparison when he says: "The chattel slavery of Africans in America for over 300 years serves as one of the saddest commentaries on man's inhumanity to man. The tales of this period of our history are so morbid that they will arouse vehement hostilities at the very thought of what occurred. The level of cruelty was incomparable to anything recorded in modern history, including the Nazi atrocities at Auschwitz which were fleeting and direct, destroying bodies, but essentially leaving the collective mind intact. The protracted and intensive atrocities of slavery have had a lingering effect, and the pain of times past continues to call from the genetic memories of those whose ancestors survived the test of slavery."

Black History Everyday - Part Two Photo. Faces and signs in the crowd for the 50th Anniversary March on Washington.

FREDERICK MONDERSON

Black History Everyday - Part Two Photo. Faces and signs in the crowd for the 50th Anniversary March on Washington.

Again, Akbar (1989: 2) continued: "As cruel and painful as chattel slavery was, it could be exceeded only by a worse form of slavery .... The slavery that captures the mind and incarcerates the motivation, perception, aspiration, and identity in a web of anti-self-images, generating a personal and collective self-destruction, is crueler than the shackles on the wrists and ankles. The slavery that feeds on the psychology, invading the soul of man, destroying his loyalties to himself and establishing allegiance to forces which destroy him, is an even worse form of capture. The influences that permit an illusion of freedom, liberation, and self-determination, while tenaciously holding one's mind in subjugation, is the folly of only the sadistic."

BLACK HISTORY EVERYDAY
PART TWO

Therefore, greedy and unscrupulous African princes and chiefs who exploited the trade in their fellow man, were working in collaboration with European merchants and slavers. According to a **Report of a Committee of the British Parliament**, "some Africans were made slaves" for committing crimes in their society. Offenses included murder, adultery, witchcraft, theft, and debt. Crimes were tried, it is said, by wise men who were respected for their age and experience. One may therefore wonder how they arrived at decisions of guilt or innocence. However, despite this, a number of writers have downplayed the role of these Africans who were really peripheral to the European involvement.

Black History Everyday - Part Two Photo. Erik Michael Dyson and Erik Monderson in the crowd for the 50th Anniversary March on Washington.

FREDERICK MONDERSON

Nevertheless, **Evidence by the House of Commons Relating to the Slave Trade** (1792: 6) indicates that: "The persons transported from Africa to the West Indies, are kidnapped or taken prisoner in wars excited by the Europeans, solely for the purpose of selling them to the traders .... They are barbarously treated in the Passage between Africa and America, and inhumanely used after their arrival there."

However, not all kings sold their people into slavery. Many rulers fought against this unjust and evil practice. Nevertheless, while reports show some kings kidnapped their subjects, the greatest numbers of such kidnapping were privately done at the hands of European slave merchants and their African cohorts. In this business it was "slash and burn" and the profit motive was most compelling. It matters not who sold whom, what matters is the plight of the suffering Africans and the beneficiaries of the trade. There were times when it was difficult to secure ship loads of captured Africans. At times like this, privateers wantonly seized individuals and sometimes they seized whole villages.

For centuries Europeans dominated the coastal areas of West Africa. They built fortresses along the coast from Senegal to Angola. From these footholds they terrorized the surrounding areas with their cannon fire. Their strong-holds gave them an unfair advantage against the Africans as well as other

BLACK HISTORY EVERYDAY
PART TWO

European competitors. Robert July in *Precolonial Africa* (1975: 234) has demonstrated how the area of procurement of slaves along the West African coast expanded: "During the earlier centuries the main sources appear to have been located along the western reaches of the Windward Coast in Senegambia, but with the eighteenth century, this preeminence had moved to the lower Guinea coast."

"Toward the end of the seventeenth century, the British Royal Africa Company had found the Ivory Coast its most profitable area of activity, while the Portuguese drew their main supplies from Angola; one hundred years later, four-fifths of all slaves taken from West Africa and close to half the total exports of the continent came from the stretch between the Gold Coast and the Cameroons. In the nineteenth century this concentration along the eastern Guinea coast continued, major supplies coming through Dahomey, the Yoruba ports of Lagos and Badagry, and the Niger Delta emporiums, these last long supported by a heavy flow of captives from Iboland."

FREDERICK MONDERSON

Black History Everyday - Part Two Photo. Address from the Podium at Sharpton and Crump's March on Washington.

E. Jefferson Murphy (1972: 284) was a bit more specific in providing names not mentioned by the previous writer, for accordingly: "Although the flow of slaves from various areas fluctuated considerably over the years, names of great slave-trading towns and localities stand out - Goree in Senegal, Guinea (Bissau), James Island (at the mouth of the Gambia), several Gold Coast towns (Assini, Elmina, Secondi, Dixcove, Anamabu, Accra), several Dahomey towns (Popo, Ardrah, Ouidah), and a host of towns and posts along what is now the Nigerian coast (Badagry, Lagos, Gwato, and Warri near Benin, Brass, Bonny, Calabar, and several small trade villages near the mouth of the Cross River). Along the coasts of what are now Cameroun and Gabon there were few major slave entrepot until the development of early Gabon, but slave ships frequently called along this area of coast. Between the mouth of the Congo and along the

BLACK HISTORY EVERYDAY PART TWO

coast of Angola down to the Benguela region there were a number of trading settlements. The export of slaves was maintained more consistently here than in almost any other part of Africa."

With all this activity going on, there is naturally the inclination to blame somebody as being responsible. In many cases the role of Africans is more often highlighted and they held responsible for selling their fellow Africans to the Europeans. This was a skillful attempt to absolve Europeans from their involvement in their trade in African. However, Stanlake Samkange (1971: 188-190) offers a number of methods whereby he considers the Europeans more responsible for the trade in Africans. In fact, Walter Rodney, decries this exchange saying it was not really trade but robbery. According to Samkange, Europeans acquired Africans for their enslavement through a number of methods, such as: "Through abducting and kidnapping individuals, the Portuguese went on to attack and capture groups .... Europeans got slaves from Africa, making war on villages and carrying the survivors into slavery.... Europeans involved themselves in African wars so as to take the vanquished into captivity .... The fourth method was sometimes employed by white slave dealers who lived among Africans. Often a trader married one of the chief's sisters and so secured the protection of his person and effects while, at the same time, gaining the right to a voice and influence in tribal affairs. The slave dealer set one African chief against another so that when they came to blows, he

FREDERICK MONDERSON

claimed the captives from both sides and sold them into slavery. One of the people we know who was captured and sold into slavery through the activities of a white slave dealer resident in Africa is **Cinque** .... it became simply a matter of looking after one's own skin, fighting, killing, capturing, and selling into slavery one's neighbors before they had a change to do the same to one."

Black History Everyday - Part Two Photo. Faces and signs in the crowd for the 50th Anniversary March on Washington.

Black History Everyday - Part Two Photo. Faces and signs in the crowd for the 50th Anniversary March on Washington.

BLACK HISTORY EVERYDAY
PART TWO

This latter individual, **Cinque**, was involved in a famous incident aboard the slaver **Amistad** that is today a major movie on the silver screen. Samkange (1971: 191-192) continued by saying: "It will be seen that of these five methods used to get slaves from Africa, only one involved the voluntary participation of Africans. Since no one can say that this last method alone yielded more slaves than the other four put together, there is no basis for claiming that Africans were as guilty as Europeans in the crime of slavery. Furthermore, as we have seen, in selling each other, Africans were doing nothing new or repugnant to their laws and customs. The only new thing they did was to sell one another to men of a different race- Europeans. Europeans treated those they bought, not according to African values and ideas, but according to notions of their own culture. This is all understandable because Africans and Europeans had different cultural backgrounds. It was not to be expected that one group would know, or, want to behave, according to the precepts of the other's culture. In this case the Africans' attitude towards people sold and bought was much more humane and civilized than that of the Europeans. How were they to know that the people they sold to Europeans would be treated as chattel and not human beings? To equate their guilt with that of Europeans when they, in fact, were incapable of even of conceiving such notions of slavery as were held by Europeans, is to be both unreasonable and unfair to Africans."

FREDERICK MONDERSON

"It is an attempt on the part of the white man to share his guilt with Africans even though they were unaware of his grotesque notion of what a slave was." He, the white man, has succeeded in brainwashing some black people in America who are now heard saying, 'I don't care a damn for these Africans. After all, it is they who, with Mr. Charlie, sold us down the river!' Let the white man carry the cross of his guilt alone. Africans will have none of it. The only thing they did, not sanctioned by traditional practice, was to assume that white men were human and to sell other Africans to them. No one has seriously contended that this assumption was wrong."

Some sources show how slaving ships used canons to bombard African villages in quest for captives. *An Historical Account ...* (1884: 27) indicates other forms of coercion: "In the year 1769, Capt. Paterson, of a Liverpool slaver, while lying off Bristol town, induced his men and natives to set fire to two villages and during the conflagration the poor blacks, crying out for help, Paterson's men seized the Negroes, branded them and made them slaves."

This conduct forced neighboring African people to succumb to a precarious method of existence: to cooperate in seizing others or in turn be shipped overseas. We are told further in *An Historical Account of the Liverpool African Slave Trade* of "villages set on fire, wars made between unoffending people, men stealers prowling about the country, a

BLACK HISTORY EVERYDAY
PART TWO

thousand subterfuges resorted to in order to kidnap the poor Negroes.... women torn from their suckling infants, son, and daughters from fathers and mothers, and humanity outraged in the name of religion."

Many Africans faced the reality of this conundrum. Firearms equally played an important part in the trade to Africa. Traders sold guns to one nation of people. Then they forced them to attack another. At times, Europeans sold guns to two warring factions then seized the victors. This is a classic example of divide and conquer to rule. It was a terrible time for the African personality! All this happened while "civilized European nations" deferred to the barbarous Slave Trade they had created. Gold and wealth betrayed the Christian admonition of brotherly love.

In time the coastal areas were depopulated, and inland forays were made to capture Africans. These raids into the interior may have penetrated for up to a thousand miles from the coast. In the TV movie Documentary: **Fight Against Slavery**, narrated by Ruby Dee and Ossie Davis, one group of captives recounted seeing "horses," meaning they had probably been far inland beyond the coastal forest region; perhaps in the Savannah. Such a distance seems reasonable since the coastal populations were sometimes totally wiped out and only large and powerful nations or tribes could unite and resist the

FREDERICK MONDERSON

might of powerful Europeans on the African coast. These people, in turn, became middle men in the traffic.

Alexander Falconbridge (1788: 12 13), a surgeon in the trade from 1780 1787, tells us, "the unhappy wretches are bought by the black traders at fairs, which are held for that purpose .... From 40 to 200 Negroes are generally purchased at a time by the black traders .... There is every reason to believe that most of the Negroes shipped from the coast of Africa are kidnapped."

Evidence of the dastardly deed could be seen on the roads and trails from the interior to the coast that were strewn with dead. Many maimed and dying specimens of Africans littered the routes. These fell under the yoke of the dreadful caravans of "slave coffles" a disgusting sight, so often seen in the American south during slavery. This could be observed before and after 1808 when this nation outlawed the trade, patterning the British who had outlawed their involvement the previous year in 1807. More sinister, these "caravans of death" with captured and hapless Africans were driven to a perilous and uncertain future when they left the shores of West Africa.

An interesting reality is indicated in "**A Few Facts Relating to the Slave Trade in Central and East Africa**," a pamphlet issued by the British and Foreign Anti-Slavery Society,

BLACK HISTORY EVERYDAY
PART TWO

(1887: 2) where Sampson Low is quoted from: *To Tanganyika in A Bath Chair.*

Here light is shed on the **Arab Slave Trade** to create comparisons of certain graphic aspects of the slave caravans in this devastation of Africa. "Every now and then I saw dark objects lying on or beside the path, and shortly afterwards became aware that they were dead bodies of helpless laggards from the various hungry caravans that had passed that way. The heat and drought had been so great that these bodies were perfectly hardened and preserved. It was a terrible sight, which suggested horrors worse than mere death in connection with the diabolical system of man hunting, and the driving of the victims in herds, on the speculation of a good percentage surviving to arrive at market. I do not mean to describe the horrors of the slave traffic, for I fear I cannot bring about the effects which so many more eloquent witnesses have failed to produce; but I must discharge my conscious of this duty to solemnly remind and warn whoever in Christian and civilized lands may read this book, given over to all the horrors of the slave traffic so often and so ably described."

FREDERICK MONDERSON

Black History Everyday - Part Two Photo. Faces and signs in the crowd for the 50th Anniversary March on Washington.

Black History Everyday - Part Two Photo. Mr. Elroy Sailor of **INSIGHT AMERICA** attending Sharpton's Washington Conference, September 9, 2016.

BLACK HISTORY EVERYDAY
PART TWO

Black History Everyday - Part Two Photo. Faces and signs in the crowd for the 50th Anniversary March on Washington.

Earlier, in 1857 Dr. Livingstone addressed the **Senate House of Cambridge** on this issue and in 1863 he wrote home noting: "Wherever we took a walk human skeleton were to be seen in every direction and it was painfully interesting to observe the different postures in which the poor wretches had breathed their last." Additionally, General Gordon, in **Few Facts** (1887: 3) expressed the view: "In three days we have caught 400 slaves, the number of skulls along the road is appalling .... I have ordered the skulls, which lay about here in great numbers, to be piled in a heap, as a memento to the natives of what the slave dealers have done to their people .... there is no reason to doubt but that seventy a day had been passing for the last year or two."

Though we have to a significant extent focused on West Africa, we must not discount the continued Arab Slave Trade on the other side of the Continent. Importantly, however, by virtue of their involvement, we know of the Arab Slave Trade. Equally too, then, European involvement settles the question that the western experience should be known as the European Slave Trade rather than the African Slave Trade. A further historical note can be appended here. In Europe's expansion naming people and places became important. Thus, we have New York, named after York in England and New Jersey after Jersey also. There are many other instances where this state affair applied when used "positively." However, when there is a "negative" connotation, particularly after historical scrutiny, the name is changed, as from European Slave Trade to African Slave Trade. It should not be this way. Let us call a "white horse a white horse," Jack! The real name should be, the European Slave Trade via the Atlantic to the New World.

Even more, we could quote Moore and Dunbar (1968: 110-111) who provide an important comparison of the trade in Africans between the Europeans and the Arabs. They write: "There are interesting similarities and contrasts between the slave trade in East and West Africa. The volume of each was enormous, but while we can make some sort

BLACK HISTORY EVERYDAY
PART TWO

of a guess at the number of slaves taken from West Africa it is extremely difficult to make an estimate for East Africa, because the volume varied and figures can only be obtained for the comparatively few final years. But we do know that the European slave trade across the Atlantic did not begin until the sixteenth century, that it did not reach its maximum until the eighteenth century, and that at the start of the nineteenth century it was abolished."

On the other hand, Moore and Dunbar (1968: 111) continued: "But the Arab slave trade across the Indian Ocean began before the Christian era and did not stop until the end of the nineteenth century, so that, although its volume in any one year did not reach the highest figure of the European slave trade, the number of Africans exported during two thousand years may well have exceeded fifteen million. The treatment of slaves by those who transported them was dreadful in both cases, but whereas about half of those captured as slaves in West Africa reached their destination, we have seen that only about one-fifth of those captured in East Africa survived. Yet those deported from East Africa who reached their destination in the Middle East were usually treated with comparative kindness and were used as domestic slaves, while those who were deported from West Africa to the American or West Indian colonies were used in gangs on plantations. Sugar is perhaps the most exhausting of all crops to harvest, and the overseers were interested in making the greatest profit in the shortest time so that they could return to England."

Continuing, he wrote: "Consequently their treatment of the slaves does not make happy reading. The Spanish alone, among European countries, made a sincere and effective attempt to treat their slaves with something like kindness. The effects of the slave trade upon Africa went deep, and even when internal warfare ended at the abolition of the slave trade, the population both east and the west remained low."

In order to help facilitate the European or Atlantic Slave Trade, a number of Africans were employed by European traders in the coastal holding stations. This connection provided quite an experience for the unfortunate and confined African, particularly after a rather trying forced march to the coast. He was certainly puzzled to see his brother "working for the man." These workers were employed as "conductors" who took care of goods coming from and human cargo going to the beach. Boys were used as "servants."

BLACK HISTORY EVERYDAY
PART TWO

Black History Everyday - Part Two Photo. Kirsten Clarke of Lawyers Committee for Civil Rights Under Law.

Black History Everyday - Part Two Photo. Faces and signs in the crowd for the 50th Anniversary March on Washington.

FREDERICK MONDERSON

Black History Everyday - Part Two Photo. Faces and signs in the crowd for the 50th Anniversary March on Washington.

Men were employed as "door keepers." Some were employed as "messengers for carrying news" to the king of the arrival of ships. The "gong gong beater" announced the opening of trade for human and material merchandise. The "trunk keeper" took care of the enslaved Africans while on shore in despicable holding centers. The "captain of the waterside" oversaw the loading and unloading of the slave ships. Each ship had six "water rollers" to supply fresh water for each voyage. "Women were used for washing and bringing water." A "viceroy" received the captain of a ship. Lastly, "porters" were used for hauling and other menial tasks.

BLACK HISTORY EVERYDAY
PART TWO

There is an interesting fact about these workers and their lack of "job security." If they did anything wrong many ended up with the same enslaved persons they helped put aboard ship. As indicated, significant players in this experience were the African privateers or black slave catchers and traders. These "independents" often sold small parcels of captives to the European traders. Sometimes they sailed their canoes alongside slavers. Unscrupulous business practice invited these "budding entrepreneurs" aboard to trade for their cargo. Celebrating, they were gotten drunk, sort of "shanghaied," robbed and thrown in with the same persons they had sold.

Falconbridge (1788: 14 15), an eyewitness in the trade provided a good example of how this unfolded as he indicated: "A black trader invited a Negroe, who resided a little way up the country, to come and see him. After the entertainment was over the trader proposed to his guest, to treat him with a sight of the ships lying in the river. The unsuspicious countryman readily consented, and accompanied the trader in a canoe to the side of the ship, which he viewed with pleasure and astonishment. While he was thus employed, some black traders on board who appeared to be in on the secret, leaped into the canoe, seized the unfortunate man, and dragging him into the ship immediately sold him."

FREDERICK MONDERSON

Black History Everyday - Part Two Photo. Faces and signs in the crowd for the 50th Anniversary March on Washington. Attorney Malik Zulu Shabazz holds copy of **The New Black Panther** with front Page article that reads "Million Man March Strikes Black!!!"

The slaving surgeon again (1788: 18) informed, "the traders frequently beat those Negroes which are objected to by the captains and use them with great severity .... Instances have happened at that place that the traders when any of their Negroes have been objected to have dropped their canoes under the stem of the belles, and instantly beheaded them, in sight of the captain."

Falconbridge tells us even further (1788: 19) of how they were handled, "having their hands tied with a

BLACK HISTORY EVERYDAY
PART TWO

kind of willow twigs and a strict watch is kept over them .... Their allowance of food is so scanty that it is barely sufficient to support nature .... The men Negroes, on being brought abroad the ship are immediately fastened together two and two, by handcuffs on their wrists and by irons riveted on their legs."

Finally, with the cargo secured, the "Middle Passage" of transshipment began. Conditions on board slave ships were intolerable. Many ships were packed beyond capacity. The dead and dying were thrown overboard sometimes. Sharks could often be observed following these "floating coffins." Since persons were shackled together, it was not surprising to wake in the morning and find one's partner had passed in the night. Even more horrifying, tropical garments did not protect these Africans from the seas' tempestuous nature. E. Jefferson Murphy (1972: 282) quotes Willem Bosman whom he credits with writing one of the few intelligent descriptions of African life along the Gold Coast, during this horrendous period. Accordingly, Bosman mentions how the slaves were assembled, sold and processed at Dahomey, before boarding ships bound for the Middle Passage. "When these slaves come to Fida [Ouidah] they are put in prison all together, they are thoroughly examined, even to the smallest member, and that naked too both men and women, without the least distinction or modesty. Those which are approved as good are set on one side; and the lame or faulty are set by as Invalids .... These are such as are

FREDERICK MONDERSON

above five and 30 years old, or are maimed in the arms, legs, hand, or feet, have lost a tooth, are gray haired, or have films over their eyes; as well those which are infected with any venereal distemper, or with several other diseases."

"The Invalids and the maimed are thrown out... the remainder are numbered .... In the meanwhile, a burning iron, with the arms or names of the companies, lies in the fire, with which ours are marked on the breast."

"I doubt not that this trade seems very barbarous to you, but since it is followed by mere necessity it must go on; but we take all possible care that they are not burned too hard, especially the women, who are more tender than the men .... we send them on board our ships at the very first opportunity before which their masters strip them of all they have on their backs; so that they come aboard stark-naked women as well as men: in which condition they are obliged to continue, if the master of the ship is not so charitable (which he commonly is) as to bestow something on them to cover their nakedness."

BLACK HISTORY EVERYDAY
PART TWO

Black History Everyday - Part Two Photo. Faces and signs in the crowd for the 50th Anniversary March on Washington.

Black History Everyday - Part Two Photo. Faces and signs in the crowd for the 50th Anniversary March on Washington.

Health conditions were equally inadequate for these voyages. The personal disposal facilities on ships were poor. The food was bad. In addition, Falconbridge's (1788: 21 22) commentary indicated, "the diet of the Negroes, while on board, consist chiefly of horse beans, boiled to the consistence of a pulp; of boiled yams and rice and sometimes of a small quantity of beef or pork .... They sometimes made use of a sauce, composed of palm oil, mixed with flour water and pepper, which the sailors call slabber sauce .... allowance of water is about half a pint at each meal."

The captives were exposed to cruel and unscrupulous sailors. Africans witnessed personal abuse of their women at the hand of harsh seamen and captains. E. Jefferson Murphy (1972) wrote: "Many Africans suffered from fevers. Others contracted diseased minds from breathing the putrid air of the ship's hold. Several became melancholy, longing for their native land. Some had flux or dysentery. Others contracted gangrene if their skins were cut in any way. Scurvy was another malady that afflicted the unfortunate Africans. Malnutrition plagued many captives and many others committed suicide, rather than face the uncertainties at the end of the ocean voyage."

Even more, in the "Middle Passage" when Africans chose to rebel, they were severely punished to set examples for others that such resistance was futile. Those who chose not to eat and hoped to die were forced fed. Their captors used specially designed metal instruments for this unpleasant task. In this respect Falconbridge (1788: 23) further added, "upon

BLACK HISTORY EVERYDAY
PART TWO

the Negroes refusing to take sustenance, I have seen coals of fire, glowing hot, put on a shovel and placed so near their lips as to scorch and burn them. And this has been accompanied with threats, of forcing them to swallow the coals, ... I have also been credibly informed, that a certain captain in the slave trade, poured melted lead on such of the Negroes as obstinately refused their food."

Many jumped overboard willingly, to be eaten by the sharks or to drown. They chose a watery grave rather than become enslaved in the New World. Their final act was one of defiance!

THE TRIANGULAR TRADE

The "Triangular Trade" is considered the effective or economic component of the Atlantic or European Slave Trade from Africa to America. Together with the "Middle Passage" and the "Institution of Slavery," history records four centuries of European and American inhumanity towards Africans. The degradation of this experience has been called a "crime against the human spirit." In fact, it was a crime to Africa, African people and humanity in general. So, we need to understand how logistics of the trade operated in a triangle, that began in Europe, involved Africa, the Americas and returned to Europe. Picton's view (1873: 222) is an apt description for he has written: "The ships sailed from

FREDERICK MONDERSON

Liverpool to the West Coast of Africa, where they shipped the slaves from depots where their living freight had been collected; thence to the West Indian islands where the slaves were sold, and the proceeds brought home in proceeds of sugar and rum."

Davidson (1966: 204-205) helps us understand this even more when he wrote: "There developed what was to become known as the triangular trade, a commercial system which greatly helped to build the continued industrial and technical progress of western Europe in the eighteenth and nineteenth centuries." Equally too, Du Bois (1971: 227-228) added his understanding of this phenomenon, particularly in the British areas of the Caribbean, when he said: "If we confine ourselves to America, we cannot forget that America was built on Africa. From being a mere stopping place between Europe and Asia or a chance treasure house of gold, America became through African labor the center of the sugar empire and the cotton kingdom and an integral part of that world industry and trade which caused the Industrial Revolution and the reign or capitalism."

The commodities were put on board ships bound for Africa and exchanged for Africans who were then shipped to the Americas. Here they were sold or exchanged with further investment being made in tropical products that were taken back to England. A handsome profit was realized all round. Again, a ship sailed outfitted for Africa with, for example, 500 British pounds of good was able to exchange this for

BLACK HISTORY EVERYDAY
PART TWO

something like three times its worth, say 1,500 British pounds of commodities in Africa, mostly humans.

In an analogous argument, according to Williams' 1944 work, *Capitalism and Slavery*, in the New World, 1,500 British pounds of African goods fetched about 4,500 British pounds when sold. This sum was reinvested in tropical commodities. The Caribbean islands produced sugar, rice, indigo and rum to be shipped to England. At home the returning entrepreneurs sold their tropical products for about 7,500 British pounds. Therefore, according to some sources, as much as 6,000 to 7,000 British pounds could be made on one such venture. Imagine several hundred ships form several ports, of one nation, operating for one, two, three, four hundred years. Multiply this by the various ports of other nations involved in the trade, with their various ports. The profits and accumulated capital were enormous and guaranteed, from enslaving persons of Africa. This then is what is meant in the argument, particularly made as introduction to the TV Documentary, **Fight Against Slavery**, narrated by Ruby Dee, when she said the Slave Trade provided one of the main streams of capital that launched the Industrial Revolution.

FREDERICK MONDERSON

Black History Everyday - Part Two Photo. Faces and signs in the crowd for the 50th Anniversary March on Washington.

Black History Everyday - Part Two Photo. Faces and signs in the crowd for the 50th Anniversary March on Washington.

BLACK HISTORY EVERYDAY
PART TWO

The role of the British nation in the Slave Trade resulted in tremendous financial gain to it. This is also a view clearly enunciated by Dr. Eric Williams' *Capitalism and Slavery*. This classic text showed how the "Triangular Trade" was fueled because "England, France and Colonial America supplied the exports and the ships; Africa the human merchandise; the plantations the colonial raw materials" worked by the human capital.

He further explained how the **Triangular Trade** gave a triple stimulus to British industry.

"The Negroes were purchased with British manufactures; transported to the plantations, they produced sugar, cotton, indigo, molasses and other tropical products, the processing of which created new industries in England; while the maintenance of the Negroes and their owners on the plantations provided another market for British industry."

Clearly, such impact of the Triangular Trade on British industry was experienced in many areas. The first important gain occurred in shipping and shipbuilding. British shipping industry benefited tremendously by building bigger and faster ships to carry more Africans. Seaport towns expanded as ports developed to handle the prodigious increase in British shipping. Also, participation in the slave trade had become a "nursery" for British seamen, Britain's merchant marine. During times of war, these seamen aided the British Navy. In addition, individuals were

FREDERICK MONDERSON

employed, wrote Williams, "in ancillary trades as carpenters, painters, boat builders, tradesmen and artisans connected with repairs, equipment and loading of slaving ships, both in Europe and America." These industries benefited tremendously.

Commissions, dock duties, and insurance increased from the trade in Africans, creating the basis to fund other enterprises.

Many British seaport towns expanded from the slave trade. Bristol, London, Liverpool, and Glasgow benefited enormously from their involvement. Port facilities expanded to accommodate the increase in shipping. Such expansion was experienced, more-so, in the latter decades of the eighteenth and early decades of the nineteenth century as the engines of industry progressed.

Wells (1902: 95) noted, in the *City of Bristol*, "the trade of the port was so great in 1725 that two new quays were built one at St. Augustine's back and one near King Street. In 1736 Corporation dues ... at 40 shillings on each 60-ton ship; dues ... worth 1000 pounds a year in those times."

Customs payment of Liverpool and Bristol for the years 1753 to 1757 were as follows

| Year | Bristol | Liverpool |

[In British Pounds]

BLACK HISTORY EVERYDAY
PART TWO

1753	170,361. 13s. 1 1/4d.	45,479 01s. 1 1/2d.
1754	156,717. 9s. 1 3/4d.	59,766 06s. 0 3/4d.
1755	177,894. 15s. 4 1/2d.	49,661 0s. 8 1/2d.
1756	155,951. 5s. 5 d.	49,976 11s. 1 1/2d.
1757	151,516. 1s. 1 1/4d.	60,263 15s. 10 1/2d.

In 1764 Bristol's contribution as a revenue producing port was, 195,000 [British] pounds and Liverpool 70,000 [British] pounds. The dues paid to the Society of Merchants by vessels of 60 tons and upwards increased from 918 British pounds in 1745 to 2000 in 1775."

More particularly, the City of Bristol boasted rather questionable beginnings for, according to Wells (1909: 381), its "first overseas trade was in white slaves, and the early prosperity of the trade was due to that nefarious traffic." In fact, Wells (1909: 382) again tells us: "Bristol men kidnapped or bought the best of the youth of both sexes whenever they could. In the Bristol market strings of young men and maidens stood tied together waiting to be bought." If this is how "merchants" treated their own people, imagine how they treated Africans who were "different."

Following John Hawkins' exploits two centuries earlier, Wells (1909: 383 84) informs: "In 1764 Charles II gave a body of London Merchants a monopoly to trade with Africa .... A flagrant injustice to the Bristol Merchant Venturers who had chartered

FREDERICK MONDERSON

rights in the trade .... Bill of Rights (1689) ... put an end to that monopoly ... gave great impetus to Bristol African Commerce. In 1696 London Merchants formed the Royal African Company tried to get the monopoly back .... The Royal African Company could not ship more than 3000 slaves per annum."

"Parliament passed an Act in 1698 virtually establishing free trade in slaves .... an Act of Parliament in 1759 threw the trade open to anybody willing to pay a registration fee of 2 [British] pounds, and thence forth Liverpool became an important slave trading port .... By 1752 Bristol was the leading port in the trade. London came second and Liverpool third."

"300,000 [British] pounds per annum from slaves, 74,000 shipped a year from Africa. The price of slaves in Jamaica were about 5 [British] pounds for boys and girls. On the West Coast of Africa, they could be bought for 20 shillings each."

In 1753 there were at least 20 sugar refineries in Bristol. John Latimer's *The History of the Society of Merchant Venturers of the City of Bristol*, (1903:178 86) recounts: "Traffic in slaves ... trade to be of the most advantage to this kingdom of any we derive, and as it were all profit; the first cost being little more than small matters of our own manufactures, for which we have in return gold, [elephant's] teeth, wax and Negroes, the last whereof is much better than the first, being indeed the best traffic the kingdom hath."

BLACK HISTORY EVERYDAY
PART TWO

"Royal African Company, monopoly of trade with Africa granted them by Charles the Second in 1764."

Black History Everyday - Part Two Photo. Faces and signs in the crowd for the 50th Anniversary March on Washington.

Black History Everyday - Part Two Photo. Senator Ted Liu at Sharpton on Dr. King's day!

FREDERICK MONDERSON

"Merchant Venturers of Bristol .... Surreptitious traffic between the West Coast of Africa and the English plantations in America. That the prosperity of the West India planters depended upon a plentiful supply of Negroes ...."

"An act was passed in 1698, leaving the trade entirely open, the first nine years of open trade the Merchants of Bristol and Liverpool dispatched no less than 160,950 Negroes to the British Plantations."

"Petition to the House of Commons in 1713, ... that the subsistence of Bristolians chiefly depended on this trade, which gave employment to great numbers of seamen, shipwrights, weavers, metal workers, and other artisans, a large part of whose manufactures were exchanged for Negroes."

"A similar Petition from the Society affirmed that many of their ships were suitable only for the African trade and they would be ruined by exclusion from it .... In 1725 the African company, ... offering the Government a loan of one-million-pound sterling if their monopoly was restored ... rejected ... the trade was solely in the hands of individual merchants or firms. A bundle of loose papers throwing a strange light on the proceedings of some captains in the Royal Navy commanding ships of war stationed on the African coast was found. It appears from these documents, which are affidavits of the masters and sailors of Bristol slave ships, that in the year 1737,

BLACK HISTORY EVERYDAY
PART TWO

whilst the deponents were trying to procure cargoes on the coast, officers and crews of three royal vessels, the Diamond, Greenwich and Spence, lying there ostensibly for the protection of the trade, were actively engaged in the purchase of Negroes, gold dust and elephant's teeth, each of the ships being provided for trafficking with large stores of cotton goods, spirituous liquors, gunpowder and other merchandise, ... while 32 pound per head was given for slaves or 4 pounds above the ordinary rate."

One affidavit stated that the Greenwich sailed for Barbados with 200 Negroes and another that the Spence, a small war sloop, carried off fifty or sixty more ... the Society cooperated with the Friends at Liverpool in forwarding a strong remonstrance to the admiralty which apparently succeeded in its object."

"The African Company... (sponsored a) determined effort in Parliament to secure the trade exclusively for themselves .... that traffic on the Slave Coast could not be protected against foreigners unless a large number of additional forts were built and garrisoned; that the government grant for that purpose (10,000 British pounds a year) was wholly inadequate; and that the charge could only be sustained by a company enjoying exclusive privileges."

"The Common Council in a Petition to the House of Commons, alleged that the trade from this port to the West Indies and America by way of Africa was the Principal and most considerable branch belonging to

FREDERICK MONDERSON

the City, and that since such trade has been free and open it has greatly increased, much better supplied with Negroes and large quantities of the manufactures of this kingdom exported."

"The average number of human beings yearly being torn from their homes had then reached the appalling total of 74,000; ... Liverpool ... that town alone was making 3000 [British] pounds per annum by the traffic."

"April 13, 1789, at a crowded meeting in the Hall, Mr. William Miles Presiding, an influential Committee was appointed to defend the traffic, "On which the welfare of the West India Island and the commerce and revenue of the kingdom so essentially depend."

So, tariff and revenue from the trade also multiplied. For example, Williams tells us, "British customs duties rose from 10,000 [British] pounds in 1634 to 334,000 pounds in 1785. Wharfage dues payable on every vessel above sixty tons, increased between 1745 and 1755."

John Latimer (1893: 270 72) mentioned how the African Company was practically insolvent and unable to raise capital without legislative help.

BLACK HISTORY EVERYDAY
PART TWO

Black History Everyday - Part Two Photo. Faces and signs in the crowd for the 50th Anniversary March on Washington.

Black History Everyday - Part Two Photo. Faces and signs in the crowd for the 50th Anniversary March on Washington.

FREDERICK MONDERSON

"(1753) in Liverpool 101, in London 135 and in Bristol 157 merchants who were members of the African Company .... Bristol list dated June 23, 1755 ... 237 members resided in Bristol, 147 in London and 89 in Liverpool .... In 1750 the price demanded of native dealers was from 28 to 32 [British] pounds a head ... that the Bristol and Liverpool shippers could carry the trade 10 or 15 percent cheaper that London."

This African Company exerted significant influence in the halls of parliament when efforts were made to regulate the trade in Africans. According to Latimer (1893: 476), the "measure was vehemently opposed by the African Merchants in London, Bristol and Liverpool."

Black History Everyday - Part Two Photo. Latino heroes at the **2nd Million Youth March**, Brooklyn, 2003.

BLACK HISTORY EVERYDAY PART TWO

Latimer tells (1893: 478) further, "the Bells of the Bristol churches rang merry peals on the news being received of the rejection of one of Wilberforce's motions .... [a Jesuit priest] Reverend Raymond Harris of Liverpool produced 'Scriptural researches on the licitness of the slave trade, showing its conformity with the sacred writings of the word of God' and of course the work was liberally patronized .... The trade was inconsistent with reason, religion and humanity."

Davidson (1971: 19-20) makes a comparison with the then capitalist schemes of things and another pariah state in the modern world in that "attitudes allowed no respect either for the victims or for the peoples from whom they came. To those who condemned the trade, British governments of the day replied that it was far too profitable to be stopped. "We cannot," said Lord Dartmouth, Secretary of State for the Colonies in 1775, "allow the colonies to check or to discourage in any degree a traffic so beneficial to the nation." The argument was persuasive: just how much so we ourselves are well placed to understand today. Nearly two centuries after Lord Dartmouth had enunciated his views on the indispensable benefits of the slave trade, another Conservative British government returned almost exactly the same reply to critics who condemned the sale of arms to the Republic of South Africa. The sale might have its unfortunate side; it was far too profitable to be stopped.

FREDERICK MONDERSON

Aggregate import of slaves to Jamaica from 1700 1750 numbered 408,101 of whom 108,000 were transferred to other islands, leaving 300,000 settled laborers. Even more significant, growth was experienced in the textile industry. Wool became an enormously profitable business. Perpetuanas, Arrangoes, Bays, Bridgewaters, and Welsh Plaines were all manufactured for sale in the Africa trade. Petitions were received by the government regarding "Suffolk, Essex, woolen traders of London, Woolen Merchants of Plymouth, Woolen Dealers of Totnes and Ashburton, Woolen Manufacturers of Kidderminster, Merchant Adventurers of Minehead" who were all involved. Eric Williams further added, "Wakefield, Halifax, Burnley, Colne, Kendal, were interested in the manufacture of woolen goods for Africa and the West Indies." Can you imagine, the brothers and sisters of Africa wearing "British wool" in the hot tropical sun? Cotton manufacture too was big business. Liverpool, Cottonopolis, Lancashire, and Manchester were heavily involved. The tremendous dependence on the Triangular Trade "made Manchester." So much so, cities not directly involved in outfitting ships for the trade were tied to and benefited from feeder industries.

According to a study by the British Privy Council in 1788, wrote Eric Williams, it was estimated that "Manchester exported annually to Africa, goods worth 200,000 pounds, 180,000 pounds of this for

BLACK HISTORY EVERYDAY PART TWO

Negroes only; the manufacture of these goods represented an investment of 300,000 pounds and gave employment to 180,000 men, women and children." Even the kids got in on the act!

The British banking industry was another significant beneficiary from the slave trade. Banks were involved full scale by accepting deposits and helping underwrite much economic development at the time. Particularly, in the Eighteenth Century, a number of banking institutions were begun as a result of the slave trade. Coupled with insurance such "infant industries" found fertile opportunities for growth, development and expansion. The names of banks in the trade included Heywood Bank, Bank of Liverpool, Banking Firm of William Gregson, and Sons, Parke and Moorland and the Manchester Bank. Then there was the Thomas Leyland Bank, the Banking Firm of Charles and Roscoe, and the North and South Wales Bank, Ltd., Hanly's Bank, the Banking Firm of Charles Caldwell, Co., and the New Bank were all involved. Lastly, named were Miles Bank and Barclay's Bank. Yes!

Ships' Bank, Arms Bank, Thistle Bank, and William Deacon's Bank, all began in and serviced the Triangular Trade. However, while many of them did not survive or moved on to other enterprises, some banks as Barclay stayed in the same business.

Insurance was needed to cover the cargo whether commodity or humanity. Lloyds of London and

FREDERICK MONDERSON

Liverpool Underwriters insured the trade. These insurance magnates also helped to finance heavy industry involved in making metal instruments such as canons, anchors and artillery. In addition, attendant metallurgical industries produced fetters, chains, padlocks, and branding irons used for psychological and other forms for behavior modification. These latter were red hot when applied to the skin of anyone. *A Historical Account of Liverpool* tells us (1884: 24) of the African "Chief Accra" who "was one of the principal men catchers and slave dealers in Old Calabar," and most used some of these same instruments.

Further (1884: 27 28) we are informed: "In the year 1769, Capt. Paterson, of a Liverpool slaver, while lying off Bristol town, induced his men and natives to set fire to two villages and during the conflagration the poor blacks, crying out for help, P's men seized the Negroes, branded them and made them slaves. Another method of obtaining slaves was by inviting traders to come on board ship to dine with the captain, ... supplied with drink, the ship be got under way, ... traders on awakening ... stripped, branded and put down the hole to share the fate of other slaves."

The slave was made to kneel down, the branding iron was red hot, then it was stamped on the poor Negro's forehead, breast, buttock or back, according to the fancy of the brander.

BLACK HISTORY EVERYDAY
PART TWO

We are told again in the same source (1884: 31 32): "as many as 800 have been stowed in the holds of these infernal ships ... remaining in for a four month's voyage to the W.I. The white man arrogating to himself the supreme privilege of being lord and master of the blacks; to buy, to sell, to torture and kill as he pleases .... Baron Montesquieu affirmed "It is impossible to allow that the Negroes are men; because, if we allow them to be men, it will begin to be believed that we ourselves are not Christians."

Black History Everyday - Part Two Photo. Faces and signs in the crowd for the 50th Anniversary March on Washington.

FREDERICK MONDERSON

Black History Everyday - Part Two Photo. Faces and signs in the crowd for the 50th Anniversary March on Washington.

In fact, Davidson (1971: 49), quoting David Kimble, in *A Political History of Ghana*, Oxford, 1963, p. 545, could write: "Africa, in ages past, was the nursery of science and literature; from thence they were taught in Greece and Rome, so that it was said that the ancient Greeks represented their favorite goddess of Wisdom - Minerva - as an African princess ... Many eminent writers and historians agree that these ancient Ethiopians were Negroes ... And why should not the same race who governed Egypt ... who had her churches, her universities, and her repositories of learning and science, once more stand on their legs and endeavor to raise their characters in the scale of the-civilized world."

Brooks (1971: 7) also added: "In antiquity scholars wrote about Africa, and their works were widely

BLACK HISTORY EVERYDAY
PART TWO

circulated. Herodotus wrote of his travels into Egypt and Kush; Pliny the Elder included Africa in his *Natural History*; Diodorus Siculus reported on Ethiopia as well as Egypt in the first century B.C., Stepahanus of Byzantium in the fifth century A.D. wrote about Ethiopia – "the earliest established country on earth .... Both Pomponious Mela's and Strabo's geographies included the known lands of Africa. And in literature there were, among many works, the fourth century romance called Aethiopicaby Heliodorus of Emesa and the later Fall of Troy by Quintus of Smyrna, both of which featured black heroes."

Closer to our own time, Charles Rollin in his *Historia Ancienne* (1730), James Cowles Prichard in the early nineteenth century, d'Olivet in his great *L'histoire Philosophique du Genere Humain* and Heeren, the eminent Gottingen historian, all studied and wrote and praised black African civilizations. And the explorers and on-site experts Cailliaud (in his Voyage a' Meroe), the brilliant Champollion in his letters, and Hopkins in his travel in Ethiopia confirmed and endorsed the views that Egyptian civilization stemmed from earlier black achievements and that the Egyptians themselves were Africans, not Asians."

Even further, in understanding there should be no differences between humankind, wrote Davidson (1967: 49-50), in quoting G. Shepperson and T. Price, *Independent Africa*, Edinburgh, 1958, p. 163: "Poor

FREDERICK MONDERSON

Resident," wrote a Nyasaland African pastor half a century before Sir Roy Welensky said his associates were busy explaining the essentially "communist" (and therefore, in Central Africa, quite new) nature of nationalism, "he thinks too much of his skin and not of his heart. What is the difference between a white man and a black man? Are we not of the same blood and all from Adam? This startles me much - is Europe still Christian or Heathen? ... If we had power enough to communicate ourselves to Europe, we would advise then not to call themselves "Christiandom" but "Europeandom." Therefore, the life of the three combined bodies [Missionaries, Government, Companies] is altogether too cheaty, too thefty, too mockey. Instead of "Give" they say "Take away from."

Industry also produced iron bars, face masks and other restraining devices used in confining the African captives during the "Middle Passage." Manufacturing industry produced copper bars and iron hoops. The hoops bound casks for rum and beer. English workers also produced copper sheathing for ships, brass pans and kettles, and iron chairs and anchors. From these involvements British iron and steel industry expanded, in view of their vanguard role during the industrial revolution sweeping that nation. In America, as the New England merchants and shippers became involved, this business too proved lucrative.

BLACK HISTORY EVERYDAY
PART TWO

In the "Triangular Trade," guns formed a regular part of every African cargo. An old saying in England was: "The price of an African is one Birmingham gun." Most of these guns, however, were not new but old, used carbines that soon broke down. In regards to firearms introduced to Africa because and during the trade as part of other traffic merchandise, Iliffe (1995: 135) argued: "Europeans have often asserted that Africans sold one another for 'mere baubles or the weapons of war.' Even in the 1680s some 40 per cent of Senegambian imports were beads and semi-precious stones. Generally, however, Europeans sold to Africans much of the same kinds of goods as they sold to American colonists. At least half of West Africa's imports during the seventeenth and eighteenth centuries were cloth, initially mostly from India or elsewhere in Africa, later mostly from Europe. Raw iron and copper were also important, as were cowrie shells (as currency) in the Bight of Benin. In the eighteenth century four items other than cloth each formed about 10 per cent of imports: alcohol, tobacco, miscellaneous manufacturers (chiefly metal goods), and firearms and gunpowder. North Europeans began to sell guns in quantity during the late seventeenth century, when cheap and more reliable flintlock muskets led states on the Gold Coast and the Bight (Gulf) of Benin to rearm their forces. A century later sub-Saharan Africa was importing nearly 200,000 muskets a year."

In addition, to underscore the worth of an African, here is evidence of a purchase from a Prince. The price paid was "'thirteen beads of coral, half a string of amber, twenty-eight silver bells, three pairs bracelet for his woman; green beads, four ounces of scarlet wood.'

Lastly, sugar refining and rum distillation industries were also big beneficiaries. Around 1750, England boasted 120 sugar refineries. "Everybody was working" to process sugar produced in the West Indies. Also, rum distillation became an important economic industry as shown, according to Eric Williams that: "Imports from the islands increased from 58,000 gallons in 1721, to 300,000 in 1730. In 1736 the figure stood at one and a quarter million gallons, and to over two million between 1765 and 1799."

The New England merchants of colonial America quickly ousted the British. These entrepreneurs began supplying enormous quantities of rum for the trade making this commodity an important medium of exchange. Imagine the manpower, resources and industry involved during the 18th and first decades of the 19th Centuries, to produce, ship and exchange something like 140 gallons of rum for 1 male African, 120 gallons for 1 female and 90 gallons for 1 pre-puberty female who, in a relatively short time, could bear offsprings to further enrich the white masters.

BLACK HISTORY EVERYDAY
PART TWO

Black History Everyday - Part Two Photo. Faces and signs in the crowd for the 50th Anniversary March on Washington.

Black History Everyday - Part Two Photo. Faces and signs in the crowd for the 50th Anniversary March on Washington.

FREDERICK MONDERSON

The above information creates an image of the economic impact of the effective dynamics of the European Slave Trade in Africans. Here profits reigned supreme over conscience and concern for fellow-humans. This all happened during the "Triangular Trade" of the infamous European Slave Trade in Africans, across the Atlantic.

In these respects, we can view glimpses of the experiences of the ancestors of today's African-Americans, particularly those celebrating **Black History Month** in February of every year. Now, I wish to reflect on the work of William Roscoe (1751 1831), poet, historian, philanthropist, and "friend of the Negro" who was born at Mount Pleasant, Liverpool. His wonderful poem is in *An Historical Account of Liverpool* (1884) is entitled "Mount Pleasant," was written in 1771 and published in 1777.

The Afric's swarthy sons their toils repeat,
Beneath the fervors of the noon tide heat;
Torn from each joy that crowned their native soil,
No sweet reflections mitigate their toil.

From morn to eve by rigorous hands opprest,
Dull fly their hours of every hope unblest,
Till broke with labors, helpless and forlorn,
From their weak grasp the lingering morsel torn,
The reed-built hovels' friendly shade denied,
The test of folly and the scorn of pride;

BLACK HISTORY EVERYDAY
PART TWO

Lift the faint head, and bend the imploring eye,
Till death in kindness from the tortured beast,
Calls the free spirit of the realms to rest,
Shame to mankind! But shame to Britons most,
Who all the sweets of liberty can boast;

Yet, deaf to every human claim, deny
that bliss to others which themselves enjoy;
Life's bitter draught with harsher bitter fill,
Blast every joy, and add to every ill,
The trembling limbs with galling iron bind,
Nor loose the heavier bondage of the mind.

Equally too, Melville Herskovits in *The Human Factor in Changing Africa* (1962: 115) tells that: "Many tales in West Africa point the moral that children should not stray from their own compounds, or answer when addressed by a stranger, a legacy from the time of child snatching by slavers. When a bullock is sacrificed for the souls of the royal ancestors in Dahomey, a goat is given for those sold into slavery. The priests chant: Oh, ancestors, do all in your power that princes and nobles who today rule never be sent away from here as slaves ... Punish the people who bought our kinsmen, whom we shall never see again. Send their vessels to Wydah harbor, ... drown their crews, and make all the wealth of their ships come back to Dahomey."

Lloyd (1972: 69) has shown: "The trade in palm oil, and slightly later in palm kernels, replaced the slave trade in the early and middle years of the nineteenth century."

Again, equally, Amin (1973: 107) in his work *Neo-Colonialism in West Africa*, quoted a Master's Thesis from the Arts Faculty at Dakar in 1970, where he explained in comparison how the region of Eastern West Africa was involved in the effort to implement agriculture and trade as part of the onslaught to wipe out the trade in humans, in the later Nineteenth Century. He wrote: "The village communities were obliged by the state - the kingdoms of Abomey and Porto Novo - to provide quotas of palm products; and villages of 'royal slaves' were subject to similar, and no doubt even heavier, levies. The 'bourgeoisie' of former slave traders - the 'Brazilian' creoles - turned similarly to legal trade. The amazing story of the growth in the fortunes of the de Souzas, d'Almeidas, da Silvas, Camposes, Sacramentos, Alcantaras, Bandeiras, Bonbozas, da Costas, Paraisos, Vieyras, Lopez, Pereiras, Moreiras, etc. goes back to this period. After 1840, the passion which had gone into the slave trade was sublimated in the palm-oil trade. They turned to business, either as middlemen or as importers, competing successfully with the European traders, and through their family alliances they obtained an increasing numerical preponderance."

In concluding this section, we can begin to make a distinction between two forms of imperialism as a pattern of European expansion, settlement and colonization. In the early years of that expansion, we

BLACK HISTORY EVERYDAY
PART TWO

encounter what has been termed "naked imperialism." Here, the Europeans, whether in Africa and in the Americas, seized, killed, maimed, destroyed and raped people and culture at will, simply to show the victims were of an inferior race and culture, as their resources were appropriated for Europe's benefit. However, in the Nineteenth Century, following first the British in 1807, the Americans in 1808, and the French in 1817, outlawing the Slave Trade, a new strategy of exploitation was implemented. This was called "enlightened" imperialism. Here, under the guise of assisting, particularly the Africans, their wealth was appropriated in a more "humane" manner. Again, all for the benefit of the changed and emerging European industrial societies.

In a comparison of economic effects of the slave trade on both African and European societies, Davidson (1961: 278) has argued: "After about 1650, with diminishing exception, African production-for-export became a mono-culture in human beings. This can be seen to have suffocated economic growth in coastal and near-coastal Africa as surely as the extension of European production-for-export of consumer goods gave the maritime nations of Europe, at the same time, their long lead in economic development."

Even further, Davidson (1961: 278-279) continued: "The reasons for this suffocation were various. It was obviously an impoverishment to send away the very men and women who would otherwise produce wealth at home. In exporting slaves, African states exported their capital without any possible return in interest or in the enlargement of their economic system. Slave exports differed radically in this respect from the more or less forced emigration of impoverished men and women from nineteenth century Europe. Thus, the millions who left Britain in those years were able to enter the mainstream of capitalist expansion, and thereby benefit the mother-country in many indirect ways."

"But the African slaves could contribute nothing except to the wealth of their masters - a wealth that never returned to Africa. Dealers in Africa undoubtedly received payment for the slaves they sold; but the nature of the payment was strictly nonproductive. The very conditions of the exchange prevented the kind of capital accumulation that could have led to a more advanced economy. Such 'capital' as the kings and prime merchants could accumulate was in mere baubles or the weapons of war."

From an economic standpoint, in short, European slaving may be rightly regarded as a primitive and particularly destructive form of colonialism: the sale of consumer goods for the raw material of slave labor.

How right he was to show that, as Rodney and so many others have shown there was no trade but robbery, exploitation, murder and inequity in the

BLACK HISTORY EVERYDAY
PART TWO

traffic in humans that is still a stain on the conscience and psyche of both victims and victimizers.

Black History Everyday - Part Two Photo. Faces and signs in the crowd for the 50th Anniversary March on Washington.

Black History Everyday - Part Two Photo. Faces and signs in the crowd for the 50th Anniversary March on Washington.

FREDERICK MONDERSON

Now, for the Blessing! Wilson (1901: 58) "**OF LIFTING UP THE FEET**" from the *Papyrus of Nu* in the British Museum No. 10,477, sheet 6.

THE CHAPTER OF LIFTING UP THE FEET AND OF COMING FORTH UPON THE EARTH. The Chancellor in chief, Nu, triumphant, saith:

Black History Everyday - Part Two Photo. Faces and signs in the crowd for the 50th Anniversary March on Washington.

"Perform thy work, O Seker, perform thy work, O Seker, O thou [who dwellest in thy house], and who [standest] on [thy] feet in the underworld! I am the god who sendeth forth rays of light over the Thigh of heaven, and I come forth to heaven and I sit myself

BLACK HISTORY EVERYDAY PART TWO

down by the God of Light (Khu). Hail, I have become helpless! Hail, I have become helpless! But I go forward. I have become helpless; I have become helpless in the regions of those who plunder in the underworld."

Wilson (1901: 58) - "**Of JOURNEYING TO ANNU**" from the *Papyrus of Nu* in the British Museum No. 10,477, sheet 13.

THE CHAPTER OF JOURNEYING TO ANNU (Heliopolis) AND OF RECEIVING A THRONE THEREIN. The Chancellor in chief, Nu, triumphant, saith:

"I have come forth from the uttermost parts of the earth, and [I have] received by apparel (?) at the will (?) of the Ape. I penetrate into the holy habitations of those who are in [their] shrines (or coffins), I force my way through the habitations of the god Remen, and I arrive in the habitations of the god Akhsesef, I travel on through the holy chambers, and I pass into the Temple of the god Kemken. The Buckle hath been given to me, it [hath placed] its hands upon me, it hath decreed [to my service] its sister Khebent, and its mother Kehkehet. It placeth me in [the eastern part of] heaven wherein Ra riseth and is exalted every day; and I rise therein and travel onward, and I become a spiritual body (sah) like the god, and they set me on that holy way on which Thoth journeyeth when he goeth to make peace between the two

FREDERICK MONDERSON

Fighting gods (i.e., Horus and Set). He journeyeth, he journeyeth to the city of Pe, and he cometh to the city of Tepu."

Wilson (1901: 59) - "**OF TRANSFORMATIONS**" from the *Papyrus of Nu* in the British Museum No. 10,477, sheet 9.

THE CHAPTER OF A MAN TRANSFORMING HIMSELF INTO WHATEVER FORM HE PLEASETH. The chancellor in chief, Nu, triumphant, saith:

"I have come into the House of the King by means of the mantis (abit) which led me hither. Homage to thee, O thou who fliest into heaven, and dost shine upon the son of the white crown, and dost protect the white crown, let me have my existence with thee! I have gathered together the great god[s], I am mighty, I have made my way and I have travelled along thereon."

Wilson (1901: 59) - "**OF PERFORMING TRANSFORMATIONS**" from the *Papyrus of Nu* in the British Museum No. 10,477, sheet 10.

THE CHAPTER OF PERFORMING THE TRANSFORMATION INTO A HAWK OF GOLD. The chancellor in chief, Nu, triumphant, saith: "I have risen, I have risen like the mighty hawk

BLACK HISTORY EVERYDAY
PART TWO

[of gold] that cometh forth from his egg; I fly and I alight like the hawk which hath a back four cubits wide, and the wings of which are like unto the mother of emerald of the south. I have come forth from the interior of the Sektet boat, and my heart hath been brought forth from the mountain of the east.

"I have alighted upon the Atet boat, and those who were dwelling in their companies have been brought unto me, and they bowed low in paying homage unto me and in saluting me with cries of joy. I have risen, and I have gathered myself together like a beautiful hawk of gold, which hath the head of a Bennu bird, and Ra entereth in day by day to hearken unto my words; I have taken my seat among those first-born gods of Nut. I am stablished, and the divine Sekhet hetep is before me, I have eaten therein, I have become a khu therein, I have an abundance therein as much as I desire the god Nepra hath given to me my throat, and I have gained the mastery over that which guardeth (or belongeth to) my head."

Wilson (1901: 60 64) **"OF TRANSFORMATION INTO A HAWK"** from the *Papyrus of Nu* in the British Museum No. 10,477, sheet 13 and 14.

THE CHAPTER OF MAKING THE TRANSFORMATION INTO A DIVINE HAWK. The chancellor in chief, Nu, triumphant, saith:

FREDERICK MONDERSON

"Hail, Great God, come now to Tattu! Make thou smooth for me the ways and let me go round about [to visit] my thrones; I have renewed (?) myself, and I have raised myself up. O grant thou that I may be feared, and make thou me to be a terror.

Black History Everyday – Part Two
Photo. Erik and Luis pose before "Old Glory" in Union Station, Washington, DC.

BLACK HISTORY EVERYDAY
PART TWO

"Let the gods of the underworld be afraid of me, and may they fight for me in their habitations which are therein. Let not him that would do me harm draw nigh unto me, or injure (?) me, in the House of Darkness, that is, he that clotheth and covereth the feeble one, and whose [name] is hidden; and let not the gods act likewise toward me. {Hail], ye gods, who hearken unto [my] speech! Hail, ye rulers, who are among the followers of Osiris! Be ye therefore silent, O ye gods, when one god speaketh unto another, for he hearkeneth unto right and truth; and what I speak unto [him] do thou also speak for me then, O Osiris. Grant thou that I may journey round about [according to] that which cometh forth from thy mouth concerning me, and grant that I may see thine own Form (or forms), and the dispositions of thy Souls. Grant thou that I may come forth, and that I may have power over my legs, and that I may have my existence there like unto that of Neb er tcher who is over [all]. May the gods of the underworld fear me, and may they fight for me in their habitations. Grant thou that I may move along therein together with the divine beings who journey onward, and May I be established upon my resting place like the Lord of Life. May I be joined unto Isis the divine lady, and may she protect me from him that would do an injury unto me; and let not anyone come to see the divine one naked and helpless. May I journey on, may I come into the uttermost parts of heaven. I exchanged speech with the god Seb, I make supplication for divine food from Neb-er-tcher; the gods of the underworld have fear of me, and they fight for me in their habitations whey they see that thou hast provided me with food, both of the fowl of the air and of the fish of the sea. I am one of those Khus who dwell with the divine Khu, and I have made my form like unto his divine Form, when he cometh forth and maketh himself manifest in Tattu. [I am] a spiritual body (sah) and possess my soul, and will speak unto thee the things which concern me. O grant thou that I may be feared, and make thou me to be a terror; let the gods of the underworld be afraid of me, and May they fight for me in their habitations. I, even I, am the Khu who dwelleth with the divine Khu, whom the god Tem himself hath created, and who hath come into being from the blossom (i.e., the eyelashes) of his eye; he hath made to have existence, and he hath made to be glorious (i.e., to be Khus), and he hath made mighty thereby those who have their existence along with him. Behold, he is the only One in Nu, and they sing praises (or do homage) unto him [when] he cometh forth from the horizon, and the gods and the Khus who have come into being along with him ascribe [the lordship of] terror unto him."

BLACK HISTORY EVERYDAY
PART TWO

Black History Everyday - Part Two Photo. Faces and signs in the crowd for the 50th Anniversary March on Washington.

Black History Everyday - Part Two Photo. Faces and signs in the crowd for the 50th Anniversary March on Washington.

FREDERICK MONDERSON

"I am one of those forms (?) which the eye of the Lord, the only One, hath created. And behold, when as yet Isis had not given birth to Horus, I had germinated, and had flourished, and I had become aged, and I had become greater than those who dwelt with the divine Khu, and who had come into being along with him. And I had risen up like the divine hawk, and Horus made for me a spiritual body containing his own soul, so that I might take possession of all that belonged unto Osiris in the underworld. The double Lion god, the governor of things which belong to the Temple of the Nemes crown, who dwelleth in his secret abode, saith [unto me]: 'Get thee back to the uttermost parts of heaven, for behold, inasmuch as through thy forms of Horus thou hast become a spiritual body, (sah) the Nemes crown is not for thee; but behold, thou hast the power of speech even to the uttermost parts of heaven.'

"And I, the guardian, took possession of the things of Horus [which belonged] unto Osiris in the underworld, and Horus told aloud unto me the things which his divine father Osiris spake unto him in years [gone by] on the day of his own burial. I have given unto thee [literally, 'Thou hast given unto me.'] the Nemes crown through the double Lion god and thou mayest pass onward and mayest come to the heavenly path, and that those who dwell in the uttermost parts of the horizon may see thee, and that the gods of the underworld may see thee and may fight for thee in their habitations. And of them is the Auhet. The gods,

BLACK HISTORY EVERYDAY
PART TWO

each and all of them, who are the warders of the shrine of the Lord, the only One, have fallen before my words. Hail! He that is exalted upon his tomb is on my side, and he hath bound [upon my head] the Nemes crown, by the decree of the double Lion god on my behalf, and the god Auhet hath prepared a way for me. I, even I, am exalted in my tomb, and the double Lion god hath bound the Nemes crown upon my [head], and he hath also given unto me the double hairy covering of my head. He hath stablished my heart through his own backbone, he hath stablished, and I shall not fall through Shu. I make my peace with the beautiful divine Brother, the lord of the two uraei, adored be he! I, even I, am he who knoweth the roads through the sky, and the wind thereof is in my body. The bull which striketh terror [into men] shall not drive me back, and I shall pass on to the place where lieth the shipwrecked mariner on the border of the *Sekhet nehen* (i.e., Field of Illimitable Time), and I shall journey on to the night and sorrow of the regions of Amenti. O Osiris, I shall come each day into the House of the double Lion god, and I shall come forth therefrom into the House of Isis, the divine lady. I shall behold sacred things which are hidden, and I shall be led on to the secret and holy things, even as they have granted unto me to see the birth of the Great God. Horus hath made me to be a spiritual body through his soul, [and I see what is therein. If I speak near the mighty ones of Shu, they repulse my opportunity. I am the guardian and I] take possession of the things which Horus had from Osiris in the underworld. I, even and I, am Horus who dwelleth in the divine Khu. [I] have gained power over his crown, I have gained power over his radiance, and I have travelled over the remote, illimitable parts of heaven. Horus is upon his throne; Horus is upon his royal seat. My face is like unto that of the divine hawk, my strength is like unto that of the divine hawk, and I am one who hath been fully equipped by his divine Lord. I shall come forth to Tattu, I shall see Osiris, I shall pay homage to him on the right hand and on the left, I shall pay homage unto Nut, and she shall look upon me, and the gods shall look upon me, together with the Eye of Horus who is without sight (?). They (i.e., the gods) shall make their arms to come forth unto me. I rise up [as] a divine Power, and [I] repulse him that would subject me to restraint. They open unto me the holy paths, they see my form, and they hear that which I speak. [Down] upon your faces, ye gods of the Tuat (underworld), who would resist me with your faces and oppose me with your powers, who lead along the stars which never rest, and who make the holy paths unto the Hemati abode [where is] the Lord of the exceedingly mighty and terrible Soul. Horus hath commanded that ye lift up your faces so that I may look upon you. I have risen up like the divine hawk, and Horus hath made for me a spiritual body, through his own soul, to take possession of that which belongeth to Osiris in the Tuat (underworld). I have bound up the gods with divine tresses, and I have travelled on to those who ward their Chambers, and who were on both sides of me, I have made my roads and I have journeyed on and have reached those divine beings who inhabit their secret dwellings, and

BLACK HISTORY EVERYDAY PART TWO

who are warders of the Temple of Osiris. I have spoken unto them with strength, and have made them to know the most mighty power of him that is provided with two horns [to fight] against Suti; and I make them to know concerning him that hath taken possession of the divine food, and who is provided with the Might of Tem. May the gods of the underworld [order] a prosperous journey for me! O ye gods who inhabit your secret dwellings, and who are warders of the Temple of Osiris, and whose numbers are great and multitudinous, grant ye that I may come unto you. I have bound up and I have gathered together the powers of *Kesemu enenet*, or (as others say), *Kesemiu enenet*; and I have made holy the Powers of the paths of those who watch and guard the roads of the horizon, who are the guardians of the horizon of Hemati which is in heaven. I have stablished habitation for Osiris, I have made the ways holy for him, I have done that which hath been commanded, I have come forth to Tattu, I have seen Osiris, I have spoken unto him concerning the matters of his first born son whom he loveth and concerning the wounding of the heart of Suti, and I have seen the divine one who is without life. Yea, I have made them to know concerning the counsels of the gods which Horus carried out while his father Osiris was not [with him]. Hail, Lord, thou most mighty and terrible Soul! Verily, I, even I, have come, look thou upon me, and do thou make me to be exalted. I have made my way through thy Tuat (underworld), and I have opened up the paths which belong to heaven and also those which belong to earth, and I have suffered no opposition therein. Exalted [be thou] upon thy throne, O Osiris! Thou hast heard fair things, O Osiris. Thy heart is glad, [O Osiris]. Thy speech (?) is stablished, [O Osiris], and thy princes rejoice. Thou art stablished like the Bull of Amentet. Thy son Horus hath risen like the sun upon thy throne, and all life is with him.

"Millions of years passeth not away. Horus is both the divine food and the sacrifice. [He] hath passed on (?) to gather together [the members of] his divine father; Horus is both the divine food and the sacrifice. [He] hath passed on (?) to gather together [the members of] his divine father; Horus is [his] deliverer, Horus is [his] deliverer. Horus hath sprung from the water of his divine father and [from his] decay. He hath become the Governor of Egypt. The gods labor for him, and they toil for him millions of years; and he hath made to live millions of years through his Eye, the only One of its Lord (or Neb s), Nebter tcher."

BLACK HISTORY EVERYDAY
PART TWO

Black History Everyday - Part Two Photo. Faces and signs in the crowd for the 50th Anniversary March on Washington.

Black History Everyday - Part Two Photo. Faces and signs in the crowd for the 50th Anniversary March on Washington.

Wilson (1901: 65 66) - **"OF TRANSFORMATION INTO A**

FREDERICK MONDERSON

GOVERNOR" from the *Papyrus of Nu* in the British Museum, 10,477, sheets 8 and 9.

THE CHAPTER OF BEING TRANSFORMED INTO THE GOVERNOR OF THE SOVEREIGN PRINCES.

The chancellor in chief, Nu, triumphant, saith: "I am the god Tem, the maker or heaven, the creator of things which are, who cometh forth from the earth, who maketh to come into being the seed which is sown, the lord of things which shall be, who gave birth to the gods; [I am] the great god who made himself, the lord of life, who maketh to flourish the company of the gods. Homage to you, O ye lords of divine things (or of creating), ye pure being whose abodes are hidden! Homage to you, O ye gods of the circuit of the flooded lands of Qebhu! Homage to you, O ye gods who live in Amentet! Homage to you, O ye company of the gods who dwell in Nut! Grant ye that I may come unto you, for I am pure, I am divine, I am a khu, I am strong, I am endowed with a soul (or I am mighty), and I have brought unto you incense, and sweet-smelling gums, and natron; I have made an end of the spittle which floweth from your mouth upon me. I have come, and I have made an end of the evil things which are in your hearts, and I have removed the faults which ye kept [laid up against me]. I have brought to you the things which are good, and I make to come into your presence Right and Truth. I, even I, know you, and I know your names, and I know your forms, which are unknown, and I come into being

BLACK HISTORY EVERYDAY
PART TWO

along with you. My coming is like unto that of the god who eateth men and who liveth upon the gods. I am mighty with you like the god who is exalted upon his resting place; the gods come to me in gladness, and goddesses make supplication unto me when they see me. I have come unto you, and I have risen like your two divine daughters upon my tables, and I drink drink offerings at eventide. My coming is [received] with shouts of joy, and divine beings who dwell in the horizon ascribe praises unto me, the divine spiritual body (Sah), the lord of divine beings. I am exalted like the holy god who dwelleth in the Great Temple, and the gods rejoice when they see me in my beautiful coming forth from the body of Nut, when my mother Nut giveth birth unto me."

Wilson (1901: 66 67) **"OF TRANSFORMATION INTO A GOD"** from the *Papyrus of Ani* in the British Museum No. 10,470, sheet 28.

[THE CHAPTER OF] MAKING THE TRANSFORMATION INTO THE GOD WHO GIVETH LIGHT [IN] THE DARKENSS. SAITH OSIRIS, THE SCRIBE ANI, TRIUMPHANT:

"I am the girdle of the robe of the god Nu, which shineth and sheddeth light upon that which belongeth to his breast, which sendeth forth light into the darkness, which uniteth the two fighting deities who dwell in my body through the mighty spell of the words of my mouth, which raiseth up him that hath fallen for he who was with him in the valley of Abtu (Abydos) hath fallen and I rest. I have remembered him.

"I have taken possession of the god Hu in my city, for I found him therein, and I have led away captive the darkness by my might. I have rescued the Eye [of the Sun] when it waned at the coming of the festival of the fifteenth day, and I have weighed Sut in the celestial houses against the Aged one who is with him. I have endowed Thoth [with what is needful] in the Temple of the Moon god for the coming of the fifteenth day of the festival. I have taken possession of the Ureret crown (Maat i.e., right and truth) is in my body; its mouths are of turquoise and rock crystal. My homestead is among the furrows which are [of the color of] lapis lazuli. I am Hem Nu (?) who sheddeth light in the darkness. I have come to give light in the darkness, which is made light and bright [by me]. I have given light in the darkness, and I have overthrown the destroying crocodiles. I have sung praises unto those who dwell in the darkness, I have raised up those who wept, and who had hidden their faces and had sunk down in wretchedness; and they did not look then upon me. [Hail, then,] ye beings, I am Hem Nu (?), and I will not let you hear concerning the matter. [I] have opened [the way], I am Hem Nu (?), [I] have made light the darkness, I have come,

BLACK HISTORY EVERYDAY
PART TWO

having made an end of the darkness, which hath become light indeed."

Black History Everyday - Part Two Photo. Faces and signs in the crowd for the 50th Anniversary March on Washington.

Black History Everyday - Part Two Photo. Faces and signs in the crowd for the 50th Anniversary March on Washington.

FREDERICK MONDERSON

Wilson (1901: 67) - **"TRANSFORMATION INTO A LOTUS"** from the Papyrus of Nu in the British Museum No. 10,477, sheet 11: **"THE CHAPTER OF MAKING THE TRANSFORMATION INTO A LOTUS**. The overseer of the palace, the chancellor in chief, Nu, saith: "I am the pure lotus which springeth up from the divine splendor that belongeth to the nostrils of Ra. I have made [my way], and I follow on seeking for him who is Horus. I am the pure one who cometh forth out of the Field."

Wilson (1901: 67) **"TRANSFORMATION INTO A LOTUS"** from the *Papyrus of Paqrer* (Naville).

THE CHAPTER OF MAKING THE TRANSFORMATION INTO A LOTUS.
Saith Osiris Paqrer: "Hail, thou lotus, thou type of the god Nefer Temu! I am the man that knoweth you, and I know your names among [those of] the gods, the lords of the underworld, and I am one of you. Grant ye that [I] may see the gods who are the divine guides in the Tuat (underworld), and grant ye unto me a place in the underworld near unto the lords of Amentet. Let me arrive at a habitation in the land of Tchesert, and receive me, O all ye gods, in the presence of the lords of eternity. Grant that my soul may come forth whithersoever it pleaseth, and let it

BLACK HISTORY EVERYDAY
PART TWO

not be driven away from the presence of the great company of the gods"

Wilson (1901: 68) **"TRANSFORMATION INTO PTAH"** from the *Papyrus of Nu* in the British Museum No. 10,477, sheets 9 and 10.

THE CHAPTER OF MAKING THE TRANSFORMATION INTO PTAH, OF EATING CAKES, AND OF DRINKING ALE, AND OF UNFETTERING THE STEPS, AND OF BECOMING A LIVING BEING IN ANNU (Heliopolis). The chancellor in chief, Nu, triumphant, saith: "I fly like a hawk, I cackle like the smen goose, and I perch upon that abode of the underworld (aat) on the festival of the great Being. That which is an abomination unto me, that which is an abomination unto me, I have not eaten; filth is an abomination unto me and I have not eaten thereof, and that which is an abomination unto my ka hath not entered into my belly. Let me, then, live upon that which the gods and the Khus decree for me; let me live and let me have power over cakes; let me eat them before the gods and the Khus [who have a favor] unto me; let me have power over [these cakes] and let me eat of them under the [shade of the] leaves of the palm tree of the goddess Hathor, who is my divine Lady. Let the offerings of the sacrifice, and the offering of cakes, and vessels of libations be made in Annu; let me clothe myself in the taau garment [which I shall receive] from the hand of the goddess Tait; let me stand up and let me sit down wheresoever I please. My head is like unto that of Ra, and [when my members are] gathered together [I am] like unto Tem; the four [sides of the domain] of Ra, and the width of the earth four times. I come forth. My tongue is like unto that of Ptah and my throne is like unto that of the goddess Hathor, and I make mention of the words of Tem, my father, with my mouth. Hymns of praise are repeated for [me] by reason of [my] mighty acts, and I am decreed to be the divine Heir of Seb, the lord of the earth and to be the protector therein. The god Seb refresheth me, and he maketh his risings to be mine. Those who dwell in Annu bow down their heads unto me, for I am their lord and I their bull. I am more powerful than the lord of time, and I shall enjoy the pleasure of love, and shall gain the mastery over millions of years."

Wilson (1901: 69) **"TRANSFORMATION INTO A BENNU BIRD"** from the **Papyrus of Nu** in the British Museum No. 10,477, sheet 10:

[THE CHAPTER OF MAKING THE TRANSFORMATION INTO A BENNU BIRD.] The chancellor-in-chief, Nu, triumphant, saith: "I came [literally "I flew."] Into being from unformed matter, I came into existence like the god Khepera, I have germinated like the things which germinate (i.e., plants), and I have dressed myself like a Tortoise. [I believe that "Turtle" is the correct

BLACK HISTORY EVERYDAY PART TWO

translation.] I am [of] the germs of every god. I am Yesterday and of the four [quarters of the world] and of those seven Uraei which came into existence in Amentet, that is to say [Horus, who emitteth light form his divine body. He is] the god [who] fought against Suti, but the god Thoth cometh between them through the judgment of him that dwelleth in Sekhem, and of the Souls who are in Annu, and there is a stream between them. I have come by day, and I have risen in the footsteps of the gods. I am the god Khensu, who driveth back all that oppose him."

Wilson (1901: 69-70)

"**TRANSFORMATION** INTO A HERON" from the *Papyrus of Nu* in the British Museum No. 10,477, sheet 10:

[THE CHAPTER OF MAKING THE TRANSFORMATION INTO A HERON. The chancellor-in-chief, Nu, triumphant, saith:] "I] have gotten dominion over the beasts that are brought for sacrifice, with the knives which are [held] at their heads, and at their hair, and at their .... [Hail], Aged ones [hail] khus, who are provided with the opportunity, the chancellor-in-chief, the overseer of the palace, Nu, triumphant, is upon the earth, and what he hath slaughtered is in heaven; and what he hath slaughtered is in heaven and he is upon the earth. Behold, I am strong, and I work mighty deeds to the very heights of heaven. I have made myself pure, and [I] make the breadth of heaven [a place for] my

FREDERICK MONDERSON

footsteps [as I go] unto the cities of Aukert; I advance, and I go forward into the city of Unnu (Hermopolis). I have set the gods upon their paths, and I have roused up the exalted ones who dwell in their shrines. Do I not know Nu? Do I not know Ta tune? Do I not know the beings of the color of fire who thrust forward their horns? Do I not know [every being having] incantations unto whose words I listen? I am the Smam bull [for slaughter] which is written down in the books. The gods cry out say: 'Let your faces be gracious to him that cometh onward. The light is beyond your knowledge, and ye cannot fetter it; and times and seasons are in my body. I do not utter words to the god Hu, [I do not utter words of] wickedness instead of [words of] right and truth, and each day right and truth come unto my eyebrows. At night taketh place the festival of him that is dead, the Aged One, who is in ward [in] the earth."

Black History Everyday - Part Two Photo. Faces and signs in the crowd for the 50th Anniversary March on Washington.

BLACK HISTORY EVERYDAY
PART TWO

Black History Everyday - Part Two Photo. Faces and signs in the crowd for the 50th Anniversary March on Washington.

Wilson (1901: 70-71) - **"OF THE LIVING SOUL"** from the *Papyrus of Nu* in the British Museum No. 10,477, sheet 9: **THE CHAPTER OF MAKING THE TRANSFORMATION INTO A LIVING SOUL, AND OF NOT ENTERING INTO THE CHAMBER OF TORTURE**; whosoever knoweth [it] shall not see corruption. The chancellor-in-chief, Nu, triumphant, saith: "I am the divine Soul of Ra proceeding from the god Nu" that divine soul which is god, [I am] the creator of the divine food, and that which is an abomination unto me is sin whereon I look not. I proclaim right and truth, and I live therein. I am the divine food, which is not corrupted in my name of Soul; I gave birth unto myself with Nu in my name of Khepera in whom I come into being day by day. I am the lord of light, and that which is an abomination unto me is death; let me not go into the chamber of torture which is in the Tuat (underworld.) I ascribe honor [unto] Osiris, and I make to be at peace the heart[s] of those being who dwell among the divine things which I love. I ascribe honor [unto] Osiris, and I make to be at peace the heart[s] of those being who dwell among the divine things which [I] love. They cause the fear of me [to abound], and they create awe of me in those beings who dwell in their divine things which [I] love. They cause the fear of me [to abound], and they create awe of me in those beings who dwell in their divine territories.

"Behold I am exalted upon my standard, and upon my seat, and upon the throne which is adjudged [to me]. I am the god Nu, and the workers of iniquity shall not destroy me. I am the first-born god of primeval matter, that is to say, the divine Soul, even the Souls of the gods of everlastingness, and my body is eternity. My Form is everlastingness, and is the lord of years and the prince of eternity. [I am] the creator of the darkness who maketh his habitation in the uttermost parts of the sky, [which] I love, and I arrive at the confines thereof. I advance upon my feet, I become a master of my vine, I sail over the sky which formeth the division [between heaven and earth], [I] destroy the hidden worms that travel nigh unto my footsteps which are toward the lord of the two hands and arms. My soul is the Soul of the souls of everlastingness, and my body is eternity. I am the

BLACK HISTORY EVERYDAY PART TWO

divine exalted being who is the lord of the land of Tebu. 'I am the Boy in the city and the Young man in the plain' is my name; 'he that never suffereth corruption' is my name. I am the Soul, the creator of the god Nu who maketh his habitation in the underworld: my place of incubation is unseen and my egg is not cracked. I have done away with all my iniquity, and I shall see my diving Father, the lord of eventide, whose body dwelleth in Annu. I travel (?) to the god of night (?), who dwelleth with the god of light, by the western region of the Ibis (i.e., Thoth)."

Wilson (1901: 72) "**OF THE SWALLOW**" from the *Papyrus of Nu* in the British Museum No. 10,477, sheet 10:

THE CHAPTER OF MAKING THE TRANSFORMATION INTO A SWALLOW.

The chancellor-in-chief, Nu, triumphant, saith: "I am a swallow. I am a swallow. I am the Scorpion, the daughter of Ra. Hail, ye gods, whose scent is sweet; hail, ye gods, whose scent is sweet! [Hail,] Flame, which cometh forth from the horizon! Hail, thou who art in the city, I have brought the Warden of his Bight therein. Oh, stretch out unto me thy hand so that I may be able to pass my days in the Pool of Double Fire, and let me advance with my message, for I have come with words to tell. Oh, open [thou] the doors to me and I will declare the things which have been seen by me.

FREDERICK MONDERSON

"Horus hath become the divine prince of the Boat of the Sun, and unto him hath been given the throne of his divine father Osiris, and set, that son of Nut, [lieth] under the fetters which he had made for me. I have made a computation of that is in the city of Sekhem, I have stretched out both my hands and arms at the word (?) of Osiris, I have passed on to judgment, and I have come that [I] may speak; grant that I may pass on and declare my tidings. I enter in, [I am] judged, and [I] come forth worthy at the gate of Neb er tcher. I am pure at the great place of the passage of souls, I had done away with my sins, I have put away mine offences, and I have destroyed the evil which appertained unto my members upon earth. Hail, ye divine beings who guard the doors, make ye for me a way, for, behold, I am like unto you."

"I have come forth by day, I have journeyed on to my legs, I have gained the mastery over my footsteps [before] the God of Light, I know the hidden ways and the doors of the Sekhet Aaru, verily I, even I, have come, I have thrown mine enemies upon earth, and yet my perishable body is in the grave!"

"IF THIS CHAPTER BE KNOWN [BY THE DECEASED], HE SHALL COME FORTH BY DAY, HE SHALL NOT BE TURNED BACK AT ANY GATE IN THE UNDERWORLD, AND HE SHALL MAKE HIS TRANSFORMATION INTO A

BLACK HISTORY EVERYDAY PART TWO

SWALLOW REGULARLY AND CONTINUALLY."

REFERENCES

Akbar, Na'im. *Chains and Images of Psychological Slavery*. New Jersey: New Mind Productions, 1989.

Baines, T. *History of the Commerce and Town of Liverpool*. London: Longman, Brown, Green and Longman, 1852.

Clarkson, Thomas. *An Essay on the Impolicy of the Slave Trade*. London: 1788

_____. 1788. *Efficiency of Regulation of the Slave Trade*.

_____. *Letters on the Slave Trade*. 1791.

Donnan, Elizabeth. *Documents Illustrative of the Slave Trade to America*: Vol. I: 1441 1700. Washington, D.C.: Carnegie Institution of Washington, 1930.

Du Bois, W.E.B. *The Suppression of the Slave Trade to America 1638 1880*.

Edinburgh Review Vol CCIII (July October, 1908: 25-44).

Evidence before the Committee of the Privy Council and Before the House of Commons Committee Relating to the Slave Trade. London: 1792.

Evidence of Robert Stokes, Esq., Before the Select Committee of the House of Lords in 1849, Regarding Regulated Slave Trade. London: James Ridgeway, Piccadilly, 1851.

FREDERICK MONDERSON

A Few Facts Relating to the Slave Trade in Central and East Africa, issued by the British and Foreign Anti-Slavery Society, 1887.

Falconbridge, Alexander. *An Account of the Slave Trade on the Coast of Africa*. London: 1788.

Fight against Slavery. Television Documentary Movie Series. Narrated by Ossie Davis and Ruby Dee.

Griggs, Earl Leslie. *Thomas Clarkson: The Friend of Slaves*. London: 1936.

Historical Account of the Liverpool African Slave Trade. Liverpool: A Bowker and Sons, Booksellers, 1884.

Illustrated London News Vol. CCXXX (January 5, 1957: 18).

Latimer, John. *The Annals of Bristol in the 18th Century*. 1893.

_____. *The History of the Society of Merchant Venturers of the City of Bristol*. Bristol: J. W. Arrowsmith, 1903.

Picton, Sir. J. A. *Memorials of Liverpool Historical and Topographical*. Vol. I. London: Longman, Green and Co, 1873.

_____. *City of Liverpool. Municipal Archives and Records from* 1700 1835. Liverpool: 1886.

Report of the Lords of the Committee of the Council Appointed for Consideration of all Matters relating to (the) Trade and Foreign Plantations, 1789. Whitehall: 1789.

Stuart Brown, A. *Liverpool Ships in the 18th Century*. London: University of Liverpool, 1932.

BLACK HISTORY EVERYDAY PART TWO

Wells, Charles. *Historic Bristol*. Bristol: 1902.

_____. *A Short History of the Port of Bristol*. Bristol: J. W. Arrowsmith, 1909.

Williams, Eric. *Capitalism and Slavery*.

Williams, Gomer. *History of the Liverpool Privateers: An Account of Liverpool Slave Trade*. London: 1897.

Wilson, Epiphanius. *Egyptian Literature*. New York: The Colonial Press, 1901.

Black History Everyday - Part Two Photo. Faces and signs in the crowd for the 50th Anniversary March on Washington.

FREDERICK MONDERSON

Black History Everyday - Part Two Photo. Faces and signs in the crowd for the 50th Anniversary March on Washington.

Black History Everyday – Part Two Photo. A stalwart **Nationalist**, here at Al Sharpton's "Power and Policy forum" on Dr. Martin Luther King's Holiday, January 20, 2020.

BLACK HISTORY EVERYDAY
PART TWO

Black History Everyday - Part Two Photo. In an old photo, Prof. George Simmonds, embraces young Dr. Fred Monderson, one of his early protégés.

FREDERICK MONDERSON
18. PROF. GEORGE SIMMONDS, "UNSUNG HERO"
BY
DR. FRED MONDERSON

On Monday October 6, 1997, scholars, students, colleagues and community residents with their children came out to the Victoria 5 Theater on 125th Street in Harlem, to honor Professor George Simmons, an unsung hero of the African American community. A parade of speakers recounted how Professor Simmonds has educated, trained and assisted so many in the most unselfish manner. This is why, so many were proud that we were able to honor this giant of a man, while he was still alive.

Black History Everyday - Part Two Photo. At the "Tribute to Prof. George Simmonds" at the Victoria 5 Theater in Harlem, "Young" Fred Monderson sat at the feet of his heroes Dr. Ben-Jochannan and with Prof. George Simmonds in full-chiefly regalia, among others.

BLACK HISTORY EVERYDAY
PART TWO

Represented in the above iconic photo, Brother William X (left, end), host and student, colleague and confidant of Dr. Simmonds, spoke of how he was encouraged to be a scholar, speaker and organizer in the interest of the welfare of Africa and African-Americans, principally motivated by Prof. Simmonds.

Black History Everyday - Part Two Photo. Faces and signs in the crowd for the 50th Anniversary March on Washington.

FREDERICK MONDERSON

Black History Everyday - Part Two Photo. Faces and signs in the crowd for the 50th Anniversary March on Washington.

Black History Everyday - Part Two Photo. Faces and signs in the crowd for the 50th Anniversary March on Washington.

BLACK HISTORY EVERYDAY
PART TWO

Black History Everyday - Part Two Photo. Elombe Brathe, "Ultimate Nationalist Soldier, stands before the iconic Red, Black and Green!

19. Dick Gregory's 'Callus on My Soul' By Dr. Fred Monderson, a Review.

What a book! We all know of the Civil Rights Movement but this book is the story of one man's involvement. Man of vision, principle, foresight, courage, "distance runner," survivor, loyal, challenger to the system, some call him a "Bear hunter" and epitome of one man becoming a majority. No wonder Ossie Davis and Ruby Dee

FREDERICK MONDERSON

said: "Dick Gregory is a product of the struggle. He is an activist. We just look like activists."

Dick Gregory's book *Callus on My Soul*, with Sheila P. Moses is an extraordinary book, a unique history of the Civil Rights Movement, a history of Civil Rights Protest by an equally exceptional individual who is a legend in this country and worldwide. A 2000 Copyright by Dick Gregory and Sheila P. Moses and originally published in Hardcover by Longstreet Press, this first Kensington Trade Paperback Printing under Dafina Books is dated 2003.

With a Dedication to the "unsung heroes and sheroes all over the world, whose names most people don't ever stop to ask: the porters, the taxi-drivers, the dishwashers, and the bell captains at the hotel; the valet at the airport, the waiters and waitresses, the cooks, the teachers, the garbage collectors and the maids." He asks that all people "pray or meditate" with him "every day at noon." Then he asks for "a special prayer for the struggling single parents, the handicapped, and those who are disabled." He also mentions "struggling farmers and the forgotten human rights workers."

Then follows **Acknowledgements** from Dick Gregory, where he mentions "soldiers we lost while writing this book" where he lists Albert Turner, Dr. Avenia Fulton, Stokeley Carmichael and James Farmer "as well as those we lost so long ago:" Dr.

BLACK HISTORY EVERYDAY
PART TWO

Martin Luther King, Jr., Medgar Evers, Viola Liuzzo, Chaney, Goodman, and Schwerner, Roy Wilkins, Dr. Benjamin Mays, Robert and John Kennedy, Malcolm X, Tom Skinner, Bob Johnson, Ralph Abernathy, Betty Shabazz, Jim Sanders, Reverend John Nettles, and those four beautiful girls from Birmingham." He also said "thanks to the good, honest, decent white folks who walked in the shadow of death with us during the movement and today."

Let me say this before I move on, when we consider all the arguments for belief in god, viz., "first cause," "first mover," "beauty of creation," we could also add Dick Gregory's profound faith and religious conviction. Fueled by the power of prayer and an unshakeable belief in god, is what I believe brought him through the many trials and tribulations he faced in fighting for the human, civil, economic and physical and emotional rights of all people.

Acknowledgements follow from Sheila P. Moses thanking several people in assisting the completion and publication of this book.

According to the **Table of Contents**, *Callus on My Soul's* 301 pages is divided into 31 Chapters and a section on "Fasting" and "Dick Gregory's Weight Loss Program." Spanning his entire life, the Chapters include: Momma, Relief, Her Last Mile, On My Way, Lily of the Valley, To Cast a Stone, Blinded by the Light, Move on Niggers, Turn Me Loose, Bombingham, Sad November, With His Armor On,

FREDERICK MONDERSON

In the Snake's Mouth, A Bullet of My Own, Black Power, Code name "Zorro," Nothing But Grace, Redskins, Going Home, The Greatest, Give Peace a Chance, Good or Evil, Happy Birthday Martin, Going the Distance, Let There Be Food, Fire With No Flame, Nothing From History, Blood On My Shoes, On Broadway, Sitting on the Couch, and Callus on My Soul.

Revisiting the old adage, "Behind Every Great man, there is a Woman," Dick Gregory could not swim his "River of Sorrows" without his beloved and god given wife Lillian Gregory. Again, bless her soul for she was "The wings under his feet," "The Wind in his Sails," "The Gasoline in his Tank," and "The Fire in His Soul." This woman Dick Gregory married who bore him 10 children and her undying love was exceptional, gentle yet stronger than steel!

Black History Everyday - Part Two Photo. Faces and signs in the crowd for the 50th Anniversary March on Washington.

BLACK HISTORY EVERYDAY
PART TWO

Though the book has no **Index**, a list of some of the names he mentions, with whom he interacted, gone to jail with, entertained alongside, confronted, prayed and fasted with, influenced, assisted, been influenced by and watched die over the years, equally gives a paltry measure of the breadth of the experience he recounts. From Mohammed Ali, Byron de La Beckwith, Harry Belafonte, Marlon Brando, George Bush, Les Brown, Tony Brown, H. Rap Brown, Lenny Bruce, Ralph Bunche, John Carlos, Jimmy Carter, Robert Chambliss, Johnny Cochran, Bull Connor, Daddy-O-Dailey, Angela Davis, Miles Davis, Ossie Davis, Ruby Dee, David Dinkins, Queen Elizabeth, Jim Ellis, Medgar and Merlie Evers, Min. Louis Farrakhan, Walter Fauntroy, Hugh Hefner, Dorothy Height, Aaron Henry, Cathy Hughes, Jessie Jackson, Eunice and John Johnson, Tom Joyner, Clyde Kennard, Coretta Scott-King, Ayatollah Khomeni and the Hostages in Iran, Irv Kupeinet, John Lewis, Coach Leyland Lingle, Abner Louima, Nelson Mandela, Bob Marley, James Meredith, Kwesi Mfume, Jackie Kennedy, Jack Parr, Adam Clayton Powell, Richard Pryor, A. Philip Randolph, Randall Robinson, Haile Selaisse, Jim Sanders, Al Sharpton, Tavis Smiley, B. Tommy Smith, Leon Sullivan, Bill Tatum, Emmitt Till, C. Delores Tucker, Maxine Walters, Oprah Winfrey, Stevie Wonder and Andy Young and Whitney Young,

FREDERICK MONDERSON

Finally, in closing a few things in the book needs to be pointed out. "Racism is a form of insanity in this country that we cannot afford to ignore …. We have to talk about it until it goes away. You have to acknowledge the presence of the tumor then cut it out. It may be painful but it will save your life." (p. 278) "Name one movement in the history of this planet in which every single leader has been murdered." "The continent of Africa is the key to the salvation of Black folks in the United States." "Gangster rap is an insult to the Black family. Take a minute to look up the definition of 'gangster' and 'rap.' Gangster means a member of a group of people banded together for some purpose, usually bad or negative. Rap means to deliver short, light blows. For our children, gangster rap means a succession of criminal messages."

"Two of the strongest forces in the history of America are and will remain the Black woman and the Black church. Gangster rap was not created by Black folks; it was created by White folks, to destroy the Black woman and the Black family. Imagine you are a Swedish woman on vacation in the United States. You get in a taxi and the Black driver is listening to a gangster rapper calling Black women bitches and whores. This is your first time in this country, and you don't know anything about Black women. Stay with me now. The next week, you go home to Sweden and two Black American women executives from Xerox with Ph. D's are there on vacation. Well, you don't see them as two Black women from

BLACK HISTORY EVERYDAY
PART TWO

corporate America - you see them as bitches and whores because that is the image that has been planted in your mind the week before by a Black gangster rapper.

So, there you have it. Dick Gregory, an extraordinary individual. Man of courage, tenacity, endurance, integrity and exceptional faith and belief in god. *Callus on My Soul* is a book that must be read, savored and understood to understand the long road Blacks have come in the United States as well as some of the obstacles still facing them.

Black History Everyday - Part Two Photo. We Shall Not be Moved March. Faces in the Crowd.

FREDERICK MONDERSON

Black History Everyday - Part Two Photo. Faces and signs in the crowd for the 50th Anniversary March on Washington.

Black History Everyday - Part Two Photo. Faces and signs in the crowd for the 50th Anniversary March on Washington.

BLACK HISTORY EVERYDAY
PART TWO

Black History Everyday - Part Two Photo. We Shall Not be Moved March. Faces in the Crowd.

Black History Everyday - Part Two Photo. We Shall Not be Moved March. Faces in the Crowd.

FREDERICK MONDERSON

Black History Everyday - Part Two Photo. Faces and signs in the crowd for the 50th Anniversary March on Washington.

Black History Everyday - Part Two Photo. Faces and signs in the crowd for the 50th Anniversary March on Washington.

BLACK HISTORY EVERYDAY
PART TWO

Black History Everyday - Part Two Photo. Faces and signs in the crowd for the 50th Anniversary March on Washington.

Black History Everyday - Part Two Photo. Faces and signs in the crowd for the 50th Anniversary March on Washington.

FREDERICK MONDERSON

Black History Everyday - Part Two Photo. A wonderful family in the audience at **CEMOTAP**.

Black History Everyday - Part Two Photo. Prof. James Blake, Chairman of the Queens Million Man March Committee, as a guest at **CEMOTAP**.

BLACK HISTORY EVERYDAY
PART TWO

Black History Everyday - Part Two Photo. Basir Mchawi hosts a Panel at **CEMOTAP**.

Black History Everyday - Part Two Photo. Appalachian State at the **Million Man March 20th Anniversary**.

FREDERICK MONDERSON

Black History Everyday - Part Two Photo. President Barack Obama all the way!

Black History Everyday - Part Two Photo. Dr. Jack Felder and activist Sonny "AB" Carson on stage addressing Middle School children.

BLACK HISTORY EVERYDAY
PART TWO

Black History Everyday - Part Two Photo. Shamgod, Sonny Carson and Atiem Ferguson at **Allah U Akbar's** funeral.

"The Universal Negro Improvement Association advocates the uniting and blending of all Negroes into one strong, healthy race. It is against miscegenation and race suicide. It believes that the Negro race is as good as any other, and therefore should be as proud of itself as others are. It believes in the purity of the Negro race and the purity of the white race. It is against rich blacks marrying poor whites. It is against rich or poor whites taking advantage of Negro women. It believes in the spiritual Fatherhood of God and the Brotherhood of Man. It believes in the social and political physical separation of all peoples to the extent that they promote their own ideals and civilization, with the privilege of trading and doing business with each other. It believes in the promotion of a strong and powerful Negro nation in Africa. It believes in the rights of men. **UNIVERSAL NEGRO IMPROVEMENT ASSOCIATION. MARCUS GARVEY, President-General. January 1, 1924.**

THE MORALS OF OUR TIME!

"It is remarkable to contemplate the deception of man, as practiced upon his brothers. The human race has degenerated into select groups of liars and thieves, who practice their profession and carry out their depredations through the media of high-sounding philosophies. Chief among the deceivers who parade as sanctified moralists and reformers are some of the leading statesmen of the white race. The white man has given us morals from his head, and lies form his heart." Marcus Garvey. *Philosophy and Opinions.*

20. MARCUS MOZIAH GARVEY BY DR. FRED MONDERSON

Today the world knows Marcus Garvey, while the people who conspired against him for the most part have gone down in oblivion and the influence he wielded, helped fan the whirlwind of African independence movements following World War II. The timelessness of his ideas still inspires young people, Pan Africanists and conscious thinking

BLACK HISTORY EVERYDAY
PART TWO

individuals who can gain from his experiences, trials, tribulations, triumphs, failures, betrayals and vision. Except for those who lived before his time, all great Black men of the 20th Century was were either influenced by Garvey or by someone whom Garvey influenced. Those modern men who have impacted upon their time unquestionably benefited from the ideas of Marcus Garvey.

A perusal of the **Table of Contents** of the book *The Philosophy and Opinions of Marcus Garvey* shows how wide was the breadth of the man's thinking, a man essentially self-taught at a time when education for Africans anywhere in the world was a hard-won sacrifice. He wrote about "Propaganda, slavery, force, education, miscegenation, prejudice, radicalism, government, evolution and the result, poverty, power, universal suspicion, dissertation on man, race assimilation, Christianity, the function of man and traitors."

Then there is "Present Day Civilization, Divine apportionment of earth, universal unrest in 1922, world disarmament, causes of wars, the fall of governments, great ideals know no nationality, purpose of creation, purity of race, man know thyself, a solution for the world peace in 1922, god as a war lord, and the image of god." Even further, "the slave trade, Negroes' status under alien governments, the Negro as an industrial makeshift, lack of co-operation in the Negro race, white man's solution for the Negro problem in America, the true solution of the Negro

FREDERICK MONDERSON

problem, white propaganda about Africa, the three stages of the Negro in contact with the white man, Booker T. Washington's program, belief that race problem will adjust itself a fallacy, examples of white Christian control of Africa, the thought behind their deeds, similarity of persecution, shall the Negro be exterminated? Africa for the Africans, the future as I see it." Finally, "Emancipation Speech, Christmas Message, Easter sermon, Convention speech and statement on arrest." These words have been so piercing and influential they were instrumental in galvanizing Kwame Nkrumah as he chaired the **5th Pan African Conference** in Manchester, England after World War II and in his struggles to free Ghana and assist in decolonization in Africa.

Black History Everyday - Part Two Photo. Faces and signs in the crowd for the 50th Anniversary March on Washington.

BLACK HISTORY EVERYDAY
PART TWO

Black History Everyday - Part Two Photo. Faces and signs in the crowd for the 50th Anniversary March on Washington.

In this country, Raymond Hall in *Black Separatism in the United States* (1978: 66) wrote offering a synopsis of Garvey and his movement. "Marcus Garvey was the UNIA's sole architect. The movement's values, in essence, reflected only slight differences from those of mainstream America. Lewis makes the point, however, that Garvey's ideological creation is paradoxical. Garvey's militant call for Black Nationalism might be too quickly called extremely radical, but its content and emphasis, all reflected 'the conventional American world view.' That is, in exhorting Blacks to be proud of their blackness and black historical achievements, 'Garvey was merely turning the white American's racial chauvinism on its head.' His ideas of justice and world order were based on the nation-state

FREDERICK MONDERSON

concept, which most Americans would embrace. His economic philosophy, like Washington's and most Americans,' was bourgeoisie. Finally, "except for its emphasis on the return to Africa, the only 'radicalism' in Garvey's thought (was) his basic assumption that black men could and would manage their affairs in the same manner as did white men."

Black History Everyday - Part Two Photo. Marcus Garvey and W.E.B. DuBois.

Assessing some aspects of Garvey's economic philosophy, Hall believed while Garvey influenced many, others also in turn influenced him. He wrote: "Clearly, Garvey proposed to bring to fruition Washington's goal of 'economic separatism' in urban America. Washington had been concerned about economic separatism - or Black independence - in the rural South, and Garvey applied his philosophy to urban America, with the **Back-to-Africa** label as an added incentive. He knew that black people had already had large doses of economic self-determination from Washington and of Back-to-

BLACK HISTORY EVERYDAY
PART TWO

Africa from Bishop Turner, Blyden, and others; he therefore had to combine the two with dynamic variables. Perhaps he saw that it was necessary to augment economic independence and Back-to-Africa with race chauvinism, pride in one's racial heritage, glorification of the African past, confidence in oneself, and other ego-bolstering tactics."

Black History Everyday - Part Two Photo. We Shall Not be Moved March. Faces in the Crowd.

Vincent Bakpetu Thompson in *Africa and Unity: The Evolution of Pan-Africanism* praises Garvey for the many slogans he coined in seeking African unity and progress. These included: "Africans for the Africans," "Renaissance of the Black RACE," "Ethiopia Awake," "Look for me in the eye of the storm," "Man love your brother," "Up, you mighty race, you can accomplish what you will." His "One God, One Destiny" sought to unite Africans and determine the road ahead. As a compliment to his "One destiny" belief Garvey declared: "Therefore, let justice be done to all mankind, realizing that if the strong oppress the weak, confusion and discontent will ever mark the path of man, but love, faith and charity toward all, the reign of peace and plenty will be heralded into the world and the generation of men shall be blessed." Yet still, he did believe passionately: "No one knows when the hour of Africa's redemption cometh. It is in the wind. It is coming. One day, like the storm it will be here. When that day comes all Africa will stand together. Any sane man, race or nation that desires freedom must first of all think in terms of blood. Why, even the Heavenly Father tells us that 'without the shedding of blood there can be no remission of sins?" Then how in the name of God, with history before us, do we expect to redeem Africa without preparing ourselves - some of us to die."

He continued: "Wake up Ethiopia! Let us work towards the one glorious end of a free, redeemed, and mighty nation. Let Africa be a bright star among the constellation of nations." Even further, the declared objectives of Garvey's Organization were stated thus: "To establish a universal confraternity among the race; to promote the spirit of pride and love; to reclaim the fallen; to administer to and assist the needy; to assist in the development of independent Negro nations and communities; to establish a central nation for the race, to establish commissaries or agencies in principal countries and cities of the world for the representation of all Negroes; to promote a

BLACK HISTORY EVERYDAY
PART TWO

conscientious spiritual worship among the native tribes of Africa; to establish universities, colleges, academies and schools for the racial education and culture of the people; to work for better conditions among Negroes everywhere." Finally, Thompson summed up Garvey's program with its four principles that are hallmarks of the Pan-African movement today; "first, the common destiny of all Africans and the need for continental unity as a prerequisite for dealing with the numerous problems; second, the 'Negro or African Personality;' third, the repudiation of all foreign rule and control and the eradication of all its vestiges which are retarding the grown of African man; and, fourth, social change including cultural regeneration and reactivation of the world's cultures."

Black History Everyday - Part Two Photo. Faces and signs in the crowd for the 50th Anniversary March on Washington.

FREDERICK MONDERSON

Clearly a visionary, Garvey hoped to create an African world state that mirrored the universalism of the Catholic Church. He argued that: "Our union must know no clime, boundary or nationality. Like the great Church of Rome, Negroes the world over must practice one faith, that of confidence in themselves, with One God, One Aim, One Destiny… the founding of a racial Empire whose only natural, spiritual and political limits shall be God and Africa at home and abroad."

Black History Everyday - Part Two Photo. We Shall Not be Moved March. Faces in the Crowd.

Certainly, his influence has been immeasurable and his name became enshrined in motifs as schools, parks, and even streets today bear the name of this Pan-African and nationalist icon who helped get us here today. However, while we can give Garvey great grades for his efforts in mobilizing "400,000,000

BLACK HISTORY EVERYDAY PART TWO

Negroes" around the world we ought to pay some attention to the mistakes he made, trusting in others who betrayed him, meeting with the Ku Klux Klan, underestimating the power of Europeans who controlled those 400,000,000 Negroes through colonialism and the role of Ethiopia and Liberia as pawns in Global white supremacy, imperialism and power politics. His Black Star Line, with traitors aboard and mismanagement, was an alligator that bled the **UNIA**, his return to Africa through the Liberia experiment was un-researched and betrayed, the "Negroes in America" who conspired and had him arrested are all causes of his failures. Nevertheless, no matter what happens, when the people believe in you, your ideas, vision or name never dies and this is why we celebrate and give Marcus Garvey such high marks today, August 17. On his arrest he remarked, "You have caged the lion but his cubs are running free out there!" Those cubs have indeed made their mark! God Bless Marcus Garvey and his timeliness as his ideas, efforts and charisma helped Black people to see the light at the end of the tunnel! **Happy Birthday Marcus Moziah Garvey!**

FREDERICK MONDERSON

Black History Everyday - Part Two Photo. Faces and signs in the crowd for the 50th Anniversary March on Washington.

Black History Everyday – Part Two Photo. Democratic Minority Leader, **Senator Chuck Schumer** at Al Sharpton' "Power and Policy forum" on Dr. King's Holiday, January 20, 2020.

BLACK HISTORY EVERYDAY
PART TWO

Black History Everyday - Part Two Photo. Faces and signs in the crowd for the 50th Anniversary March on Washington.

FREDERICK MONDERSON

Black History Everyday - Part Two Photo. New York State Assembly speaker Hastie addresses the audience at Rev. Sharpton's "Power and Policy Forum."

Black History Everyday - Part Two Photo. Faces and signs in the crowd for the 50th Anniversary March on Washington.

BLACK HISTORY EVERYDAY
PART TWO

Black History Everyday - Part Two Photo. We Shall Not be Moved March. Faces in the Crowd.

Black History Everyday - Part Two Photo. We Shall Not be Moved March. Faces in the Crowd.

21. FREDERICK MONDERSON
OFFICIAL VIEW OF CIVIL RIGHTS
BY DR. FRED MONDERSON

With the recent loss of Coretta Scott King, Rev. Augustus Jones, of Bethany Baptist Church in Brooklyn, his brother Attorney Clayton Jones, Rosa Parks, and the litany of civil rights leaders as Sonny Carson, Kwame Toure, Jitu Weusi, Fannie Lou Hamer, Frederick Douglass, Paul Robeson, W.E.B. DuBois, and so many more, their history and legacy need be emphasized. In this, we must continue their efforts to secure economic, political and educational empowerment, influence and remain ever vigilant against all efforts at disenfranchisement, racial discrimination and denial of human and civil rights.

It is interesting in order to assess the works of these stalwarts, we must reflect back on the history of the Civil Rights struggle and in so doing, and help focus on the future direction of the movement, so the next generation must keep the pressure on.

Every measure of the progress made by African-Americans in America was won by unending effort in the name of Human Rights, political or voting rights, and Civil Rights with the struggle for economic rights still looming on the horizon. This essay, however, seeks to trace the struggle for Civil Rights that gained credence after the Civil War when

BLACK HISTORY EVERYDAY PART TWO

African-American gains began to be measured in tangible legislation and unequalled valor and determination, all at a heavy cost.

Albert P. Blaustein and Robert T. Zangrando in *Civil Rights and the American Negro* (1968: vii) puts it best when they affirmed: "As we organized this material, we were confronted with the overriding effects of the pattern of white dominance on the Negro Minority. The white majority has been virtually the sole decision-maker regarding the Negro's destiny. Characterized in part by hostility to the Negro and in part by ambivalence about itself and its feelings towards the Negro, the dominant white majority in each historical period pulled back from the point of extensive reform. Through some process of myopic self-deception and wishful thinking, the dominant majority repeatedly convinced itself that it had done right by the Negro-that the minority was pleased with the reform. At its best, this is sheer hypocrisy on the part of the white majority; at its worst, it is the breeding ground for unrelenting anger and frustration on the part of the Negro."

However, prior to the civil war there was no such thing as civil right for Black-Americans. On the other hand, Congress passed seven **Civil Rights Acts** during the **Reconstruction Era**, represented in the Thirteenth, Fourteenth and Fifteenth Amendments, (1866-2875) with two of limited historical significance while all five were of crucial

FREDERICK MONDERSON

importance regarding the struggle for equality by Blacks in this country.

The Thirteenth Amendment was passed January 1, 1865 and ratified December 6, 1865, abolishing slavery and stated in Section I: "Neither slavery nor involuntary servitude, except as a punishment for crime whereof the party shall have been duly convicted, shall exist within the United States, or any place subject to their jurisdiction."

Section II read "Congress shall have power to enforce this article by appropriate legislation."

The Fourteenth Amendment defined national and state citizenship; protected citizens' rights; and promised to its citizens "equal protection of the laws." In Section 1 it says: "All persons born or naturalized in the United States, and subject to the jurisdiction thereof, are citizens of the United States and of the state wherein they reside. No state shall make or enforce any law, which shall abridge the privileges or immunities of citizens of the United States; nor shall any state deprive any person of life, liberty, or property, without due process of law; nor deny any person within its jurisdiction the equal protection of the laws."

The **Civil Rights Act of 1866** - Passed April 9 and re-passed that year over President Johnson's Veto, was entitled: "An Act to protect all Persons in the United States in their Civil Rights, and furnish the

BLACK HISTORY EVERYDAY PART TWO

Means of their Vindication." It held: "That all persons born in the United States and not subject to any foreign power, excluding Indians not taxed, are hereby declared to be citizens of the United States; and such citizens, of every race and color, without regard to any previous condition of slavery or involuntary servitude, except as a punishment for crime whereof the party shall have been duly convicted, shall have the same right, in every State and Territory in the United States, to make and enforce contracts, to sue, be parties, and give evidence, to inherit, purchase, lease, sell, hold, and convey real and personal property, and to full and equal benefit of all laws and proceedings for the security of person and property, as is enjoyed by white citizens, and shall be subject to like punishment, pains, and penalties, and to none other, any law, statute, ordinance, regulation, or custom to the contrary notwithstanding."

Black History Everyday - Part Two Photo. Dr. Fred Monderson in younger days.

FREDERICK MONDERSON

Black History Everyday - Part Two Photo. Dr. Fred Monderson displays the last three of his books (4) chronicling the tenure of President Barack Obama.

The **Civil Rights Act of 1866;** The **Civil Rights Act of 1870;** The **Civil Rights Act of 1871;** The **Civil Rights Act of 1875;** The **Civil Rights Act of 1883**; according to Plano and Greenberg in *The American Political Dictionary* (1962: 332) were "Laws passed by congress after the Civil War to guarantee the rights of blacks. The public-accommodation provisions of the 1875 law were declared unconstitutional by the Supreme Court in the Civil Rights Cases, 109 U.S. 3 (1883), as a federal invasion of privacy rights. Other provisions of these laws were struck down by the courts or repealed by Congress. Today, a few major provisions

BLACK HISTORY EVERYDAY
PART TWO

remain from the acts of 1866 and 1871. One makes it a federal crime for any person acting under the authority of a state law to deprive another of any rights protected by the Constitution or by laws of the United States. Another authorizes suits for civil damages against state or local officials by persons whose rights area abridged. Others permit actions against persons who conspire to deprive people of their rights."

Black History Everyday - Part Two Photo. Bronx Congressman Adriano Espaillat addresses the audience at Rev. Al Sharpton's "Power and Policy Forum" on Dr. King's Holiday, January 2020.

FREDERICK MONDERSON

Black History Everyday - Part Two Photo. Brother Walter Brown joins those protesting with "Hands Up!"

The significance of this landmark collection of legislation, meant: "The failure of the post-Civil War Acts reflected the general attitude of the time that the national government had a limited role to play in the enforcement of individual rights. The remaining provisions served occasionally as a weapon in the hands of national officers to restrain state officials who violated the constitutional rights of persons in their charge. Today, as the national government expands its role in the protection of individual rights, particularly in the area of race relations, these laws have taken on new importance. Of particular significance are: (1) the Supreme Court's ruling in *Jones v. Mayer*, 392 U.S. 409 (1968), holding that the 1866 law, enacted under authority of the Thirteenth Amendment ban on slavery, bars public and private

BLACK HISTORY EVERYDAY
PART TWO

discrimination in the sale or rental of housing, and a subsequent ruling that a private school may not, under the 1866 law, deny admission to black students (*Runyon v. McCrary*, 427 U.S. 160 [1976]); (2) the Court's virtual elimination of restrictions on the right of individuals to sue state and local governments and their officials under the Act of 1871 for alleged violations of constitutional rights or of federal laws in *Maine v. Thiboutot*, 448 U.S. 1 (1980); and (3) the Court's 1987 rulings that open the right to sue under the 1866 law to a wide variety of ethnic groups, including Arabs and Jews (*Saint Frances College v. Al-Khazrati*, 107, S. Ct. 2022; *Shaare Tefila Congregation v. Cobb*, 107 S. Ct. 2019). In 1980, Congress authorized the Attorney General to bring suit against states to protect the rights of institutionalized person such as those in hospitals, jails, or juvenile facilities."

In 1895, the Assembly of the State of New York passed, "An Act to protect all citizens in their Civil and Legal Rights" taking effect immediately where Section I said: "That all persons within the jurisdiction of this State shall be entitled to the full and equal accommodations, advantages, facilities and privileges of inns, restaurants, hotels, eating-houses, bath-houses, barber-shops, theaters, music halls, public conveyances on land and water, and all other places of public accommodations or amusement, subject only to the conditions and limitations established by law and applicable alike to all citizens."

FREDERICK MONDERSON

Section II says, "That any person who shall violate any of the provisions of the foregoing section by deny to any citizens, except for reasons applicable alike to all citizens of every race, creed or color, and regardless of race, creed, and color, the full enjoyment of any of the accommodations, advantages, facilities or privileges of said section enumerated... shall be fined not less than one hundred dollars nor more than five hundred dollars, or shall be imprisoned not less than thirty days."

Section III says no citizen, "shall be disqualified to serve as grand or petit juror in any court of this state on account of race, creed or color,"

The **Civil Rights of 1957** - "The first civil rights law passed by congress since Reconstruction," Plano and Greenberg held, "designed to secure the right to vote for blacks. Its major feature empowers the Department of Justice to seek court injunctions against any deprivation of voting rights, and authorizes criminal prosecutions for violations of an injunction. In action, the Act established a **Civil Rights Division**, headed by an Assistant-Attorney- General in the Department of Justice, and created a bipartisan **Civil Rights Commission** to investigate civil rights violations and to recommend legislation." The significance of this measure insisted, "The **Civil Rights Act of**

BLACK HISTORY EVERYDAY
PART TWO

1957 marked a major breakthrough in positive federal action in the field of civil rights. The Act is based on the theory that if blacks are protected in their voting rights, they will be in a better position to seek reform in other areas of discrimination. It is supplemented by voting provisions in the Civil Rights Acts of 1960 and 1964 and by the Voting Rights of 1965."

Its major Section 131 (b) reads: "No person, whether acting under color of law or otherwise, shall intimidate, threaten, coerce, or attempt to intimidate, threaten, or coerce any other person for the purpose of interfering with the right of such other person to vote or to vote as he may choose, or of causing such other person to vote for, or not to vote for, any candidate for the office of President, Vice President, presidential elector, Member of the Senate, or Member of the House of Representatives, Delegates or Commissioners, from the territories or possessions, at any general, special, or primary election held solely or in part for the purpose of selecting or electing any such candidate."

(c) "Whenever any person has engaged or there are reasonable grounds to believe that any person is about to engage in any act or practice which would deprive any other person of any right or privilege secured by subsection (a) or (b), the Attorney General may institute for the United States, or in the name of the United States, a civil action or other proper proceeding for preventive relief, including an application for a permanent or temporary injunction, restraining order, or other order. In any proceeding hereunder the United States shall be liable for costs the same as a private person."

The **Civil Rights Act of 1960** - is "An Act to Enforce Constitutional Rights, and for other Purposes" Title II reads: "Flight to avoid prosecution for damaging or destroying any building or other real or personal property; and, illegal transportation, use of or possession of explosives; and, threats or false information concerning attempts to damage or destroy real or personal property by fire or explosives."

In fact, Plano and Greenberg (1989: 333) held this **Civil Rights Act of 1960** was: "A law designed to further secure the right to vote for blacks and to meet problems arising from racial upheavals in the South in the late 1950s. The major provision authorizes federal courts to appoint referees who will help blacks to register after a voter-denial conviction is obtained under the 1957 Civil Rights Act, and after a count finding of a 'pattern or practice' of discrimination against qualified voters. Other provisions: (1) authorize punishment for persons who obstruct any federal court order, such as a school desegregation order, by threat or force; (2) authorize criminal penalties for transportation of explosives for the purpose of bombing a building; (3) require preservation of voting records for twenty-two months, and authorize the Attorney General to

BLACK HISTORY EVERYDAY
PART TWO

inspect the records; and (4) provide for schooling of children of armed forces personnel in the event that a school closes because of an integration dispute."

Black History Everyday - Part Two Photo. Faces and signs in the crowd for the 50th Anniversary March on Washington.

Black History Everyday - Part Two Photo. Faces and signs in the crowd for the 50th Anniversary March on Washington.

FREDERICK MONDERSON

The significance of this measure, Plano and Greenberg continued, "Continuing the pattern established in the **1957 Civil Rights Act**, Congress sought to strengthen the voting rights of citizens and reached out into other problem areas. The **Civil Rights Act of 1964** and the **Voting Rights Act of 1965** supplement the **Acts of 1957 and 1960**."

Section 201 No. 1074 (a) Whoever moves or travels in interstate or foreign commerce with intent either (1) to avoid prosecution, or custody, or confinement after conviction, under the laws of the place from which he flees, for willfully attempting to or damaging or destroying by fire or explosive any building, structure, facility, vehicle, dwelling house, synagogue, church, religious center or educational institution, or public or private, or (2) to avoid giving testimony in any criminal proceeding relating to any such offense shall be fined not more than $5000 or imprisoned not more than five years, or both."

Section 203 No. 837 (b) Whoever transports or aids and abets another in transporting in interstate or foreign commerce any explosive, with the knowledge or intent that it will be used to damage or destroy any building or other real or personal property for the purpose of interfering with its use for educational, religious, charitable, residential, business, or civic objectives or of intimidating any person pursuing such objectives, shall be subject to imprisonment for

BLACK HISTORY EVERYDAY
PART TWO

not more than one year, or a fine of not more than $1000, or both; and if personal injury results shall be subject to imprisonment for not more than ten years or a fine of not more than $10,000, or both; and if death results shall be subject to imprisonment for any term of years or for life, but the court may impose the death penalty if the jury so recommends."

One of the most fascinating pieces of literature from the **Civil Rights Era** is Dr. King's "**Letter form a Birmingham Jail**" which he wrote on April 16, 1963 to "MY Dear Fellow Clergymen" in which he explained "Why We Can't Wait" outlining the concerns, causes and strategies of his "Direct Action" as also a response to his critics who accused him of being an "outsider" who came to Birmingham, Alabama, to incite others.

"But more basically, I am in Birmingham because injustice is here. Just as the prophets of the eight century B.C left their villages and carried their 'thus saith the Lord' far beyond the boundaries of their home towns, and just as the Apostle Paul left his village of Tarsus and carried the Gospel of Jesus Christ to the far corners of the Greco-Roman world, so I am compelled to carry the gospel of freedom beyond my own home town. Like Paul, I must constantly respond to the Macedonian call for aid."

"Moreover, I am cognizant of the interrelatedness of all communities and states. I cannot sit idly by in

FREDERICK MONDERSON

Atlanta and not be concerned about what happens in Birmingham. Injustice anywhere is a threat to justice everywhere. We are caught in an inescapable network of mutuality, tied in a single garment of destiny. Whatever affects one directly, affects all indirectly. Never again can we afford to live with the narrow, provincial 'outsider agitator' idea. Anyone who lives inside the United States can never be considered an outsider anywhere within its bounds."

"You deplore the demonstrations taking place in Birmingham. But your statement, I am sorry to say, fails to express a similar concern for the conditions that brought about the demonstrations. I am sure that none of you would want to rest content with the superficial kind of social analysis that deals merely with effects and does not grapple with underlying causes. It is unfortunate that demonstrations are taking place in Birmingham, but it is even more unfortunate that the city's white power structure left the Negro community with no alternative."

"In any nonviolent campaign there are four basic steps: collection of the facts to determine whether injustice exists; negotiation; self-purification; and direct action. We have gone through all these steps in Birmingham. There can be no gainsaying the fact that racial injustice engulfs this community. Birmingham is probably the most thoroughly segregated city in the United States. Its ugly record of brutality is widely known. Negroes have experienced grossly unjust treatment in the courts.

BLACK HISTORY EVERYDAY
PART TWO

There have been more unsolved bombings of Negro homes and churches in Birmingham than in any other city in the nation. These are the hard, brutal facts of the case. On the basis of these conditions, Negro leaders sought to negotiate with the city fathers. But the latter consistently refused to engage in good-faith negotiation."

"I must make two honest confessions to you, my Christian and Jewish brothers. First, I must confess that the past few years I have been gravely disappointed with the white moderate. I have almost reached the regrettable conclusion that the Negro's great stumbling block in his stride toward freedom is not the White Citizen's Council or the Ku Klux Klanner, but the white moderate, who is more devoted to 'order' than to justice; who prefers a negative peace which is the absence of tension to a positive peace which is the presence of justice; who paternalistically believes he can set the timetable for another man's freedom; who lives by a mythical concept of time and who constantly advises the Negro to wait for a 'more convenient season.' Shallow understanding from people of good will is more frustrating than absolute misunderstanding from people of ill will. Lukewarm acceptance is much more bewildering than outright rejection."

"I had hoped that the white moderate would understand that law and order exist for the purpose of establishing justice and that when they fail in this purpose, they become the dangerously structured

FREDERICK MONDERSON

dams that block the flow of social progress. I had hoped that the white moderate would understand that the present tension in the South is a necessary phase of the transition from an obnoxious negative peace, in which the Negro passively accepted his unjust plight, to a substantive and positive peace, in which all men will respect the dignity and worth of human personality. Actually, we who engage in nonviolent direct action are not the creators of tension. We merely bring to the surface the hidden tension that is already alive. We bring it out in the open, where it can be seen and dealt with. Like a boil that can never be cured so long as it is covered up but must be opened with all its ugliness to the natural medicine of air and light, injustice must be exposed, with all the tension its exposure creates, to the light of human conscience and the air of national opinion before it can be cured."

"When I was suddenly catapulted into the leadership of the bus protest in Montgomery, Alabama, a few years ago, I felt we would be supported by the white church. I felt that the white ministers, priests and rabbis of the South would be among our strongest allies. Instead, some have been outright opponents, refusing to understand the freedom movement and misrepresenting its leaders; all too many others have been more cautious than courageous and have remained silent behind the anesthetizing security of stained-glass windows."

BLACK HISTORY EVERYDAY
PART TWO

"I have heard numerous southern religious leaders admonish their worshipers to comply with a desegregation decision because it is the law, but I have longed to hear white ministers declare: 'Follow this decree because integration is morally right and because the Negro is your brother.'"

Black History Everyday - Part Two Photo. Faces and signs in the crowd for the 50th Anniversary March on Washington.

Black History Everyday - Part Two Photo. Faces and signs in the crowd for the 50th Anniversary March on Washington.

FREDERICK MONDERSON

"Before closing I feel impelled to mention one other point in your statement that has trouble me profoundly. You warmly commend the Birmingham police force for keeping 'order' and 'preventing violence.' I doubt that you would have so warmly commended the police force if you had seen its dogs sinking their teeth into unarmed, nonviolent Negroes. I doubt that you would so quickly commend the policemen if you were to observe their ugly and inhuman treatment of Negroes here in their city jail; if you were to watch them push and curse old Negro women and young Negro girls; if you were to see them slap and kick old Negro men and young boys; if you were to observe them, as they did on two occasions, refuse to give us food because we wanted to sing our grace together. I cannot join you in your praise of the Birmingham Police Department."

"Perhaps Mr. Connor and his policemen have been rather nonviolent in public, as was Chief Pritchett in Albany, Georgia, but they have used the moral means of nonviolence to maintain the immoral end of racial injustice. As T.S. Eliot has said: "The last temptation is the greatest treason: To do the right deed for the wrong reason."

This letter, setting out Dr. King's principles for **Direct Action** ultimately led to the August 1963 "March on Washington" where he made his "I have a Dream Speech" at the Lincoln Memorial. Many people have seen and used the "Dream" aspect of his

BLACK HISTORY EVERYDAY PART TWO

great speech rather than the fundamental essence of its purpose, which was poverty and injustice.

The **Civil Rights Act of 1964** - was entitled "An act to enforce the constitutional right to vote, to confer jurisdiction upon the district courts of the United States to provide injunctive relief against discrimination in public accommodations, to authorize the Attorney General to institute suits to protect constitutional rights in public facilities and public education, to extend the **Commission on Civil Rights**, to prevent discrimination in federally assisted programs, to establish a **Commission on Equal Employment Opportunity**, and for other purposes."

This was, according to Jack C. Plano and Milton Greenberg's *The American Political Dictionary* (New York: Holt, Rinehart and Winston, Inc., 1962, 1989: 333-334) who states: "A major enactment designed to erase racial discrimination in most areas of American life. Major provisions of the Act: (1) outlaw arbitrary discrimination in voter registration and expedite voting rights suits; (2) bar discrimination in public accommodations, such as hotels and restaurants, that have a substantial relation to interstate commerce; (3) authorize the national government to bring suits to desegregate public facilities and schools; (4) extend the life of the Civil Rights Commission; (5) provide for the withholding of federal funds from programs administered in a discriminatory manner; (60 establish the right to equality in employment opportunities; and (7) establish a Community Relations Service to help resolve civil rights problems. The Act for bids discrimination based on race, color, religion, national origin, and, in the case of employment, sex. Techniques for gaining voluntary compliance are stressed in t he Act, and the resolution of civil rights problems through state and local action is encouraged. Discrimination in housing is not covered by the law, but is prohibited by the Civil Rights Act of 1968."

The significance of the **Civil Rights Act of 1964** is seen as "the most far-reaching civil rights legislation since Reconstruction. It was passed after the longest debate in Senate history (eighty-three days) and only after cloture was invoked for the first time to cut off a civil rights filibuster. Compliance with the Act's controversial provisions on public accommodations and equal employer opportunity has been widespread. Title VI of the Act, which authorizes the cut-off of federal funds to state and local programs practicing discrimination, proved to be the most effective provision of the Act. For example, a dramatic jump in southern school integration took place when the national government threatened to withhold federal funds from schools failing to comply with desegregation orders. All agencies receiving federal funds are required to submit assurances of compliance with the 1964 Act. Hundreds of grant-in-aid programs are involved,

BLACK HISTORY EVERYDAY
PART TWO

amounting to 20 percent of all state and local revenues. The Supreme Court upheld the public accommodations provisions of the law as a legitimate exercise of the commerce power provisions of the law as a legitimate exercise of the commerce power of Congress (Heart of Alabama Motor v. United states, 379 U.A. 241 [1964])."

The **Civil Rights Acts of 1968** was crafted as - "A Law which prohibits discrimination in the advertising, financing, sale, or rental of housing, based on race, religion, or national origin and, as of 1974, sex, but provided limited and ineffective enforcement powers. A major amendment of the Act in 1988 extended coverage to the handicapped and to families with children and added enforcement machinery through either administrative enforcement by the department of Housing and Urban Development (HUD) or by suits in federal court, with the choice of forums left to either party in the dispute. The law covers about 90 percent of all housing. Major exclusions are owner-occupied dwellings of four units or less and those selling or renting without services of a broker. Other provisions of the **1968 Act** provide criminal penalties for interfering with the exercise of civil rights of others, or for using interstate commerce to incite riots."

The significance of this legislation, according to Plano and Greenberg 1989: 334-335) meant: "Residential segregation was the last and most

FREDERICK MONDERSON

sensitive civil rights issue faced by Congress. The 1968 Act was passed in the wake of the assassination of Dr. Martin Luther King, Jr., and after a filibuster was overcome in the Senate. Discrimination in housing isolates minorities, intensifies school segregation problems, and deprives even economically successful blacks from full enjoyment of housing opportunities. Most housing discrimination results from private acts of bankers, real estate agents, and individual landowners rather than governmental action. Shortly after enactment of the **Civil Rights Act of 1968**, the **Supreme Court** ruled in *Jones v. Mayer*, 392 U.S. 409 (1968), that the **Civil Rights Act of 1866** outlawed all racial discrimination in housing. The **Court** reconciled the 1968 law with the 1866 law by noting that the law covers religion and national origin, in addition to race, and provides for enforcement machinery."

Black History Everyday - Part Two Photo. Rev. Al Sharpton and the National Action Network is so helping to "Keep the Dream Alive."

BLACK HISTORY EVERYDAY
PART TWO

Black History Everyday -Part Two Photo. Drs. Jeffries sits next to Fredricka Bey and Professor Blake at CEMOTAP'S Presentation on Dr. King and Malcolm X's influences.

"The difference between the Universal Negro Improvement Association and the other movements of this country, and probably of the world, is that the Universal Negro Improvement Association seeks independence of government, while the other organizations seek to subordinate the Negro as a secondary consideration in a great civilization, knowing that in America the Negro will never get his constitutional rights. All those organizations which are fostering the improvement of Negroes in the British Empire know that the Negro in the British Empire will never reach the height of his constitutional rights. What do I mean by constitutional rights in America? If the black man is to reach the height of his ambition in this country – if the black man is to get all of his constitutional rights in America – then the black man should have the

FREDERICK MONDERSON

same chance in the nation as any other man to become president of the nation, or a street cleaner in New York.

Black History Everyday - Part Two Photo.
"**KWANZAA** - more than a holiday, it's a lifestyle," is the message.

"The leadership of the Negro of to-day must be able to locate the race, and not only for to-day bot for all times. It is in this desire to locate the Negro in a position of prosperity and happiness the future that the Universal Negro Improvement Association is making this great fight for the race's emancipation everywhere and the founding of a great African government. Every sober-minded Negro will see immediately the reason why we should support a movement of this kind. If we will survive then it must be done through our own effort, through our own energy. No race of weaklings an survive in the days of tomorrow, because they will be hard and strenuous days fraught with many difficulties." Marcus Garvey. *Philosophy and Opinions.*

BLACK HISTORY EVERYDAY PART TWO

22. MARCUS GARVEY AND THE UNIA
BY
DR. FRED MONDERSON

Marcus Garvey brought a new impetus to the needs and aspirations of Black people in America from his Harlem, New York based Universal Negro Improvement Association. Founded in 1914 in Jamaica, West Indies, under a philosophy of Black "redemption" and "self-improvement," the **UNIA** soon became a force to be reckoned with in the United States, where the masses flocked to join, precisely because of its message of hope and pride. Foremost, Garvey felt, only the Black man can save the Black man! Naturally and for many reasons, he had his detractors or critics! Yet, calling the devil white, Garvey denounced White America for the tribulations of slavery and its aftermath the had visited upon the Black man. Still, white liberals were impressed by his self-help philosophy and even the KKK was "happy" that he wanted to take Blacks "Back to Africa." Many "Negroes" held him in contempt because he favored "Black."

FREDERICK MONDERSON

Black History Everyday - Part Two Photo. Faces and signs in the crowd for the 50th Anniversary March on Washington.

Black History Everyday - Part Two Photo. A **KWANZAA TABLE** of first fruits and candles.

BLACK HISTORY EVERYDAY
PART TWO

Black History Everyday - Part Two Photo. Faces and signs in the crowd for the 50th Anniversary March on Washington.

Black leaders were especially critical, accusing him, says WEB DuBois, of being a "visionary" and A. Philip Randolph, according to Bradford Chambers in *Chronicles of Black Protest* (1968: 165) accused him of "outright exploitation of the black man." Nevertheless, it's interesting how time and history has put Garvey in proper perspective. DuBois later praised Garvey, while A. Philip Randolph despite his enormous Civil Rights efforts, had been retired to the "old folks' home" of history to pass out his days. Garvey, on the other hand, has remained to this day, a vibrant and motivating symbolic icon as the people, in time, got to know the man and his ideas. His red, black and green flag remains a living symbol of Black Nationalist aspirations.

FREDERICK MONDERSON

Marcus Moziah Garvey, born in Jamaica on August 1, 1887, was impressed with the work of Booker T. Washington after reading *Up from Slavery*. He wrote Washington with the intent of setting up a Tuskegee-like school in Jamaica. Booker T. invited him to come to America in 1915 but by the time he arrived in 1916, the Tuskegee icon had died. Nevertheless, Garvey settled in Harlem, New York, and began to plant the seeds of **UNIA** there in 1917. By the time of the **Versailles Peace Conference of 1919** ending World War I (1914-1918) Garvey boasted he had set up 19 branches of the UNIA throughout the United States. Within those few years, the movement had lit a fire under the downtrodden and Garvey's star began to rise.

John Hope Franklin in *From Slavery to Freedom* (Sixth Edition) (1987: 320) explained: "The basis for Garvey's wide popularity was his appeal to race pride at a time when Negroes generally had so little of which to be proud. The strain and stress of living in hostile urban communities created a state of mind upon which Garvey capitalized. He called upon Negroes, especially the ones of the darker hue, to follow him. Garvey exalted everything black: he insisted that black stood for strength and beauty, not inferiority. He asserted that Africans had a noble past, and he declared that Negroes should be proud of their ancestry. In his newspaper, *The Negro World*, he told Negroes that racial prejudice was so much a part of the civilization of the whites that it was futile to appeal to their sense of justice and their high-

BLACK HISTORY EVERYDAY
PART TWO

sounding democratic principles. With an eye to the growing sentiment favoring self-determination of dependent peoples, Garvey said that the only hope for Negro-Americans was to flee America and return to Africa and build up a country of their own. On one occasion Garvey cried out: 'Wake up Ethiopia! Wake up Africa! Let us work toward the one glorious end of a free, redeemed and mighty nation. Let Africa be a bright star among the constellation of nations." However, while he sent missions to Africa to explore land options, no one was ever repatriated back to Africa. Equally importantly, many of the people who surrounded Garvey, it can be pointed out, worked against him and his people's best interest.

Notwithstanding, Garvey was a master analyst, tactician, orator and man of action! Apprenticed in his youth as a printer, Garvey began printing his newspaper, *The Negro World* to get his message out and this certainly helped in expanding membership in the UNIA. After his travels in Latin America and Europe and then coming to America, he became acutely aware of the plight of Africans worldwide. Perhaps he looked in the mirror as Malcolm X would later say. According to Franklin (1987: 323) Garvey asked: "Where is the black man's Government?" "Where is his King and Kingdom?" "Where is his President, his Country, and his Ambassador, his Army, his Navy, his Men of Big Affairs?" I could not find them and then I declared "I will help to make them." That was the cataclysmic moment, when looking in the mirror, one sees the messiah!

FREDERICK MONDERSON

Garvey then created titles to fit the positions of "men of big affairs." The nobility he created included: "Knights of the Nile," "Knights of the Distinguished Service Order of Ethiopia," and "Dukes of the Niger and Uganda." He also created the "Count of the Congo." His auxiliary organs included the "Universal Black Cross Nurses," the "Universal African Motor Corps," and the "Black Eagle Flying Corps" and to promote commerce between Africa and America, the **Black Star Line**.

Nonetheless, and again, many of the people who worked for him made the **Black Star Line** his "Achilles Heel." The captains, for the most part, sabotaged the ships so that they required more and more resources to operate and this became a drain, siphoning off resources for other projects.

Black History Everyday - Part Two Photo. Iconic Colors of **KWANZAA**!

BLACK HISTORY EVERYDAY
PART TWO

However, within four years after its founding in Harlem in 1917, the **UNIA** held its 1921 convention and Garvey put on a spectacular show of pomp, pride and performance.

Bradford Chambers' in *Chronicles of Black Protest* (1968: 165) offers commentary on Garvey's "Back to Africa Movement" in which he wrote: "The 1921 convention of the **UNIA** in New York was a prime example of Garvey's use of pageantry. Led by Garvey, in a uniform of purple, green and black - with gold-braid trimmings and a helmet crowned with flowing white feathers - 50,000 Garveyites and partisans from Harlem marched down Lenox Avenue. With flags and bands, they paraded to Madison Square Garden for a mass rally. There they proclaimed Garvey the Provisional President-General of Africa. Splendid was the pomp and ceremony of the occasion. There was an invocation by the black archbishop of the "African Orthodox Church," which Garvey created (complete with a "Black Holy Trinity," a black "Christ of Sorrow," and a "Black Madonna"). Also, on display were contingents from the "African Legion," the "Black Cross Nurses," the "African Motor Corps," and the "Black Eagle Flying Corps." Garvey also had assistants in his role as President-General of Africa.

Even further, Bradford (1968: 166) continued: "He told his followers that black men's only hope was to build an independent nation in Africa where they

FREDERICK MONDERSON

could choose their own leaders. He criticized interracial organizations such as the **NAACP** for their lack of concern for the ordinary black, and urged black people to do something for themselves."

Naturally, Garvey like all great revolutionary visionaries who challenged behemoth systems of oppression, was betrayed, jailed, deported and died alone in London in 1940, far from his beloved **UNIA** in Harlem.

Black History Everyday - Part Two Photo. With the **NAKO** (National Association of Kawaida Organizations) Emblem in full display, "The Band Plays on!"

John Hope Franklin and Isidore Starr in *The Negro in 20th Century America* (1967): 110) quoted Garvey in which he states: "To fight for the African redemption

BLACK HISTORY EVERYDAY
PART TWO

does not mean that we must give up our domestic fight for political justice and industrial rights. It does not mean that we must become disloyal to any government or to any country wherein we were born. Each and every race outside of its domestic national loyalty had a loyalty to itself; therefore, it is foolish for the Negro to talk about not being interested in his own racial, political, social and industrial destiny. We can be as loyal American citizens as British subjects as the Irishman or the Jew, and yet fight for the redemption of Africa, a complete emancipation of the race."

Black History Everyday - Part Two Photo. Faces and signs in the crowd for the 50th Anniversary March on Washington.

FREDERICK MONDERSON

Black History Everyday - Part Two Photo. Faces and signs in the crowd for the 50th Anniversary March on Washington.

Franklin (1967: 112) outlined the main points of the **Preamble of the UNIA** as stated by Garvey. "The Universal Negro Improvement Association and African Communities League is a social, friendly, humanitarian, charitable, educational, institutional, constructive, and egalitarian society, and is founded by persons, desiring to the utmost to work for the general uplift of the Negro peoples of the world. And the members pledge themselves to do all in their power to conserve the rights of their noble race and to respect the rights of all mankind, believing always in the Brotherhood of man and the fatherhood of God. The motto of the organization is: **One God! One Aim! One Destiny!** Therefore, let justice be

BLACK HISTORY EVERYDAY
PART TWO

done to all mankind, realizing that if the strong oppress the weak confusion and discontent will ever mark the path of men, but with love, faith and charity towards all the reign of peace and plenty will be heralded into the world and the generation of men shall be called blessed."

Franklin (1967: 112) further added that the declared objectives of the association are: "To establish a **Universal Confraternity** among the race; to promote the spirit of pride and love; to reclaim the fallen; to administer to and assist the needy; to assist in civilizing the backward tribes of Africa; to assist in the development of **Independent Negro Nations and Communities**; to establish a central nation for the race; to establish Commissaries or agencies in the principal countries and cities of the world for the representation of all Negroes; to promote a conscientious Spiritual worship among the native tribes of Africa; to establish Universities, Colleges, Academies and Schools for the racial education and culture of the people to work for better conditions among Negroes everywhere."

In a speech delivered at Liberty Hall, New York City, on November 25, 1922, Garvey outlined "The **Principles of the Universal Negro Improvement Association**" as presented in *The Philosophy and Opinions of Marcus Garvey* (New York: Atheneum, 1971: 93-100)

FREDERICK MONDERSON

"Over five years ago the Universal Negro Improvement Association placed itself before the world as the movement through which the new and rising Negro would give expression of his feelings. This Association adopts an attitude not of hostility to other races and peoples of the world, but an attitude of self-respect, of manhood rights on behalf of 400,000,000 Negroes of the world ...."

"We represent a new line of thought among Negroes. Whether you call it advanced thought or reactionary thought, I do not care. If it is reactionary for people to seek independence in government, then we are reactionary. If it is advanced thought for people to seek liberty and freedom, then we represent the advanced school of thought among the Negroes of this country. We of the UNIA believe that what is good for the other fellow is good for us. If government is something that is worthwhile; if government is something that is appreciable and helpful and protective to others, then we also want to experiment in government. We do not mean a government that will make us citizens without rights or subjections without consideration. We mean the kind of government that will place our race in control, even as other races are in control of their own governments ...."

BLACK HISTORY EVERYDAY
PART TWO

Black History Everyday - Part Two Photo. The **MAN** himself, Founder of **KWANZAA**, Dr. Maulana Karenga and his constant companion.

"I desire to remove the misunderstanding that has been created in the minds of millions of people throughout the world in their relationship to the organization. The Universal Negro Improvement Association stands for the Bigger Brotherhood; the Universal Negro Improvement Association stands for human rights; not only for Negroes, but for all races. The Universal Negro Improvement Association believes in the rights of not only the black race, but the white race, the yellow race and the brown race. The Universal Negro Improvement Association believes that the white man has as much right to be considered, the yellow man has as much right to be considered as the black man of Africa. In view of the fact that the black man of Africa has contributed as much to the world as the white man of Europe, and brown man and yellow man of Asia, we of the Universal Negro Improvement Association demand that the white, yellow and brown races give to the black man his place in the civilization of the world. We ask for nothing more than the rights of 400,000,000 Negroes ...."

"We of the Universal Negro Improvement Association ... desire to bring together the 15,000,000 of the United States, the 180,000,000 in Asia, the West Indies and Central and South America, and the 200,000,000 in Africa. We are looking toward political freedom on the continent of Africa, the land of our fathers."

"The difference between the Universal Negro Improvement Association and the movements of this country, and possibly the world, is that the Universal Negro Improvement Association seeks independence of government, while the other organizations seek to make the Negro a secondary part of existing governments. We differ from the organizations in America because they seek to subordinate the Negro as a secondary consideration in a great civilization, knowing that the Negro in America will never reach his highest ambition, knowing that the Negro in America will never get his constitutional rights .... You and I can live in the United States of America for 100 years, and our generations may live for 200 years or for 5,000 more years, and so long as there is black and white population, when the majority is on

BLACK HISTORY EVERYDAY PART TWO

the side of the white race, you and I will never get political justice or get political equality in this country ...."

"We are not preaching a propaganda of hate against anybody. We love the white man; we love all humanity because we feel that we cannot live without the other. The white man is as necessary to the existence of the Negro as the Negro is necessary to his existence. There is a common relationship that we cannot escape. Africa has certain things that Europe wants, and Europe has certain things that Africa wants and if a fair and square deal must bring white and black with each other, it is impossible for us to escape it. Africa has oil, diamonds, copper, gold and rubber and all the minerals that Europe wants, and there must be some kind of relationship between Africa and Europe for a fair exchange, so we cannot afford to hate anybody."

"Whosoever's the cause of humanity stands in need of assistance; there you will find the Negro ever ready to serve."

"He has done it from the time of Christ up to now. When the whole world turned its back upon the Christ, the man who was said to be the Son of God, when the world spurned him and spat upon Him, it was a Black man, Simon, the Cyrenian, who took up the cross. Why? Because the course of humanity appealed to him. When the black man saw the suffering Jew, struggling under the heavy cross, he

FREDERICK MONDERSON

was willing to go to His assistance, and he bore the cross up to the heights of Cavalry. In the spirit of Simon, the Cyrenian, 1900 years ago, we answered the call of Woodrow Wilson, the call to a larger humanity, and it was for that we willingly rushed into the war ...."

Black History Everyday - Part Two Photo. Faces and signs in the crowd for the 50th Anniversary March on Washington.

Black History Everyday - Part Two Photo. Faces and signs in the crowd for the 50th Anniversary March on Washington.

BLACK HISTORY EVERYDAY
PART TWO

"We have not forgotten the prowess of war. If we have been liberal minded enough to give our life's blood in France, in Mesopotamia and elsewhere, fighting for the white man, whom we have always assisted, surely we have not forgotten to fight for ourselves, and when the time comes that the world will again give Africa an opportunity for freedom, surely... black men will march out on the battle plains of Africa, under the colors of the red, the black and the green."

"We shall march out, yes, as Black-American citizens, as Black-British subjects, as Black-French citizens, as Black Italians or as Black-Spaniards, but we shall march out in answer to the cry of our fathers, who cry out to us for the redemption of our own country, our motherland, Africa."

"We shall march out, not forgetting the blessings of America. We shall march out, not forgetting the blessings of civilization. We shall march out with a history of peace before and behind us, and surely that history shall be our breastplate, for how can man fight better than knowing that the cause for which he fights is righteous? How can man fight more gloriously than by knowing that behind him is a history of slavery, a history of bloody carnage and massacre inflicted upon a race because of its inability to protect itself and fight? Shall we not fight for the glorious opportunity of protecting and forever more establishing ourselves as a mighty race and nation,

FREDERICK MONDERSON

never more to be disrespected by men? Glorious shall be the battle when the time comes to fight for our people and our race."

"We shall say to the millions who are in Africa to hold the fort, for we are coming 400,000,000 strong."

Black History Everyday - Part Two Photo. Culture, culture, culture at **KWANZAA** celebration in New York!

Thus, Garvey was indeed an immortal African thinker whose timely appearance on the world stage became a wind beneath the Black man's sails and helped propel him, with not simply the wherewithal to improve himself in the significant parameters of social development but in much more. He instilled a new and forward reaching type of thinking that has helped him reach higher and higher heights. As a publisher, Garvey wrote and inspired his people on every conceivable subject from Propaganda, slavery, force, education, miscegenation, prejudice,

BLACK HISTORY EVERYDAY PART TWO

radicalism, government, evolution and its results, poverty, power, universal suspicion, dissertation on man, race assimilation, Christianity, the functions of man, and traitors and an even wider area of subject matter.

Truly the man was a visionary well ahead for his time, a great thinker and man of action, whose success still propels Blacks and perhaps it was inevitable that he be betrayed and brought down. Convicted and handcuffed on his way to Atlanta Federal Prison, he uttered, "You have caged the lion, but the cubs are still running around out there. So, look for me in the whirlwind!" And as equally inevitable, "Truth crushed to earth shall rise" and Garvey's aspirations and visions for the Black man is alive and well today under the Red, Black and Green, a symbolic motif with great potential for inspiration and action!

FREDERICK MONDERSON

Black History Everyday - Part Two Photo. Stalwarts receiving their accolades at **CEMOTAP**.

"By burying the 'Runaway Samuel Carson' in Ghana, West Africa, we will Open the "Door of Return" as a site of pilgrimage and point of departure for Africans seeking their Roots in Africa." Sonny Carson at *The Bones Committee.*

"We now have the names of hundreds of Black Veterans who were buried in the Brooklyn Navy Yard, a segregated Black Cemetery, with the earliest name dating back to 1801. If people today could trace and establish their connection to these veterans, the Navy probably owes them money, with compounded interest! Some of these names were published in the Brooklyn, New York *Afro Times*, part of the *Daily Challenge* family newspaper. Sonny Carson on "The Bones."

BLACK HISTORY EVERYDAY PART TWO

Black History Everyday - Part Two Photo. More Culture, dancing.

23. HAVE WE FORGOTTEN SONNY CARSON? BY DR. FRED MONDERSON?

"A people who have forgotten their past, are like a tree without roots."

Have we forgotten Sonny Carson? If so, we have also forgotten Queen Mother Moore, Fannie Lou Hamer, Barbara Jordan, Sojourner Truth, Mary McLeod Bethune, Dick Gregory, Rosa Parks and Coretta Scott King! Of course, Jitu Weusi, Rev. Shuttlesworth, Rev. Abernathy, Bill Lynch, all should remain actively in our memories.

FREDERICK MONDERSON

Naturally, we have not forgotten Martin Luther King, Jr., or Malcolm X. Equally, others have not forgotten these giants, for they too promote Martin Luther King Sale and Malcolm X Sale. What a pity!

Black History Everyday - Part Two Photo. Faces and signs in the crowd for the 50th Anniversary March on Washington.

Black History Everyday - Part Two Photo. Faces and signs in the crowd for the 50th Anniversary March on Washington.

Why has not a sale day set aside for Sonny Carson on May 18; Paul Robeson; Kwame Nkrumah; Marcus Garvey, August 17; WEB DuBois; Jackie Robinson;

BLACK HISTORY EVERYDAY PART TWO

Countee Cullen; Claude McKay; Langston Hughes; Booker T. Washington; Frederick Douglass; Martin Delaney; Henry Highland Garnett; David Walker; Nat Turner; Crispus Attucks; and so on. So, if we're promoting sales let's remember everyone.

Imagine, since Black people spend so much on the two afore-mentioned sale days; imagine how much more they would spend if sale days were promoted on the birth and death days of the above. After all, isn't it about money?

Nevertheless, and naturally, since some may think this is an exercise in futility, I beg to differ. It is, however, to prove a point that some of our leaders' names are not commercially lucrative. Hence, we must struggle to retain control of their image, persona and philosophic outlook and revolutionary perspective for such represents pillars aiding our situation. After all, it was the great Theophile Obenga, Dr. Cheikh Anta Diop's Research Associate who advised, we must forever echo the names and works of our great ancestors for herein lies our strengths needed to confront the oppressor's constant challenges, day after day!

Sonny Carson remained obdurate in his revolutionary outlook and demands for Black liberation through economic emancipation, educational advancement and social upliftment particularly in its most creative expressions. He adamantly opposed the prison industrial complex for its evisceration of the

FREDERICK MONDERSON

psychological aspirations of Black manhood, trampled upon constantly on a day to day basis.

Sonny was, however, acutely aware, our people contribute much to their travail by boldly walking into traps set by their captors.

Sonny "AB," "Abubadika" Carson, was equally and unalterably opposed to the scourge of drugs in our community; police brutality; racism; inferior education; joblessness; the paucity of respectable and admirable leaders and leadership. That is, creating a void of role models the young can pattern themselves after. He despaired young people do not have sufficient credible contemporary heroes to emulate. This is, he recognized, despite sports figures, actors and musicians, who are constantly fed to the young on a false and deceptive premise.

In fact, one of the major fights Sonny had with the musical giant, Sony, ET. Al., is their fostering the portrayal of Blacks as gangsters through the lyrics of their promoted music. Unfortunately, as our demands for Black ownership in the music industry proved successful, the lyrics never got better. It's like Rev. Al Sharpton said in his **Eulogy** for James Brown, "How did we get from 'Say it loud, I'm Black and proud' to 'Bitches and hos?'"

Championing creative and clean musical lyrics in his "Tone it down" admonition, Sonny Carson proved a multi-issue activist. Granted, he got bad-publicity for

BLACK HISTORY EVERYDAY
PART TWO

the Ocean-Hill-Brownsville struggle to decentralize the New York City school system owing to its improper representation of Blacks and Hispanics in teaching and administrative positions, he remained steadfastly an education advocate. He was concerned with the plight of derelict landlords, poor housing, and lack of ownership of the economic infrastructure of the Black community. As such, particularly when merchants dealt egregiously with Black patrons, he led economic boycotts that were not universally praised. Sonny Carson founded, was a founding member or advocated the founding of several organizations. The **Restoration Corporation** in Bedford-Stuyvesant that spawned economic revitalization of this hub of the Black community is one such entity. He was active in the evolution from Malcolm-King College into Medgar Evers College. Despite this at one of its graduation ceremonies he complained. He said: "I thought I was in a Greece. Where are the drums that connect with the African heritage?"

In 1968, after the assassination of Martin Luther King, the then Mayor John Lindsey personally appealed to Sonny Carson as a leader of substance to quell any acts of looting and violence. And, Sonny accepted the challenge.

Sonny Carson founded the **Committee to Honor Black Heroes** and set about changing the names of streets, Viz., Malcolm X Boulevard,

FREDERICK MONDERSON

Martin Luther King Boulevard and Harriet Ross Tubman Avenue. He also changed school names such as Malcolm X and was instrumental I naming Toussaint L'Ouverture and fortunately a host of others were in the pipeline before his demise. He also founded **Black Men Against Crack** and the **Black Men's Movement**. Despite his advocacy against police brutality and misconduct, many top brass in the Police Department respected Sonny for his principled activism.

Sonny Carson's **Final Triumph** came when the U.S. Navy discovered the remains of Sonny's ancestor Samuel Carson, "The Runaway," who served and died in the Mexican-American War in 1845. He was buried in the Brooklyn Navy yard, for long a segregated Black cemetery. That is, until 1926 when manty bones were reinterred to the Cyprus Hills national Cemetery in the Brooklyn-Queens part of Brooklyn. Utilizing one of his strengths, Sonny set up the "Bones Committee" that met for nearly 2 years and finally resolved to repatriate "The runaway" creating "The Door of Return" into Ghana, West Africa. In this, he created a memorial site of pilgrimage for African-Americans seeking their cultural and ancestral roots in Africa.

The farcical display of New York City Council denying the naming of a street in Bed-Stuy for Sonny Carson is more of a shame on their part. As one writer wrote: "The Revolution was in the hearts and minds of the people," and so whether it was the street or the

BLACK HISTORY EVERYDAY
PART TWO

park, the name resonates in the minds and hearts of the people. The Community Board 3 voted and today Bed-Stuy is called "Abubadikaville" and Linden Boulevard Park is called Sonny Carson Park!

Now, with all the challenges facing Blacks today, not discounting many who act foolishly, if we think about it, only Al Sharpton is out there as a true activist. Hence, we cannot afford to forget Robert "Sonny" Carson, AB, "Abubadika," and what he stood for in terms of Black elevation and advancement, educational upliftment, creative but respective musical lyrics, decent housing, and full-employment for Blacks, while saying no to police brutality, racism and racial profiling. May the spirit of Sonny Carson prevail.

Black History Everyday – Part Two Photo. Dr. Rosalind Jeffries at the Podium at **CEMOTAP's** Dr. King and Malcolm X's Presentation on January 25, 2020.

FREDERICK MONDERSON

Black History Everyday - Part Two Photo. Councilwoman Letitia James, Lt.-Governor David Patterson, Councilman Al Vann and Dr. Rosado.

Black History Everyday - Part Two Photo. Faces and signs in the crowd for the 50th Anniversary March on Washington.

BLACK HISTORY EVERYDAY
PART TWO

Black History Everyday - Part Two Photo. Faces and signs in the crowd for the 50th Anniversary March on Washington.

"History will one day have its say; it will not be history taught in the United States, Washington, Paris or Brussels, however, but the history taught in the countries that have rid themselves of colonialism and its puppets. Africa will write its own history, and both north and south of the Sahara, it will be a history full of glory and dignity." **Patrice Lumumba**. *Last letter to wife Pauline Lumumba* [1960]

"Time is on the side of the oppressed today, it's against the oppressor. Truth is on the side of the oppressed today, it's against the oppressor. You don't need anything else." **Malcolm X**. *Speech* [May 29, 1964]

FREDERICK MONDERSON

24. REFLECTIONS ON BLACK HISTORY IN BROOKLYN - A DECADE AGO
BY
DR. FRED MONDERSON

On a cold and wintry Friday night February 9, 2007, when most people are either snuggled at home or out enjoying the luxury of dining out or partying, history was made at a Brooklyn Power meeting held at the **Hope City Empowerment Center**, 650 Washington Avenue, between Dean and Bergen streets. The featured speaker, Lieutenant Governor David Patterson, came to the Borough to celebrate **Black History Month** as part of the **Black Brooklyn Empowerment Convention's Economic Development Cluster** on the theme of "The New York State Budget" in which he sought to outline the state of affairs in Albany and speak to an agenda that is designed to help empower Blacks in Brooklyn and New York State.

BLACK HISTORY EVERYDAY
PART TWO

Black History Everyday - Part Two Photo. Dr. Maulana Karenga, author of **KWANZAA** addresses the Festival Celebration in Brooklyn, New York.

Reflecting back on the June 17, 2006 **Black Brooklyn Empowerment Convention (BBEC)** convened to ratify solutions to address critical issues impacting Blacks in Brooklyn, this gathering was part of a continuation of the Economic Development Cluster's purpose of "galvanizing business leaders, educators, administrators, elected officials and community leaders to develop and implement tangible solutions for overcoming barriers to economic development, housing and workforce development." As a result, and seldom, would one see so many elected officials from federal, state and city offices, as well as professional and concerned people gathered in one place signifying a sort of

FREDERICK MONDERSON

coming of age of Black political power in Brooklyn with the potential for grooming future leaders, both male and female, and implementing meaningful strategies for change and advancement of the cause of African people.

Seated together behind the Microphone were Honorable David Patterson next to City Councilman Albert Vann, Assemblywoman Annette Robinson, State Senator Erik Adams, Councilwoman Letitia James, and Congresswoman Yvette Clarke. Across from these were Assemblyman Karim Camara, Senator Kevin Parker, Councilwoman Darlene Mealey, Assemblyman Darrel Towns, Assemblyman Hakeem Jeffries, Rev. Fine, Pastor of 82-year-old Beulah Baptist Church on St. Johns Place, at whose outreach center the event was held, and Dr. John Flateau of Medgar Evers College. The riveted audience was numerous, with folks standing in the rear and along the aisles. They all seemed to have a sense that we should forever thank Dr. Carter G. Woodson for being the "Father of Black History."

Congresswoman Yvette Clarke was introduced by the Hostess Letitia James and she began by quoting a famous line from Charles Dickens' *A Tale of Two Cities* (1859), 'It was the best of times, it was the worst of times' and insisting on the need for retooling and reassessing as a means of empowerment, she began praising the audience as being talented, gifted and skilled and insisted we assess and utilize the tremendous resource potential we have at our

BLACK HISTORY EVERYDAY
PART TWO

disposal. The audience, I am sure are aware that we ourselves must bring about the change we want to see. Saying in public she will vote 'No to War, Yes to the new Resolution circulating in Congress and No to further Funding" for the War in Iraq, she expressed disappointment at the poverty of the President's recent State of the Union Message. He never addressed the state of poverty in the country, the challenges of the people of the Gulf Coast, nor any significant domestic agenda, but laid great emphasis on the war in Iraq.

Black History Everyday - Part Two Photo. Faces and signs in the crowd for the 50th Anniversary March on Washington.

FREDERICK MONDERSON

Black History Everyday - Part Two Photo. Faces and signs in the crowd for the 50th Anniversary March on Washington.

Black History Everyday - Part Two Photo. Faces and signs in the crowd for the 50th Anniversary March on Washington.

BLACK HISTORY EVERYDAY
PART TWO

Black History Everyday - Part Two Photo. Dr. Rosado, Assemblyman Al Vann, Harry L. Wells and Erik Monderson at the Black History in Brooklyn affair.

Praising the accomplishment of Congresspersons, Charles Rangel, John Conyers and Maxine Waters and those on whose shoulders we stand today, she insisted 'These are action times' and we must make sure our children inherit a better America and opportunity than she and her generation did. She

FREDERICK MONDERSON

criticized the financial waste in Washington, DC. She sounded the clarion call for imperatives around Health Care, Medicare and praising the Brooklyn community for being monumental, she saw the need for a commitment to see the community grow and blossom. To accomplish this, we must all be activists, build coalitions, network and work for change. However, this can only come about if many are committed to give time, energy and sweat equity. Being elected Congresswoman of the 11th CD, Yvette Clarke made history in the Borough that gave birth and nurturing to Shirley Chisholm, Jackie Robinson, and Michael Jordan. Many were surprised that the Lieutenant Governor, son of Basil Patterson, former New York State Secretary of State, was born in Brooklyn though raised in Harlem.

Black History Everyday - Part Two Photo. Assemblyman Karim Camara, Assemblyman Darrel Towns, Rev. Fine, Dr. Flateau, Senator Kevin Parker and Kaziem Woodbury.

BLACK HISTORY EVERYDAY
PART TWO

In an audience full of people of substance were Princess James, Priscilla Maddox and Nijoni Granville of Community Board 8 in Crown Heights in whose district the meeting was held. Gloria Dulan Wilson of the *Daily Challenge* and *Black Star News*, Harry L. Wells, Author: *Ten Successful Start-Ups*, Matthew Huggins of Ameriplan, USA, Evadyne Smith and Mia Smith-Mallory, Linnette Grant, Jesse Scott, Duke Saunders, Bob Law, Elira Petrie, Dr. Lois Blades-Rosado, Assistant Dean, Executive Director of Brooklyn Educational Opportunity Center of the State University of New York and the Host Kaziem R. Woodbury, Special Assistant to the Executive Director of the Brooklyn Educational Opportunity Center of the State University of New York. Cynthia Davis and Kevin Alexander, Tiffany Tucker of Redemption, and New York State Commissioner of Education Dr. Sheila Tranumn were in attendance. There were many, many more whose names are not here!

Lloyd and Hillary Porter of **Bread Stuy** helped with the cakes, Ms. Jennifer the Chef did her thing in preparing the buffet, Tracy D. Hughes of the **Rum Cake Factory** brought her goodies, sound was afforded by the **Brooklyn Borough President's office** and security was provided by **Black Veterans for Social Justice** whose President Mr. Job Mashiriki and wife were in the audience. Ronald McLaney among many others was

FREDERICK MONDERSON

in attendance. Justices L. Priscilla Hall and Larry D. Martin of the New York State Supreme Court were there and are also running for re-election to that 14-year position. They are naturally seeking Black Brooklyn support in their re-election bid. Mrs. Hasoni Pratts Chief of Staff of Assemblyman Karim Camara and also Lauren Baranco Assistant Chief of Staff to the Assemblyman Camara as well as GiGi Davis-Elliott, Community Affairs Coordinator to Councilwoman Letitia James are numbered among the many in attendance.

State Assemblyman Darrel Towns, Chair of the Black, Hispanic, Puerto Rican and Asian Caucus, recognizing that 'Racism is alive and well in America' said, "We are not where we want to be, but thank God we're not where we were." Recognizing the "Modern Day struggle of equal Rights" he touched upon the health crisis facing the African-American community and the broken families resulting from this dilemma. Recognizing the significance of the gathering, he said "We have a lot to celebrate but our work is not done." Therefore, the prescription for this work is continuous activism to combat the ills facing our people. I think it was Percy Sutton of Harlem who said, "If we did not have Al Sharpton, we would have to invent him." This view sort of underscores the critical nature of our situation. Remember, Malcolm X said you want that leader, that savior, that individual who will do that terrific job, "Well, look in the mirror!"

BLACK HISTORY EVERYDAY
PART TWO

Black History Everyday - Part Two Photo. Faces and signs in the crowd for the 50th Anniversary March on Washington.

Black History Everyday - Part Two Photo. Faces and signs in the crowd for the 50th Anniversary March on Washington.

FREDERICK MONDERSON

Councilman Al Vann in introducing the Lieutenant-Governor spoke of the unbelievable expectations of our people once we put people in power. Nevertheless, he did recognize that David Patterson: "Made history by the position he accomplished" he said, "but he will make history by what he also does."

Black History Everyday - Part Two Photo. Councilman Al Vann, Dr. James Flateau of Medgar Evers' DuBois Center and Assemblyman Darrel Towns.

The Lieutenant-Governor began by recounting the camaraderie of the **Black Caucus** in Albany and Article 15A, regarding "Equity in Awarding Contracts to Minorities and Women." He mentioned that in 1994, Blacks received 1788 contracts from the state but that figure was now down to 309. The authorities who dole out the contracts

BLACK HISTORY EVERYDAY
PART TWO

disproportionately shortchange minorities and these are some of the numbers he quoted. Women who make up 50 percent of the population got only 2 percent of the contracts in New York State. You have to first Pre-Qualify then be offered the contracts. Asians who made up 8 percent of the Pre-Qualified population received 1 percent of the contracts; Hispanics made up 10 percent of the Pre-Qualified contractor pool received .74 of 1 percent of contracts; African-Americans who comprised 10 percent of those Pre-Qualified for contracts received .66 or two thirds of 1 percent of contracts; and women .17 of 1 percent. He vowed to "Change this program." He insisted further, "This program was a pre-condition of me running for Lieutenant-Governor." The **MWBE** (Minority, Women, Business, Enterprise) Program was treated like a ward of those who doled out contracts. He also added: "The Democratic Party does not understand business in minority communities."

In a calm and eloquent manner, he outlined the paucity of encouragement for black businesses. Of the top 200 across the country, 24 are in Michigan and these are affiliated with the automobile industry. There are 17 in Georgia, 15 in Texas and the state with the best opportunities for Blacks is Florida. The Governor of Florida, Jeb Bush, is a Republican. North Carolina, Georgia, Alabama are run by Republicans and Blacks fare better economically there than elsewhere, particularly where Democrats run things. There are three times more African-

FREDERICK MONDERSON

American businesses in North Carolina, Georgia and Alabama than in New York. What is the Democratic Party doing? He recognized that "Black contractors in Harlem are fronting for white entities." His take is that "Our whole business complex has to take on a new dynamic." He pointed out that when the Port Authority of New York and New Jersey built the JFK complex, Blacks and Hispanic contractors got 19 percent of the pie. He outlined further that there are 27 state agencies with no goals and only 4 were in compliance. The MWBE had 75 employees and this is down to 9 now. All this will change starting this Monday, the 12th of February, birthday of Abraham Lincoln.

Black History Everyday - Part Two Photo. Young Luis listens attentively to Dr. Maulana Karenga deliver the Kwanzaa Message.

BLACK HISTORY EVERYDAY
PART TWO

In retrospect, this notion of contract allocation is synonymous with what the attorney Michael Hardy said regarding the upgrading and reinvestment of the Javits Convention Center in Mid-Manhattan. This is a multi-billion-dollar enterprise as well as the rebuilding of the World Trade Center towers: "The people who load the trucks, deliver the supplies, remove the supplies from the trucks, and are building these structures do no look like us!" So where is our share? Where is the Black contractors' share of the pie? We do know they are qualified. Who is keeping tabs on this development?"

Significantly, the Lieutenant-Governor commented on an even more prevalent problem, depending on where you sit or stand. In New York state, a single dollar passes through 36 Jewish hands; in the Italian community 20 hands; 4 in the Chinese community; 2 in the Japanese; 1 ¼ in the Hispanic community and in the African American community ¾ of 1 time. Wow!

New York City lost 19 ½ percent of African-American families in the last 12 years. They have gone south to Alabama, Memphis, and so on. This is a shrinking of our political force. It is a collapse of our economic, political and social force. We must fix this as well as make place for younger people with ideas who are being left out. Elders must recognize and advance young talent. He did point out that in 1884, North Carolina had a Black Lieutenant-Governor.

FREDERICK MONDERSON

Today we have Black Lt.-Governors in New York and Maryland as well as a Black Governor in Massachusetts. Much has been said about the notion of voting. Jesse Jackson, once back from Africa said: "We win when we're involved;" others have said: "We make a difference when we vote;" and even more important: "If you don't vote, you don't count." Therefore, in this enlightened age, let us remember Sean "Puffy" Combs: "Vote or die!" Sadly, in the 2016 election P. Diddy advised, "Hold the Vote!" and so, we end up with President Donald J. Trump.

In essence it's like Franz Fanon said in his book *The Wretched of the Earth*: "Each generation must discover its destiny and either fulfill or betray it."

Pointing out further that if you're alone you will accomplish very little. Mr. David Patterson recommended that Blacks begin networking. While praising the accomplishments of the "old guard" he pointed out they were hamstrung by the limitations of their time. He said that regarding the New York State Pensions, Carl McCall did very little in terms of awarding contracts to minorities. Today, Bill Thompson, the City Comptroller has made great strides by awarding 5 percent contracts to Blacks and his goal is 10 percent.

BLACK HISTORY EVERYDAY
PART TWO

Black History Everyday - Part Two Photo. Faces and signs in the crowd for the 50th Anniversary March on Washington.

Black History Everyday - Part Two Photo. Faces and signs in the crowd for the 50th Anniversary March on Washington.

FREDERICK MONDERSON

He insisted we need qualified Blacks in leadership roles in politics, business, education, health care, and in churches. Vowing that he is going to make changes in his position as Lieutenant-Governor, Honorable David Patterson promised "The sons and daughters of people who came here are now going to set America free."

John Flateau spoke of "Gender Equality" and that Blacks were in Brooklyn 400-500 years ago. He pointed out that big tobacco and sugar were active in Brooklyn, in those big buildings down by the waterside, being fed raw materials from the Caribbean region.

State Assemblywoman Annette Robinson exclaimed its "Truly, truly a great day" in regard to the election and coming of the Lieutenant-Governor to Brooklyn. She said that "We're coming together in Brooklyn. We're getting it together. We can create wealth in our community. We must make sure the dollar turns over more in our community."

Hakeem Jeffries praised the kick-off of **Black History in Brooklyn** with David Patterson just as Shirley Chisholm and Jackie Robinson had brought Black fame and integrity to the Borough of Brooklyn. He quoted Malcolm X that we will not have "Full political liberation until we're economically free."

BLACK HISTORY EVERYDAY
PART TWO

Senator Kevin Parker offered praises to Councilman Al Vann, the elder statesman of Brooklyn politics who offered "leadership and mentorship" to many who served their communities.

Assemblyman Karim Camara determined it was a "Grand, historic day." In praising the Lieutenant-Governor, he explained, Mr. Patterson moved from being a State Senator with a constituency of 19,000 to one of Lieutenant-Governor with a constituency of 19,000,000. "We must remember, politics without economics is the symbol of power without substance. If we have no economic base, we have no power!"

Significantly, what some people seemed to take from that meeting was the realization that all things are possible for people who have a plan and consistently work it.

Lerone Bennett said: "Don't expect to win by next Monday evening."

Adam Clayton Powell, Jr.: "Keep the faith Baby."
Tavis Smiley: "When you make Black-America great, you make America great!"

For those who came out this was a wonderful experience to be educated, network and show support for the betterment of Black Brooklyn.

FREDERICK MONDERSON

"There is little difference between the Antebellum South and the New South. Her white citizens are wedded to any method however revolting, any measure however extreme, for the subjugation of the young manhood of the race. They have cheated him out of his ballot, deprived him of civil rights or redress therefore in the civil courts, robbed him of the fruits of his labor, and are still murdering, burning and lynching him." **Ida Bell Wells-Barnett**. *Southern Horrors*: *Lynch Law in All its Phases* [1892]

"If someone else's apology is a prerequisite for your healing, you may never get well." *Essay*. **Essence** [*November* 2006]

25. SHAMELESS "ANTE BELLUM" LEGISLATORS BY DR. FRED MONDERSON

As speaker Boehner and Senator McConnell publicly flagellate President Obama accusing him of jeopardizing their children's future, these two legislators should be asked "Are you teaching your children to be as reprehensible as you are?" Unfortunately, these two men have presided over a climate of racial hatred and disrespectful treatment of

BLACK HISTORY EVERYDAY PART TWO

President Obama, so that today obscure lawmakers are emerging from the political woodwork to demonstrate that infamous Joe Wilson "You Lie" mentality. Now, seemingly individuals shamelessly acting as "Ante Bellum" legislators are championing sending the President to jail! Congratulations Speaker John, your people have descended to the sub-sewer of human indecency and have "damaged your foot," as the "chickens have indeed come home!" Point is, after such commendable circus performances, your people probably call and congratulate each other then sleep well knowing they have done in "The Nigger in the White House."

It is amazing how much of a laughing stock America has sunk into as in a "barrel of crabs." When we tout the superiority of American culture abroad your political behavior seems hypocritical and emboldens our enemies who mimic Republican leaders in their propaganda repertoire. A credible question is "Are we as rotten as we profess or is it because Mr. Obama is a Black man whose race has been enslaved, down-trodden and brutalized in this society?"

Since "old ideas die hard," Republican behavior today is not much different from Ante Bellum days when slave owning legislators looked disdainfully upon and harshly treated native born Blacks as this colony transformed itself through a revolution under the **Declaration of Independence, Articles of Confederation**. Subsequently the

FREDERICK MONDERSON

United States Constitution, viable though not perfect in its initial implementation requiring some 26 Amendments as the nation expanded, is still considered a work in progress struggling to have rights guaranteed to Black not negated.

It is interesting how Mr. Jim Henson, the first President under the **Articles of Confederation** is for the most part not given his proper place as he guided the nation experiencing the initial pains of its birth. This deafening silence, somewhat different in its recognition more intensely equates with the treatment meted out to the first African-American President of the Republic under the **Constitution**. Intermediate between these two Black-American leaders, presidents and legislators either impugned or ignored the African-American, backbone of an emerging Republic, who, up to today fights its many wars that, in contradiction, protects individuals who today practice Ante Bellumism!

First as unpaid laborers, then victims of "share cropping" exploitation and a largely ignored unemployed Black labor force as the nation progressed from Agrarian through Industrial and post-Computer ages, disrespect for Black has remained a premium mindset by influential members in this nation. Wayward and callous policemen show contempt and disrespect for Blacks and Black Lives. Nevertheless, **BLACK LIVES MATTER!** Still, such behaviors in concert, regardless of the academic

BLACK HISTORY EVERYDAY
PART TWO

and intellectual achievements and political standing; where even the lowest class white person strives to manifests the falsity of white supremacy. But so many know the truth! Or, as Biggie sang, "If you didn't know, Now you know!"

Strange, in a nation that takes pride in its history, champions of liberality and ethical and humanistic principles have remained, for the most part, silent on the significance and ramifications of important, yet troubling, milestones in this nation's growth. Whether the 1787 **Three Fifth Clause**; the **1820 Missouri Compromise**; the **1850 Compromise**; the **1857 Dred Scott Decision**; "**Grandfather Clause**;" and the 1896 **Plessey v. Ferguson** decision, merchants of discrimination and racial hatred exploited these legislative milestones whether for political or economic gain. Fortunately, some results of the Civil War sought to reinvigorate a semblance of humanity in the perception of America as a nation on a mission. Sad to say, however, while Radical Republicans, not to be confused with others of the same genre today, championed the Black cause and legislated resulting in the 13th, 14th and 15th **Amendments to the Constitution**, the defeated and disaffected South struggled and re-emerged thanks to the **Compromise of 1877** that ended **Reconstruction**. This legislative betrayal in vengeance gave birth to and emboldened the Ku Klux

FREDERICK MONDERSON

Klan, Knights of the White Camelia, White Citizens Council, etc., to show their true nature as acts of terrorism against African-Americans through lynchings, tar and feathering, disrespecting, intimidation, killings, trickery and denial of political expression escalated especially in the period called "The Nadir;" that is 1870-1920, particularly. Caught in the throes of gushing wealth as the nation entered the industrial age and expanded across the North American continent in Manifest Destiny, the federal government ignored the plight of its most vulnerable and authentic citizens. Odious groups as the Klan became the face of America!

Amidst Jim Crow and other forms of terrorism, promoting economic and social advantages of white privilege in the Southern "Lynching States," as Teddy Roosevelt charged up San Juan Hill with "Blacks watching his back," these warriors got no respect for their heroism. Confronted by racial riots at home, they were first to be sent abroad to save the world for democracy in 1917. Having fought abroad and return home fighting, Republicans abandoned these supporters who instantly became Democrats and changed American political history. In an age of **New Dea**l, they were still generally ignored in the labor force until A. Philip Randolph threatened to "March on Washington" in 1941. Government acquiescence in job offers became more real and the armed forces became desegregated after World War Two.

BLACK HISTORY EVERYDAY
PART TWO

Black History Everyday - Part Two Photo. Faces and signs in the crowd for the 50th Anniversary March on Washington.

Black History Everyday - Part Two Photo. Faces and signs in the crowd for the 50th Anniversary March on Washington.

The 1954 **Brown v. Board** decision simply antagonized the hornets' nest of racial oppression

FREDERICK MONDERSON

spawning the **Civil Rights Movement** where Black supermen and women challenged the might of American racial prejudice. The **1963 March on Washington** was to address the need for jobs and the plight of the poor, Black and White! As events unfolded, the Black Community paid a heavy price in leadership and suffering to achieve the **Civil Rights** and **Voting Rights Act** and their protections in the 1960s and beyond.

Today, every one of those hard-fought for gains are challenged and being eroded as Republicans re-emerge in the political process in state houses across the nation as in the post-Reconstruction era. The fight to remove Blacks from Congress, post-Civil War joblessness can be equated with the inequity of "share-cropping peonage" and marginalization, gerrymandering, even political chicanery as well as denial of voting rights through all manner of schemes have been ongoing. Today, the same trickery and chicanery warns we must be constantly on guard against members of the Republican Party who have exchanged hoods for business suits and esquire titles. A Christian line asks 'Where were you when they took and persecuted our Lord?' The answer, "I was under my sheet; I mean hood," literally and figuratively Clearly, much of this is occurring under the cloak of blatantly false propaganda to mislead.

For example, on Saturday, November 22, 2014, **National Action Network** South Brooklyn

BLACK HISTORY EVERYDAY
PART TWO

Chapter with Queenie Huling presiding sponsored an **Affordable Care Act** - "Obamacare" Open Enrollment Forum at the Coney Island Branch Library. New York State Assemblyman (D-46) Alex Brook-Krasny mentioned a Kaiser Family Foundation Study indicating "60 percent of Republicans support the 6-most important clauses on Obamacare." **Strange they support Affordable Care Act but object to Obamacare**! Asked if they supported expanding pre-existing conditions, they responded yes. Did they support carrying children up to age 26? Yes! Did they support Obamacare, no! The pending contradiction is, if the Republicans now in the congressional majority repeals Obamacare, as they have long tried, will they retain those provisions which benefit their constituencies. If they do, then this is indeed hypocrisy of the highest order and the bane of political chicanery.

Despite what Republicans may propagandize about Obama Care, President Obama is a visionary who realized the need, since 60 percent of bankruptcies occur because of health care costs. This lack of insurance coverage more particularly affected people of color and immigrants as well as poor whites who are not exempt from the debilitating challenges of health care costs.

FREDERICK MONDERSON

According to the **New York State Health Care** Navigator Pierre Devaud, who works for the Brooklyn Chamber of Commerce, another Republican misrepresentation is that the Affordable Care Act is government insurance but it is not. It is private insurance! The measure, falsely dubbed "Obamacare," yet provides ten essential health benefits providing quality and affordable access to health care to those covered, which means a lot to poor folks.

Wide-ranging with some ninety plans to choose from, in 2013, one million New Yorkers registered for this program. Many qualifying for some subsidy to assist their payment. In several Southern States, legislators prevent their constituencies from accessing these benefits! For example, a single individual making $46,000.00 or less per year is eligible for financial assistance to offset the costs as well as a family of four making $96,000.00 or less?

All this is complicated but you have to hand it to Republicans as masters of deception and misrepresentation to hoodwink their base. However, try as they may, the "little men can never tie truly Gulliver" because not only are his moves legal, his credibility unblemished, his work ethic unmatched and his humanity unparalleled. Mr. Obama is a cut above the opposition, the Republicans, that is!

BLACK HISTORY EVERYDAY PART TWO

"Every act of racial terror, with its vastly increasing sophistication of style and escalation in human loss, is itself an acknowledgment of improved knowledge of respect for the potential of what is feared, an acknowledgment of the sharpening tempo of triumph by the victimized." **Wole Soyinka** [Akinwande Oluwole Soyinka. *Noble Lecture [December 8, 1986]*

"The imprimatur that is being sought here today sends a sign out to the rest of this country that the peculiar institution has not been put to bed for once and for all; that indeed, like Dracula, it has come back to haunt us time and time and time again; and that, in spite of the fact that we have made strides forward, the fact of that matter is that there are those who would keep us slipping back into the darkness of division, into the snake pit of racial hatred. **Carol Moseley Braun**. *Speech to the U.S. Senate during vote on patenting the Confederate flag* [July 22, 1993]

FREDERICK MONDERSON

Black history Everyday – Part Two Photo. CEMOTAP's Members offer show of support for Probation for Delbert Africa.

26. THE SCOURGE OF RACIAL HATRED BY DR. FRED MONDERSON

As a student of the esteemed Professor Dr. Leonard James at New York City Technical College of the City University of New York, Brooklyn, among hundreds, perhaps thousands, we were taught a **Methodology of History** very different from the usual. Not foremost the question of when something happened but what happened, how it happened, why it happened and last but not least, when it happened. There were also other variables

BLACK HISTORY EVERYDAY
PART TWO

such as the ability to make Critical Comparative Historical Analyses and the role such factors as Internal and External developments play in creating outcomes that are favorable or unfavorable.

One such ingredient as part of the Methodology, **Internal and External**, can be applied to a discussion of the question of racism in America, today an issue many believe needs attention but never gets. Many will agree, decisions of great significance need a point, place or time of departure in order to arrive at a satisfactory assessment or conclusion even answer to the question under study. In that case, the External and Internal components of the Methodology can be applied to the phenomenon of recent events in Charleston, South Carolina. Interesting, the tragedy of Charleston raised the issue of "heritage" and its dynamics as manifested in history, hate and racism. And purported harmony among citizens, while in fact, deep-seated racism simmers beneath a sheer veneer full of ugly puss, and if pricked can easily explode and ooze. That is to say, heritage should truly be considered on both sides of the racial equation.

FREDERICK MONDERSON

Black History Everyday - Part Two Photo.
Faces and signs in the crowd for the 50th Anniversary March on Washington.

Black History Everyday - Part Two Photo.
Faces and signs in the crowd for the 50th Anniversary March on Washington.

BLACK HISTORY EVERYDAY
PART TWO

Sad to say, the Charleston Church martyrs proved a catalyst and drove a number of subsequent developments to the surface, chief of which were the viciousness of the church massacre with intent to incite a race war; the realization, even a "holy place" is not immune from such violence; a profound and true belief in the goodness of God and the forgiving nature of the "victims;" the bold and courageous vision to recognize the existence of prevalent racism and hatred masquerading as heritage and the actions to speak out against such harmful negativity; a realization, removal of the Confederate Flag was not only easy but soothing; and most important, this entire phenomena is only the "tip of the Iceberg," and must be urgently addressed to help America shed the shackles of this devastating psychological "ball and chain" that stifles its moral compass especially in all its prevalence across the South.

Strange, but this boiling cauldron is not really new and can be easily traced in a series of developments emerging from as late as 2008, even if we, in this respect not give much attention to the previous age through which the foundation of all this rests. From the time Barack Obama declared for the Presidency, in 2008, the scab of American racism was pricked and slowly but profoundly it began oozing the puss of a sin that has long stained the conscience of this nation. Winning the Presidency, all manner of opposition declared in response to a Black man leading the nation. From militias who began arming to the teeth for a race war fabricated in their own minds and belabored to impressionable youth and seasoned racists alike; to Dylann Roof following in this putrid path seven years later who massacred in and stained a holy place, was actually a race-war misfiring dud, unable to spark the mischievous intent; and from an Arizona pastor who prayed for Barack Obama's death to "Daddy Cruz" who wanted to "Send Obama back to Kenya," but when Obama offered him Cuba, his place of birth, he declined. Then we had Mitch McConnell who failed to "make Obama a one-term president" and "Waterloo DeMint" who surrendered his seat, to "You Lie" Wilson and "Stupid" Grassley who could only languish while Obama won twice in the Supreme Court. We could only conclude across that wide spectrum of anti-Obama and anti-Black sentiments many "South Carolina Flag and motifs Syndromes" of "hate" and "racism" stand camouflaged in business suits across the nation, drenched in perfumes to cover the stench of racial hatred they harbor.

In the 2012 Presidential Election all the Southern or "Lynching" states voted for Mitch Romney but ostensibly they voted against the Black guy. These slave owning Confederate or rebel states could not countenance, given their history, of "being on a Black man's plantation." However, it was more than that and it can be argued, the unforgiving nature of losing the Civil War, giving birth to the Ku Klux Klan ideology and practice of lynching and terrorism of Black folk, denial of due process and the right to vote and hold office in a climate of Jim Crow practicing

BLACK HISTORY EVERYDAY
PART TWO

separate and unequal, amplifying "white privilege" and having discrimination and terror as its hallmarks, reflect a fiery hatred not easily quenched even with the passage of time. Hence, the hatred and racism the South Carolina legislators identified in association with the Confederate flag is a well-camouflaged fact abounding denials, notwithstanding.

Given that ideas and practices masked as beliefs and heritage are extremely difficult to surrender and given all of the above, and the fact a good man such as Mr. Obama could not win a Southern state, then the "Carolina Syndrome" is effectively masked and deep seated as especially represented in the 2012 vote.

Recently *The New York Times* newspaper featured an article about a Southern legal eagle who documented some 3,953 lynchings and racial killings across much of this nation's Southern landmass extending from 1877 to 1950.

The gentleman vowed to memorialize these "Heritage Sites" with a marker. Equally, and given that such cultural markers will blemish a lily-white topography, resistance in the "Carolina Confederate Mold" is expected but the nation must confront the problem. After all, after apartheid, South Africa held a "Truth Commission" in which all forms of evil behaviors were confessed and laid out. Some such effort is needed in America to expose then forgive its past.

FREDERICK MONDERSON

Granted these days, some business entities have raised the issue of divesting from states publicly promoting the "Confederate Brand," the first and most profound question that arises becomes, "Is this an economic epiphany or a moral obligation?" If the first, then it is a strategic decision to forestall the consequences of an economic boycott of such a state. If the later, it is a realization on the part of some to divest of the racial albatross this baggage of heritage brings at a time when the consequences exert a stiff penalty in moral and material payments. Second, "With slave trade and slavery, 19th Century racial terrorism and 20th Century lynchings among other unspeakable acts evident in history, do residents who live in the potential marker site states have the courage, strength, conviction and wisdom to forgive, themselves, for that history of unspeakable acts?"

Therefore, still more questions can be posed, given the legacy of slavery and resistance and the prevalence of a Confederate culture across the South, which after all, was a defense of slavery. Thus, the first question is, "Must there be another horrendous act before hate loses?" Rodney King asked pointedly, "Can we all get along?" Should the old legacy of hatred, terrorism and racism remain in the chess and trotted out ever-so-often? The contradiction is, young people want a united country with equality for all given there are so many, internally and externally, who envy and plot against the goodness of this nation and such an attainable outlook can be manifested as

BLACK HISTORY EVERYDAY
PART TWO

represented by the forgiving nature of the victims of the "Charleston Mother Emanuel Church Massacre" who refused to be chained to tit-for-tat hatred.

The irony is, this is a praying nation, so "Do we have the courage to confront the malady" allowing the force of change to emanate from within our Christian values and institutions?" "Can we truly teach multiculturalism in our schools?" "How do our practices and teachings affect the young who long for a tranquil future?" To address the myriad problems, we must move beyond and address the inequality that has plagued our nation for the longest. That is rich over poor; white over black; man over woman; war hawks over peace doves; rural versus urban; employed and unemployed for as Lincoln admonished, "A house divided against itself cannot stand." It should not be only when catastrophe strikes do the nation come together for a minute.

FREDERICK MONDERSON

Black History Everyday - Part Two Photo. Faces and signs in the crowd for the 50th Anniversary March on Washington.

Black History Everyday - Part Two Photo. Faces and signs in the crowd for the 50th Anniversary March on Washington.

Americans are thought to be able to do anything but "Can these physicians heal themselves?"

Then again, contrary to misguided beliefs that though Africans are a god-fearing, praying and forgiving people, we are by no means cowards. Aristotle made the contradictory mistake in ancient times when in his

BLACK HISTORY EVERYDAY
PART TWO

Physiognomonica he declared "Egyptians and Ethiopians are cowards because they are black!" What the great scientist did do, first is affirm the ancient Egyptians and Ethiopians were Black Africans. Second, and unfortunately, he misjudged the martial prowess of the Back man evident from the many wars they fought down through the ages. Thus, the great philosopher and scientist was both right and wrong on the same issue.

Internecine warfare for the burgeoning wealth of the Nile Valley; Old Kingdom pharaohs represented as smiting the Bedouin at Serabit el Khadem; Mentuhotep II pacifying and uniting the land to establish the Middle Kingdom; Senusert establishing his boundary at Egypt's southern border in Nubia during the 12th Dynasty; Sekenenra-Ra unleashing a protracted 50-year war of liberation in the 17th Dynasty and his son Kamose and grandson Ahmose expelling the Hyksos, finally founding the 18th Dynasty and New Kingdom. Whether Amenhotep I, Thutmose I's efforts or Thutmose III's 17 successful military campaigns executed in brilliant military strategy first on the "Plains of Megiddo" and annually thereafter; Rameses II dominating at Kadesh; Merenptah, "My country, right or wrong;" Rameses III against the "Peoples of the Sea;" the Ethiopians Khasta and Piankhi invasion of Egypt "For the Ancestors," Shabaka, Shabataka and Taharka at Thebes and in Palestine, all happening before "Alexander the Great." Then there was Hamilcar, Hasdrubal and Hannibal Barca challenging the Roman Empire; the Haitians at the Revolutionary

FREDERICK MONDERSON

War "Battle of Savannah;" the Buffalo Soldiers on the American Plains; Samori Toure against the French in West Africa; Yaa Asantewaa against the British in Ghana; Shaka Zulu against the Boers in South Africa; and one could ask the Italians about the "Battle of Adowa" in 1896. Let us not forget Blaise Diagne recruiting 100,000 West Africans to stem German obliteration of French Manhood in World War I; Black Americans "Charging up San Juan Hill" protecting Teddy Roosevelt's "Rough Riders" and Black Americans overseas fighting "to save the world for democracy." Haile Selaisse stood against the Second Italian coming; the Tuskegee Airmen fought brilliantly in World War II; the feared Black soldier in Vietnam and our boys in the Gulf, Afghanistan and Iraq are remarkable examples of modern military prowess. We cannot also forget the thousands of Black Veterans buried in the Brooklyn Navy Yard including Samuel Carson who died in the Mexican War and in being repatriated to Ghana, West Africa, opened the "Door of Return" exit to unspeakable Middle Passage slave trade and New World slavery so long closed instead of the "Door of No Return" dating back centuries.

Thus, the malicious should know, African-Americans" would rather pray than fight; remaining fully aware that Machiavelli admonished, "Any man who wishes to make a profession of Goodness must naturally come to grips with many who are not good. Thus, he must learn how to be good and not good and

BLACK HISTORY EVERYDAY
PART TWO

use and not use this knowledge as the situation warrants."

Therefore, Americans must girdle themselves in a forging mold reminiscent of the "Charleston martyrs' families" and work for the betterment of the nation, not their narrow racially motivated and stained self-interest. In every respect, the old labor movement's admonition "United We Stand, Divided We Fall" should be our watchword as we face the future particularly in view of the many futuristic policies and practices put in place by Barack Obama, the 44th President, designed to send a message to America's global enemies, "Don't tred on us!"

"We can love what we are, without hating what – and who – we are not." **Kofi Annan**. Noble Lecture

Black History Everyday - Part Two Photo. "We are Trayvon Martin" and Attorney Michael Hardy at the Podium at Rev. Sharpton's "Power and Policy forum."

FREDERICK MONDERSON

"There is no medicine to cure hatred." *Ashanti saying*

27. MOOD OF THE COUNTRY BY DR. FRED MONDERSON

The mood of America is at an important crossroad, which means turning left at the fork promises encounter with a simmering cauldron of inequality of wealth and inequity before the law that will not bode well for this country. The right turn will go far in pursuing the very best for this country, the clear skies, smooth sailing, respect and equality in person and opportunity that will make all Americans stand proudly against every thought, action and deed that contravenes and threatens the American way of life, the fundamental principles the nation seeks to perfect, whether such is from foreign or domestic threats. But we must remember, a threat to justice, equality and freedom anywhere in America is a threat to justice, equality and freedom of person or expression everywhere in America!

Revisiting President George Walker Bush's Inauguration Address 14 years ago in 2005, he insisted racism as practiced in this new century is not in the nation's best interest and all must work to eradicate this scourge which has festered since the foundation of the nation. Three years later Barack Hussein Obama, an African-American dared to

BLACK HISTORY EVERYDAY
PART TWO

declare for the Presidency. He waged a well-orchestrated campaign in the most unbelievable and relentless fashion winning the day and becoming the 44th President of the United States.

Black History Everyday - Part Two Photo. Faces and signs in the crowd for the 50th Anniversary March on Washington.

Black History Everyday - Part Two Photo. Faces and signs in the crowd for the 50th Anniversary March on Washington.

FREDERICK MONDERSON

At the 2009 **Inauguration** of this first African-American President, the Civil Rights Icon Reverend Jesse Jackson remarked, "Barack Obama represents the very best of the Civil Rights Movement and the best of what we have to offer." In addition, the then Mayor of Newark, New Jersey, Cory Booker expressed an emerging and prevailing view, "We have now entered a post-racial period in our nation's history." As time and events have shown since then, the level of respect and protections for Black men plummeted with the reported deaths of Trayvon Martin, Michael Brown, Eric Garner, Gurley, Reece, etc. New York City Police Commissioner Bratton introduced a "Broken Windows" program to replace "Stop and Frisk" because crimes were rampant in Black and minority communities! Many see gross unemployment disparities between Black and White labor with Black youth being even more disproportionately affected, and this viewed as a principal cause of criminal behavior. However, all of this has been undergirded by the harshest, unjustified and unconscionable treatment of President Obama, where individuals encouraged and perpetuated an insidious climate of racial hatred and disrespect towards the highest elected official in the land. Even further, this attitude has emboldened public and private individuals to say and do things while men of stature, position and conscience remain silent, all the while the world watches and wonders at such hypocrisy.

BLACK HISTORY EVERYDAY
PART TWO

From the inception, this latter behavior has been characterized first by militias propagating false information about Mr. Obama's initial intent, significantly arming their groups and conducting military drills in preparation for a race-war they falsely envisioned. The "Birther" movement fiasco used by Donald Trump as a platform to launch his Presidential campaign, unending Congressional disrespect, perennial sabotage by the "Party of No" of every Presidential legislative initiative of Mr. Obama proposed and every time the issue of race as a discussion topic, the answer is "Let's not discuss such!" When the President injects a statement about a seeming racial issue commentary states he should not because he is the President of "all the people." Yes, but "all the people say nothing" to the Mitch McConnells, John Boehners, Michele Bachmanns, Joe Wilsons, DeMints, Donald Trumps, Chuck Grassleys, "Black Protester with Guns" and "men of the cloth" such as his pastor praying for the President's death and the Papa Cruzs who want to "Send Barack Obama back to Kenya!"

Today, *The New York Times*, "the paper of record," is reporting on Campbell Robertson's "History of Lynchings In the South Documents nearly 4000 Deaths" that identified and intends to publish some 3,959 names of individuals lynched in 12 Southern states with the intent to further place markers on each location where such dastard deeds were perpetrated in an inglorious history of this nation from 1878 to 1950.

FREDERICK MONDERSON

About two years ago, CBS **Channel 2** reported on an FBI investigation of an unsolved Civil Rights murder where the perpetrator is still alive but no one is talking except the victim's family. The report mentioned "more than 100 unsolved civil rights era murders" and that many persons who ran for office in associated areas had either to belong to or espouse "Klan Ideology" especially while running in "White Primaries." Clearly, there is a connection between such requirements and activities in the "Lynching States" and their metamorphic descendants now commanding state houses and national political forums.

Without a doubt, the national groundswell of protest and demonstrations following the Trayvon Martin murder, the Ferguson Rebellion, the Eric Garner protest movement at home and abroad by young, old members of all races sends a powerful message, people want change in the way this nation "regards and does business" towards its citizens, particularly the most vulnerable. They certainly don't want "new wine in old wineskins."

In addition, and most important, published in 1944, Gunnar Myrdal did a study entitled "**An American Dilemma**" in which he showed how "Southern Prisons," especially, part of today's "Prison Industrial Complex," were used to keep Blacks in line, even having them inform on others in order to exert control over their communities. Not

BLACK HISTORY EVERYDAY
PART TWO

much has changed in respect to Jesse Jackson railing against the state of South Carolina, a state with some 36 state prisons and 1 state college!

While today we recognize the psychological and social emasculation a rampant prison system is having on Black men and women and their impact on families at home, the report on lynching also identified this mechanism as a replacement tool during the Depression Era when lynching was ruled "Illegal!" Question is, at what point was lynching legal?

Fact is, slave trade, slavery, Jim Crow, Segregation, racism, lynching, tar and feathering, share-cropping, terror as intimidation, denial of the right to run for office and to vote, redlining, police brutality and insensitivity, and all such odious practices are simply terror tactics waged against African-American citizens because of their race which is not only wrong, ungodly but certainly illegal under law and perpetrators should be punished!

Black History Everyday - Part Two Photo. Faces and signs in the crowd for the 50th Anniversary March on Washington.

FREDERICK MONDERSON

"By the time the fool has learned the game, the players have dispersed." *Ashanti Proverb*
"Goodness sold itself, badness flaunted itself about." *Swahili Proverb*

28. HATERS WILL HATE!
BY
DR. FRED MONDERSON

Recently one of those racists was fired from her job after posting extremely unflattering comments about Michelle Obama while praising Melania Trump for her beauty even boasting of having voted for President-Elect Donald Trump. This person, a white woman sought to extoll Melania Trump as the "Second coming of Jackie Kennedy" while seeking to delegitimize Michelle Obama in similar fashion as Melania's husband Donald trump had sought, for years, to delegitimize Barack Obama the twice elected President of the United States.

Somehow this weird comparison brings to mind an event that transpired sometime at the end of the Eighteenth Egyptian dynasty. Thutmose III's grandson Amenhotep III, "the magnificent" had ruled for nearly 30 years and as was practice in those days, "political marriages" were arranged to solidify political, trade and cultural ties among nation states. Well, the Syrian king Dushrata wanted to create such

BLACK HISTORY EVERYDAY
PART TWO

an alliance so he sent his daughter Thadukippa to wed the old king, who, at the time had as his "great wife" Queen Tiye, a beautiful Black of Nubian-Ethiopian heritage.

And so, the Syrian princess arrived, wealthy as she was, with an entourage of some 300 hand-maidens. Now, Queen Tiye, the love of Amenhotep's life, very influential at Court, a sort of "power behind the throne," though she sat in equal with her husband on that magnificent pedestal. While not opposed to the marriage alliance idea more than likely she suggested the princess marry the young prince Amenhotep IV, the next in line to be king, who would, in the not too distant future, launch the Amarna Revolution. This Queen Tiye, however, was so enamored by Amenhotep III he built her a palace called Malcata equipped with all the most fabulous trappings and furnishings. In addition, he dug a lake, Birket Habu for her to sail her craft leisurely as time permitted. This latter was simply because this "power behind and seated beside the throne" was intensely involved in matters of state and was often busy. When ambassadorial dignitaries came calling to conduct state business, Queen Tiye was the one they sought and dealt with. Not only did Amenhotep III initiated the idea of using scarabs as royal seals to communicate decrees, he had one issued proclaiming his marriage to Tiye and had her represented as equal beside him on the throne as queen. Thus, very early in time, we see a Black woman proximate to near godly status expressing tremendous influence from the seat of power of the most significant nation on the face of the earth which is nothing short of remarkable.

And so, Thadukhippa's arrival with her entourage with the presumed understanding she would not be the "great wife" for that position was already occupied. So, Queen Tiye acquiesced and proclaimed "My husband is taken, marry my son" which she did. In time, Amenhotep IV succeeded to the throne with his wife Thadukippa at his side. Her name, however was difficult to pronounce and the powers that be replaced it with Nefertiti, "the beautiful one cometh." However, while Nefertiti was dubbed "the beautiful one cometh" her counterpart and mother-in-law Queen Tiye was called "the most beautiful one cometh." Suffice to say, Nefertiti came into a beautiful family and was welcomed. There seems no conflict between her and Queen-Tiye. In fact, evidence does indicate after Amenhotep IV launched the Amarna Revolution and erected the city of Amarna, Tiye lived with the couple.

The Amarna Revolution, some have argued, was Tiye inspired through her Nubian-Ethiopian roots. Nevertheless, while it was creative for forays into new cosmological beginnings and innovative art and architecture techniques, it was a challenge and damaging to the old religious order generally thought to be corrupt in its administrative functioning. Most important, the young religious revolutionary saw a conflict between the old dominated god Amon and

BLACK HISTORY EVERYDAY PART TWO

his newly revealed god the Aton. When protestation failed, he tried violence and this has had its consequences. One scholar argued, using Christ's teachings laid down in a peaceful, love thy neighbor manner, if Amenhotep had simply laid down his teachings short of violence it would take-hold and would probably have survived its initial intent of revealing the true reality of nature as he professed his god to represent. However, in using violence against Amon, an established religious system continuing the most ancient practices, the young upstart and his religion bred violence in its layout and in return evident in the "Restoration" and subsequent developments.

Nevertheless, as indicated Nefertiti fit well with her in-laws who, during the revolution may have returned to Malcata at Thebes. Professor John H. Clarke, however tells, perhaps Queen Tiye's last rebellious pronouncement exclaimed against her son's now vocal and violence-prone critics. "You may disagree with my son's religious beliefs and policies, but if you harm one hair on his head, I will send you to the infernal regions." This was an African woman of power exercising influence in speaking truth as she envisioned it manifested at her say so.

Now, despite the many insidious ramblings, ancient and modern, Nefertiti stuck with her man being shown alongside him worshipping their god, the Aton. She bore him six daughters some of whom were shown alongside them in their pious religious display of worship.

Now, Amenhotep IV took lots of flack, ancient and modern, for the religious revolution his artistic and architectural innovations brought about and his ahead of time revelations regarding principles of science that Theophile Obenga, Dr. Cheikh Anta Diop's associate, deemed "surprisingly scientifically correct." One criticism in particular made by modern haters is that Amenhotep, Ikhnaton, Akhnaton, whom some have claimed was physically deformed was incapable of fathering the six daughters Nefertiti bore for her husband. Even more damaging, another Black man, his wife and their integrity under assault. In this insidious slash and burn assault, these critics crossed the line by not simply criticizing Akhenaton but impugning the integrity of his wife. Such an argument by extension holds, not only did Nefertiti cheat on her husband, this had to go on for some time through the duration of six births, he must have known about it and accepted a cheating wife. Yet, he is often shown admiring his offsprings. Nonetheless, he was seen in public and in art representation having his wife alongside as he communicated and prayed with his god.

Strange that Western and American art lovers would extoll Nefertiti's beauty, yet allow such a criticism that impugns her integrity as mother, lover, religious combatant and historic figure so prominently in a great movement for socio-religious change amidst an

BLACK HISTORY EVERYDAY
PART TWO

artistic explosion receiving rave reviews more than three thousand years later.

Black History Everyday - Part Two Photo. Faces and signs in the crowd for the 50th Anniversary March on Washington.

Now, this modern insidious hater, fired for posting the disrespectful, hate-filled and damaging diatribe not to Michelle Obama, but exposing her own hatred, while confessing her unabashed pride in voting for Donald Trump. In fact, she casts Melania into the spotlight. In comparing Melania to "Jackie Kennedy" in an attempt to prejudge her successes as First Lady of the United States, while attempting to denigrate Michelle Obama insists Melania's tale be told.

FREDERICK MONDERSON

But first, Michelle Obama is a descendant of slaves who went from the plantations shack to the big White House. She is an attorney of remarkable accomplishment while Melania "married into money." Michelle's legal expertise held a respectable job while Melania "modelled, exposing the wares." Upon becoming First Lady, Michelle Obama travelled the world with her husband, as a consummate "ambassador" wowing her contacts and counterparts from Queen to other similarly disposed "global nobility," particularly as a fashionista who floored the press and those who cover such personalities, she earned the nomenclature "Mighty Michelle."

Michelle Obama writes her own material, defends it and her remarks are sensationalized. Melania, well, she delivers or as "The Donald" has said, "Melania delivered the same speech" that failed the "fact check" test. As First Lady, Michelle Obama "ruled the kitchen" while Melania "couldn't take the heat and got out." Remembering the "Bush shoe throwing incident" and given no such thing happened to Barack Obama or Michelle, one must wonder when some critic throws "Melania's shoes at Donald."

BLACK HISTORY EVERYDAY
PART TWO

Black History Everyday - Part Two Photo. While "Chief" Parker Barkim gives Sonny Carson the "Walk" into the **Drummer's Grove** at Prospect Park, the "Big Drummer Ashram drums" in a ceremony to honor Runaway Enslaved Samuel Carson preparing to leave for Ghana to "**Open the Door of Return**" for African-Americans seeking "Roots" in Africa.

FREDERICK MONDERSON

Black History Everyday - Part Two Photo. Luis, Dr. Jack Felder in the center and Cherise Maloney listen attentively at a **CEMOTAP** lecture.

"Render therefore to all their dues; tribute to whom tribute is due; custom to whom custom; fear to whom fear; honor to whom honor. Owe no man anything, but to love one another." *Holy Bible Corinthians*

"Before honor is humility." Holy Bible Proverbs

29. HONORING A GIANT BY DR. FRED MONDERSON

CEMOTAP attracted a tumultuous turnout at the Dr. Robert Johnson Life Center, to honor and celebrate the 72nd Birthday of **Dr. Leonard Jeffries**, historian, scholar, activist, author, healer, on Saturday, January 24, 2009, at 2: 00 pm.

BLACK HISTORY EVERYDAY PART TWO

Sister Betty Dobson did the Welcome; Sister Yvonne Hill, the Prayer; Dr. James McIntosh 'Who is this African Man and Why do we Honor him? Brother James Small 'A Tribute from a Spiritual Son;' and Dr. Leonard Jeffries himself, offered a 'Blessing of the Food by the Honoree.'

After the **Introductory Music** by "Mark and the Music Messengers," Birthday tributes were offered by Attorney Alton Maddox, Dr. Adelaide Sanford, Sister Frederica Bey and Brother Gil Noble. After a music interlude, and collection of gift envelopes, Sister Viola Plummer boasted: 'I roasted him five years ago.' Then there were highlights of 'My life with Leonard' by his wife Dr. Rosalind Jeffries, and then the Honoree offered 'Thank you my friends.'

Dr. James Macintosh, **Master of Ceremonies**, provided a glowing and well-deserved tribute to Dr. Leonard Jeffries that set the stage for a night of great praise and earnest outpouring of love and respect and accolades for a giant and great warrior chieftain. In referring to his subject, he began by saying: "Marcus Garvey said 'Men in earnest are not afraid of consequences.'" Then he quoted Claude McKay's poem "**If We Must Die**."

This literary classic of the **Harlem Renaissance** appropriately epitomizes the condition and struggles of the great one who never

FREDERICK MONDERSON

shied away from great engagements. The poem **IF WE MUST DIE** was read as follows:

"If we must die, let it not be like hogs
Hunted and penned in an inglorious spot
While round us bark the mad and hungry dogs
Making mock at our accursed lot.

"If we must die, O let us nobly die
So that our precious blood may not be shed
In vain; then even the monsters we defy
Shall be constrained to honor us though dead!

"O kinsmen we must meet the common foe!
Though far outnumbered let us show us brave
And for their thousand blows deal one death blow.

"What though before us lies the open grave
Like men we'll face the murderous, cowardly pack
Pressed to the wall, dying, but fighting back!"

Then Dr. Macintosh quoted the English poet Rudyard Kipling who believed "Even a broken clock is correct two times every day;" before he glowingly synopsized why he was honoring and supporting Dr. Jeffries.

"If you can hear the truth you've spoken
Twisted by knaves to make a trap for fools
Or watch the things you gave your life to broken
And stoop and build 'em up with worn-out tools

BLACK HISTORY EVERYDAY
PART TWO

"If you can meet with triumph and disaster
And treat those two imposters just the same
If you can fill the unforgiving minute
With sixty seconds' worth of distance run
Yours is the Earth and everything that's in it
And which is more, you'll be a Man my son."

Black History Everyday - Part Two Photo. We Shall Not be Moved March. Faces in the Crowd.

Saying that Kipling and his types have had to recognize Dr. Jeffries was a man, is the reason **CEMOTAP** was honoring this giant, celebrating his 72nd Birthday.

Even more, Dr. MacIntosh offered some important reasons why Jeffries could be considered for the honor are: "Not just because he rose out of the

FREDERICK MONDERSON

Newark Public School system; not because he became President of his graduation class at Sussex Avenue School; or graduated with honors from Barringer High school; not because he graduated from Lafayette College (in Easton, Pennsylvania), or joined operation crossroads, or lead trips to Senegal; not because he left law school to get the background in Political Science that he would need to serve his life's mission; not because he married Nana Essie Abibio, Queen Mother of Education, Development and Social Services of the Edina Traditional Area in Elmina; not because he has travelled back and forth to Africa 40 times (actually 100 times); or has been building a hotel for our people on the motherland; or taught thousands of students in and out of the class room about mother Africa and the greatness of African Civilization. Not because he has nurtured other giants such as Brother James Smalls; not because he has loyally supported U.A.M. Brother Alton and Sister Leola Maddox during their bleakest hours; or helped Dr. John Henrik Clarke establish the African Heritage Studies Association. Or that he has helped set up the Black Studies Program at San Jose; not because he has lectured at Harvard, Yale and First World Alliance. He was being honored, not because he was installed as the Division Chief of Agogo, Ghana; not because he fought to change the curriculum of NYC schools or did so many other great things. But, we honor him because he is a man who has stood for African people; because he represents the very best of what it means to be an African man, a complete man with the kindness and

BLACK HISTORY EVERYDAY
PART TWO

humility for his people and possess a fierce warrior spirit for any who would harm his people. This is why we celebrate Dr. Jeffries."

Black History Everyday - Part Two Photo. Faces and signs in the crowd for the 50th Anniversary March on Washington.

Black History Everyday - Part Two Photo. Faces and signs in the crowd for the 50th Anniversary March on Washington.

FREDERICK MONDERSON

Prof. James Smalls confessed about the influence Dr. Jeffries has had on the evolution of his cultural consciousness, from his days as a student at City College and up to today. Prof Smalls said, he learned from Dr. Jeffries the importance of economics, politics and culture. Then he added, "your culture is at the core of your spirituality. African spirituality is its most profound attribute." Looking at the audience, he reminded them as to the reason they were in attendance: "You're here because you see god in him. His spiritual-beingness. True revolutionaries exist in the spirit." Then he admonished them, "You must restore your spiritual religiosity. If you can't kill the African spirit, you can't kill the African revolution."

Next it was Regent Dr. Adelaide Sanford who gave a tremendously glowing tribute emphasizing the gentle, creative, omnipotent power of Dr. Jeffries, the author of a portion of the Curriculum of Inclusion that told the African-American story. He has a nobility of spirit, great magnanimity, majesty, dignity, pride, is an extra-dimension of the creator, centered on the reality of who we are. He is also brilliant, gracious in the face of confusion, steps over the debris, and rises from the ashes. Then she turned to the audience and confessed, "I be loving you!"

Gil Noble of **Like It Is**, likened Dr. Jeffries to someone mirrored in Dr. Martin Luther King's

BLACK HISTORY EVERYDAY PART TWO

declaration that, "A man can't ride your back, unless it's bent." He confessed, in his day, no Black History was taught in school so he had to learn Black History from those like Dr. Jeffries. Therefore, he was there to salute the honoree's sojourn on this planet.

Alton Maddox exclaimed Dr. Jeffries "Takes the burden off of us." Thus, "We will celebrate Dr. Jeffries' birthday every month this year, on the 19th. Fredericka Bey, visiting from New Jersey, was equally eloquent in her praise of the man who has given so much.

Sister Viola Plummer spoke to Dr. Jeffries of the "African spirit you embody. The African-ness that made you who you are – never to bow down."

Dr. Rosalind Jeffries explained some aspects of her life with Leonard. Upon their marriage, she confessed of not being prepared for sharing her husband with the struggle. She had no preparation for what to expect. Yet, she boasted, "I got a giant, genius, magnanimous man, possessing a tender streak; tender, loving, full of absolute truth. He lives on the cutting edge of things and this is dangerous." Jokingly, she continued, "He did not want to be born. They used forceps to pull him out. He is a genius and godly being."

FREDERICK MONDERSON

Black History Everyday - Part Two Photo. We Shall Not be Moved March. Faces in the Crowd.

Finally, it was Dr. Leonard Jeffries' turn to address those who came to acclaim him. He began by pointing to Wade Nobles' dictum: "Power is the ability to define reality and to have other people accept it as if it was their own." Then he opened up, "We are the creation. It was an African victory. African primacy created the evolution of society. The cradle of civilization. There were no Europeans in the origins; no Europeans in evolution; no Europeans in civilization." Then he explained the role of the Ethiopians who comprised the 25th Egyptian Dynasty and were the only kings who ruled the entire distance of the Nile Valley. Dr. John Clarke labeled this time, "The last great Black walk in the Sun!" He Dr. Jeffries also took that journey of 1000 miles of glory from Khartoum to Cairo for the "Nourishment of the

BLACK HISTORY EVERYDAY
PART TWO

mind. This is what sustains me," he confessed. Finally, he informed "My wife is my rock and my best friend." Today I say, "My Wife Carmen is my Crowning Glory!"

Black History Everyday - Part Two Photo. Faces and signs in the crowd for the 50th Anniversary March on Washington.

Black History Everyday - Part Two Photo. Faces and signs in the crowd for the 50th Anniversary March on Washington.

FREDERICK MONDERSON

Black History Everyday - Part Two Photo. Faces and signs in the crowd for the 50th Anniversary March on Washington, August 2013.

Black History Everyday - Part Two Photo. Faces and signs in the crowd for the 50th Anniversary March on Washington.

BLACK HISTORY EVERYDAY
PART TWO

Black History Everyday - Part Two Photo. Faces and signs in the crowd for the 50th Anniversary March on Washington.

30. ABOUT THAT 96 PERCENT
BY
DR. FRED MONDERSON

During the time Donald Trump was waging his campaign in the 2016 Presidential Election, even after he had exposed his racist underbelly in the "Birther Falsity;" expressed his "proclivity for grabbing women by the genitals;" accused Mexicans of being rapists; mocked a disabled reporter; accused an American born federal judge of Mexican heritage of potential bias in a case he was presiding in; had unflattering things to say about Megyn Kelly and

FREDERICK MONDERSON

Rosie O'Donnell; Mr. Trump had the unmitigated gall and temerity to proclaim, by the next, 2020, election 96 percent of African-Americans would vote for him. Evidence seems to indicate Donald Trump is so contaminated from his disgusting description of African nations, there he relishes in a false sense of clarity and fragrance, others see odiousness and disgust.

While President Trump may boast of having the greatest memory, he yet has lapses in remembering things such as the "Stormy Daniels" debacle despite being smacked on the bottom with her TIME magazine. Naturally Mr. Trump forgot "in ancient times," he and his dad were sued by the Federal Government for racist practices in their real estate dealings. When the "Central Park Jogger's" unfortunate incident broke, Donald Trump practically "lynched" the "Central Park Five" by taking out a full-page AD in The New York Times newspaper. Strange, at that time and for convenience, *The Times* was not "fake news." There he insisted on all manner of horrible resolutions such as "They should be executed" and "Bring Back the Death Penalty, Bring Back Our police." Yet, after their lengthy years in prison and being declared innocent, New York City offered a settlement for wrongful imprisonment. Mr. Trump objected to the payment in compensation.

Not only is Donald Trump labeled a bigot, liar and racist, an "idiot," "professional liar," but those in his

BLACK HISTORY EVERYDAY
PART TWO

camp, 99 percent of Republicans, including Kelly-Ann Conway, Sarah Huckabee Sanders, and the untold numbers who "enable him," rationalize his behavior, defend his actions in words and deeds, even believe his untruths are not really what they actually are. Given he has told his supporters, "Don't believe what you see. Don't believe what you hear. Don't believe what you read. This is not what is happening." Does this mean Trump's supporters are blind, deaf and dumb who "See no evil, hear no evil, speak no evil" against him. Can they be painted with the same filthy and disgusting brush he deserves? Strange that many have criticized Sarah Huckabee Sanders for enabling, even lying, for President Trump and while her father, Rev. Huckabee criticizes so many but won't say a word regarding his daughter's daily misleading at the White House briefing. They both are included in Hillary's "basket of deplorables."

While people of goodwill strive to correct the nation's misdirection, the President continues to move the nation off the page. This pseudo-leader; clocked at 4720 (now nearly 13,000) lies and misstatements in 18 months (not fully 3 years) in office, some half-a-dozen per day, has no remorse about his truthlessness because he never apologizes and if he ever does as with "Birther" it is generally not genuine. Sadly, the "moral majority" and others who supports and enables the Trump aberration have not only lost the moral high ground in religious, political and ethical discussions, but as history will

FREDERICK MONDERSON

acknowledge, they are mired yet and falsely, relishing in the cesspool that has infested the White House. With the exception of Fox News, all commentators are agreed the behemothic Trump administration is a "culture of corruption." Unfortunately, that misogynous leader, having been "played like a fiddle" by North Korea's Kim Jung Un; considered a "chump" by China; laughed at by Vladimir Putin as Ohio governor John Kasich has demonstrated in a tweet, and because he is supported by a few blacks, viz., Carson, Dennard, West, Darrell Scott, and, oh yes, that "Blacks for Trump" individual who acts clownish and is probably very underpaid. Notwithstanding, Mr. Trump foolishly stated and still believes, "96 percent of African-Americans" are ill-informed enough and don't care about his record but will flock to the polls to vote for an "equal opportunity abuser." Oh well, time will tell.

Black History Everyday - Part Two Photo. **We Shall Not be Moved March**. Faces in the Crowd.

BLACK HISTORY EVERYDAY
PART TWO

Now, gauging the ante-bellum mentality of many in the Trump's base whose ancestors helped encourage the reality of the 3/5 Compromise; cultivated and managed slave farms in an institution of degradation, destitution and death; that gave support and strength to the reality of the Dred Scott Decision; relished in Jim Crow practices and benefited from the "Grandfather Clause;" perpetuated share crop peonage that essentially created economic enslavement; either participated in KKK and Knights of the White Camelia intimidation, terrorism and death or sanctioned such, that resulted in some 3,973 lynchings from 1870 to 1950; many of those benefitted from the "White Primary" and Southern disfranchisement of Blacks aided through literacy tests, poll taxes and denial of the secret ballot. These and similar machinations as that of the "Bull Connors" and his cohorts unrestricted functioning brutality in an age of more than 100-unsolved Civil Rights murders; thinking individuals expect Mr. Trump will be proven wrong in his expectation of Black support.

FREDERICK MONDERSON

Black History Everyday - Part Two Photo. Faces and signs in the crowd for the 50th Anniversary March on Washington.

Black History Everyday - Part Two Photo. Faces and signs in the crowd for the 50th Anniversary March on Washington.

The putative record indicates there have been 43 white men as President and once Barack Obama, an African-American, secured the democratic nomination then elected to the Office, Donald Trump and associated ilks unfolded and perennially perpetuated their "Birther" falsity seeking to delegitimize the man and his presidency. Thus, there resulted many fronts of assault on the integrity of Mr.

BLACK HISTORY EVERYDAY
PART TWO

Obama and his administration; yet he persevered because people of goodwill, black and white, prayed for him and showered good vibes on his efforts. This tremendous spiritual support strengthened his resolve and helped bring about his divine mission of rescuing a ship of state adrift, yet many fail to acknowledge this effort particularly because a Black President brought it about.

Miscreant behaviors represented in the person of "Joe the Plumber;" "Tea party" gatherings displaying signs and sounds portraying Mr. Obama as a "witch doctor" and chanting "kill the Nigger;" putrid dribbles of the Sarah Palins, Joe Wilsons, Jim DeMints, Allen West, "Black Protester with Guns" and his "Pastor praying for Obama's death;" the "White House Protester" in shorts and with "middle finger in the air" helped perpetuate a climate of systemic racism, hatred and disrespect toward President Obama. Let us not forget Mitch McConnell's racist and failed diatribe "I intend to make Barack Obama a one-term resident;" all aided by the obstructionist Republican "Party of No's" chokehold on the federal legislature. Much of this Donald Trump inherited and actively exploited in pursuing his agenda. What a conglomeration of persons acting negatively against an individual, a black man; extraordinary in many ways, still his superior intellect best them time and time again. And so, one has to wonder about the conspiratorial nature of their intent. Nonetheless, Obama persevered in rescuing the nation from a debilitating recession and its devastating economic impact, a besmirched nation's image abroad, and having to contend with two wars raging in Iraq and Afghanistan. The perverted state of mind disguised in racist machinations became manifest when, after the 2012 Presidential Election witnessed during October 6, 2013, *The New York Times* newspaper published an article entitled "A strategy long in planning" that involved Mitch McConnell, Ed Meese and top Republican operatives aided by some 20-CEOs of Republican NGOs particularly targeting the Affordable Care Act, maliciously misnomered "Obamacare."

Countering the treasonous behavior and intent and unleashing religious and ethical soul-force with spiritual power because of its sincerity, resoundingly enabled grand-mothers through their prayers to consistently undergird Obama and strengthen his faith in face of the many challenges and doubt. Persevering, he is today considered and has been Polled the greatest American President in modern times.

Many saw the conspiracy as early as 2008 but the 2012 actions involving the same actors was documented proof of a crime against the Presidency. These were conspirators who clearly failed in their primary effort of restricting Obama's election and re-election.

BLACK HISTORY EVERYDAY
PART TWO

Fast forward to 2018 and in preparation for the gubernatorial mid-term election in Florida, surprises emerged in the Primary contest. Just before, President Trump appeared before Republican preachers seeking their support to counter the "coming Democratic wave" expected at the mid-term November election by saying, "If Democrats win control of Congress there will be violence." He probably referred to those anti-Obama forces who support him and will be toppled from their questionable perch to this end. This master manipulator invoked fear in the minds of these pastoral leaders creating a religious, political and ethical dilemma for them and their followers tethered to a man with such terribly negative impeccable credentials.

Today, the nation currently has 50 governors, one for each state. All of a sudden one African-American, Andrew Gillum, the Democratic contender emerged victorious in the Florida primary. He was instantly attacked by both Mr. Trump and the Republican standard bearer for governor, Ron DeSantis. The sad thing is, practically before the final voter count was in, Mr. Trump's attack on Gillum emboldened Mr. DeSantis who referred to Mr. Gillum as "articulate." White men are never addressed as "articulate." More significant, he also used the term "monkey" in referring to the results of a potential vote for Mr. Gillum.

FREDERICK MONDERSON

For years, decades and more, ill-intentioned individuals have used the term "monkey" to refer to African-Americans. Monkeys have hair on their chests and while a few African-Americans do have hair on their chests, most whites do have this monkey distinguishing physical characteristic. Early in his first tenure, the *New York Post* published a political cartoon showing two New York policemen "shooting Mr. Obama" characterized as a monkey or ape. Even more recent, Roseann Barr lost her TV show by referring to Valerie Jarrett, an Obama aide, as a "monkey." The disturbing reality, like the dog running after its master, this Trump clone DeSantis seems well-trained in "lowness." However, and significantly, as Michelle Obama laid it down, "When they go low, we go high." Gillum did just that and stuck to the issues of Health Care, Joblessness, infrastructure repairs, climate change, clean air, Women's Rights' etc. Amidst all this and unquestionably, Barack Obama can be considered an aristocrat, political, ethical and intellectual, because of his elegance of mind and nobility of spirit, as well as being "frighteningly prepared" to execute his extraordinary work ethic. This is a somewhat similar "presidential timber" that characterized Senator John McCain. Donald Trump, on the other hand, is a low class, billionaire with white supremacist tendencies and, as he struggles to "hold back the dawn," his world is coming apart based on the possibility of criminality linking him and his associates. That is why he will forever be a subject of historical discussion but as villain not hero.

BLACK HISTORY EVERYDAY
PART TWO

Sadly, African-Americans who have struggled across this nation for equality in human and civil rights; consistently profiled "while Black;" been victimized through poor education, joblessness, lack of quality health care and efforts of consistent political disfranchisement; and as Ayana Pressly a new personality on the scene who spoke against the Trump "firehose of insult and assault" we must insist all persons "fight, organize and mobilize." All this, despite being misrepresented by a few Blacks who "see the world differently" and support Donald Trump unquestionably. The question then becomes, 'Will these thinking Black-Americans rush to vote, 96 percent of them, for a man described as a crook, bigot and racist?' Some even question Mr./ Trump's patriotism over his business interest. Such is hardly the case for as John Anthony West indicated, "the snowball goes down the hill only until its momentum is expended."

FREDERICK MONDERSON

Black History Everyday – Part Two Photo. Attention focused on the speaker at the Podium at the "Power and Policy forum" on Dr. King's Birthday.

Black History Everyday - Part Two Photo. **We Shall Not be Moved March**. Faces in the Crowd.

BLACK HISTORY EVERYDAY
PART TWO

31. KILLING DR. KING, AGAIN
BY
DR. FRED MONDERSON

On April 4, 1968, Dr. Martin Luther King, Jr., a "drum major for justice," was assassinated as backlash to his involvement in the civil rights movement then underway. However, on April 4, 2019, pens of perniciousness in the *New York Post*, in an Editorial and Front-page article, attacked to vilify the Rev. Al Sharpton as he hosted this year's "Keepers of the Dream Convention." Despite all the platitudes of peace, equality and progress in this nation, where profit, privilege and power run rampant, the day this saintly man was murdered should be a day of commemoration and penance simply because Dr. King sought to help mold and propagate the best in "The better angels of America." Instead, we get the gall of the *New York Post*, rather than calling upon the United States' President to help elevate the high moral ideals Dr. King sought to cultivate in the American character, the *Post* attacked to vilify the last man standing who hoists aloft standards of equality and justice so righteousness can indeed roll down like a mighty stream in order to realize America's true identity, purportedly "the last hope for humanity." Sadly, in today's environment we see more "last" than "hope."

FREDERICK MONDERSON

Black History Everyday - Part Two Photo. Faces and signs in the crowd for the 50th Anniversary March on Washington.

Black History Everyday - Part Two Photo. Faces and signs in the crowd for the 50th Anniversary March on Washington.

BLACK HISTORY EVERYDAY PART TWO

What makes the *Post* mischaracterization of Rev. Sharpton on this "holy day" of reflection through civil, political and social activism, is unquestionably a reminder of how American elements can be unforgiving, vindictive and destructive. After all, that killing and silencing through vilification of Black leadership has been centuries in the making. From the beginning, Denmark Vesey, Gabriel Prosser, Nat Turner, Henry Highland Garner, Frederick Douglass, Booker T. Washington, Marcus Garvey, Patrice Lumumba, Stephen Beko, Malcolm X, Toussaint L'Ouverture, Maurice Bishop, Odinga, Chokwe Lumumba, Richard Green, Harold Washington, Medgar Evers, have all been victimized by Pen, Pressure and Projectiles. Thus, in killing Black leaders and visiting a new form of slavery on Black citizens evident in the practices of civil and institutional racial discrimination, police brutality, Incarcerated Criminal Justice vindictiveness, poor housing, inadequate and poor education, poor health care, negative stereotyping and desecration of Black places of worship in burning, bombing and killing, one wonders, "Is the nation progressing or regressing?" Without question, Dr. King had been a constant victim of personal attacks and in the Press as well. Therefore, the attack on Sharpton is simply a continuation of the same sick maliciousness because he is continuing the work of the great martyr. Yet and significantly, despite those atrocities, Blacks in general refuse to be burdened by the albatross of hate and racial animus so readily perpetrated by the oppressor class particularly among those they

FREDERICK MONDERSON

influence even incite, especially in today's climate seeking to "Make America Great Again." All this transpires amidst a materialist culture of lies, hate, racism, vindictiveness and untrustworthiness.

Notwithstanding, while oppressive forces kill or persecute Black leaders, we celebrate and commemorate these martyrs, commending their courage and steadfastness in commitment to principled behavior in challenge to orchestrated and ongoing oppression and injustice.

As such, **2019 National Action Network Convention** – "400 years since the first Enslaved Africans were Brought to America," individuals who attended and participated, held Sharpton in high esteem as he in turn beamed in the brightness of his brain child represented in the "Keepers of the Dream" memorial, the past's vile mischaracterization, notwithstanding.

Thus, we recognize, the politicians who came to present at NAN's annual convention, do so for a number of reasons. Chief of which, despite the vilification, *The New York Post* Editorial sought to visit on Al Sharpton and in this case, even lumping Jesse Jackson and Barack Obama, the established sponsors and supporters unqualifiedly recognize, Reverend Sharpton is significantly a national leader with demonstrated credentials. The reality here is, though politicians may make pronouncements for public consumption, after the cameras depart, only

BLACK HISTORY EVERYDAY
PART TWO

Sharpton remain standing alongside the victims visited by the many injustices. This is especially so regarding the people Dr. King sought to help in his efforts to transform America.

Therefore, the attack on Sharpton is understood and welcome. Such a display is thus a modern example of the 2019 Convention theme, paralleling the 1619-2019, 400-years of oppressive onslaught against African people on these shores.

Second, owing to his lengthy travels beginning as an 8-year old preacher and the travails along the dusty road of civil and social rights activism; wise politicians, Democrats, sadly not Republicans, realize, "When Sharpton speaks people listen;" but more important Sharpton's people, enlightened, listen and can and do mobilize for action. That is not simply his supporters, but more important the oppressor and those who feign support as well for they realize how formidable a champion of the people Sharpton really is. More to the point, as the people's representative, Sharpton can and does hold the decision makers' feet to the fire. Holding them accountable, they come not simply for his endorsement since he seldom publicly takes such a stand, but they are permitted a platform to pitch their programs of promised legislative action or to indicate what enacted legislation will benefit Sharpton's constituency, the American people, irrespective. Also, those returning come to report to the people what stated goals they have accomplished.

FREDERICK MONDERSON

Black History Everyday - Part Two Photo. We Shall Not be Moved March. Faces in the Crowd.

Again, rather than castigate Sharpton, the *New York Post* should vigorously investigate the nearly 10,000 lies or misstatements (now 13,000) President Trump has uttered which they purposely ignore and the impact the administration's behavior is having on the nation, the view from abroad, and most important on the minds of the young living through these turbulent times. In fact, rather than vilify Al Sharpton whose father was a slave owned by an ancestor of a great segregationist Strom Thurmond; Barack Obama whose wife Michelle Obama is a descendant of slaves; Jesse Jackson, whose heritage is equally of the slave experience; and the question as to why and how these great men emerged to play significant roles in the Reconstruction of the nation, truly investigative reporting should champion the work of such great

BLACK HISTORY EVERYDAY
PART TWO

Black leaders, whose efforts have certainly benefitted America and Americans. Instead, the little people at the *New York Post*, an institution bristling in "fake News" vindictive reporting and racial mischaracterization, should come to realize, on April 4, 2019, as they vilified Rev. Al Sharpton the thousands in attendance did not buy the *Post* that day. Therefore, mobilizing and getting out the vote and demonstration of wise and targeted spending of Black dollars should be the effective projectiles that pressure poison pen proponents.

Black History Everyday - Part Two Photo. Faces and signs in the crowd for the 50th Anniversary March on Washington.

FREDERICK MONDERSON

Black History Everyday - Part Two Photo. Faces and signs in the crowd for the 50th Anniversary March on Washington.

32. COUP VERSUS CONSPIRACY
BY
DR. FRED MONDERSON

In his false characterization of the Muller Report as "No Collusion, No Obstruction," Mr. Trump described the investigation as a "coup, a takedown" by angry democrats which failed! The interesting thing about Mr. Trump's "base" especially after he declared, "If I shoot someone on Fifth Avenue, I would not lose a vote;" the reality seems to be, if he further indicates "Today is Sunday," even though it is Thursday, the base would agree with him. More important, however, and if we examine a statement made in court regarding Mr. Trump shooting on Fifth Avenue, the question then become further, "If he

BLACK HISTORY EVERYDAY PART TWO

shoots more than one person in a rampage, who does what?"

Nevertheless, an equally and meaningful comparison that makes a point is as follows: Some years ago, *Newsweek* Magazine featured a cover article entitled, "Why are Obama's Critics so dumb!" Perhaps the same can be said for Mr. Trump's base who loves him beyond reason especially after he told them, "Don't believe what you hear. Don't believe what you read. Don't believe what you see, that's not happening. Believe me!" So, he conned these people and kept referring to critical media as "fake news" while accepting the false factory mill "Fox News" as genuine because they praise him and stroke his ego. Even when the man is lying, he is lying! Chances are, the base only listens to Fox News and "right wing media," and so are hopelessly uninformed about events. I'm reminded of the commercial showing the couple and their dog sitting in the living room with the flood water rising and they, reading their newspaper, remained seemingly oblivious to what was happening.

The *Washington Post* newspaper's **Fact Check** apparatus assessed Mr. Trump committed more than "10,000 lies or false statements" in his first two years in office. Now it is nearly 13,000 lies or misstatements. The Trump people belittled Michael Cohen because he told a lie or three and is going to jail for it. They claim he was under oath when he testified in Congress, which is true. Mr. Trump told thousands of lies. He did not testify under oath to the Muller Inquiry, 'Does that make his testimony questionable and therefore "Collusion" not correct?

The morals of Mr. Trump's base and evangelicals in particular is such they do not see a problem with his lying. Trump has stained the once "sacred" Oval Office with his behavior and these people are still committed to "four more years." At the current rate for the remainder of his term he may double the lies. Given the same rate of lying, over a second term, he would out-perform the Dow Jones industrials with his falsity. Thus, since Mr. Trump's base and especially evangelicals do not see his behavior as problematic, then as Christians seeking heavenly redemption, one has to wonder how this religious right would square such behaviors with Saint Peter!

A glaring contradiction in Mr. Trump's interpretation of the Muller Report is the fact Muller cleared him of "Collusion" which is ok to a point; but does not clear him of "Obstruction" which is not ok, by Trump's unstated reckoning, since he falsely touts the opposite. That is, the President continues to say saying to his followers, "No Collusion, No Obstruction, Folks!" Recently James Comey, the former head of the FBI reminded, a Russian once affirmed, "If you keep repeating a lie it becomes the truth!"

Sad to say, Mr. Trump's accept this false characterization despite the numerous assessments to

BLACK HISTORY EVERYDAY
PART TWO

the contrary. All this notwithstanding, Mr. Trump, in decrying the Muller Report, characterized the findings as a "Take down, a coup" against his presidency that "failed."

Strange that an evangelical pastor proposed giving Mr. Trump 2 years in office as "Reparations" for the "hardships" created as the Muller investigation proceeded. How sad that "Men of the Cloth" could entertain such over the cliff views. I'm again reminded of the Florida "Koran burning Pastor" and the Arizona "Pastor praying for Obama's death." The contradiction rests in the fact, when Mr. Trump addresses his political rallies, he boasts of appointing Supreme Court and other federal judges, passage of the biggest tax cut in history, takes credit for Wall Street gains and lower unemployment figures because he is "doing a good job." To cap it off, his questionable boast of "No Collusion, No Obstruction" despite interpretations to the contrary, one wonders what has the country come to. All this notwithstanding, two issues are tremendously important as per the above. All the while Mr. Trump enjoyed being president; he golfed; visited Mar-O-Lago and enjoyed all the attendant amenities of his office while saying "to hell with the emoluments clause!"

More important, Chief Justice Thomas once remarked, "there are no Republican or Democratic judges, only United states Courts judges." Still

FREDERICK MONDERSON

Donald Trump boasts of "his judges." If so, are these judges compromised in their rulings going forward?

Nevertheless, and first, how ridiculously misplaced is the idea of Reparations for Mr. Trump when denied to the African-American community claiming such having been victimized in being subject to slave trade, slavery, racial terrorism, institutional and all forms of discrimination. That is, providing free labor under duress for this nation's building enterprises. All such behaviors contributed to extreme forms of psychological, economic, and educational social maladies resulting in deleterious and irrepressible deprivation and lacerations on the psyche of the legitimate claimants for Reparations who were oppressed simply because of their race, which is Black. Thus, given the totality of the Muller Report, the pastor's suggestion and Mr. Trump's claims, these are all outrageously simplistic and false.

Black History Everyday - Part Two Photo. Brother Emanuel in full effect.

On the one hand, President Barack Obama was victimized by the "real coup and conspiracy" that

BLACK HISTORY EVERYDAY
PART TWO

failed as perpetuated by Mitch McConnell and a number or high-ranking Republicans who sought to sabotage the man and his legally elected and constituted administration. The animus and racial prejudice galvanized against Mr. Obama was principally because of his race, however rationalized, notwithstanding. On the other hand, the Muller Report brought indictments and convictions, jail time, against and to several high-ranking individuals connected to the 2016 Trump Campaign. Mr. Obama was never subject to the shamefulness that characterizes Mr. Trump's behaviors. That is, not simply the indictments against his top operatives but the "almost criminal behaviors" against the "best" people in his administration who had to resign or be fired.

Black History Everyday – Part Two Photo. Majority leader in the New York Legislature at Sharpton's "Power and Policy Forum."

FREDERICK MONDERSON

Black History Everyday - Part Two Photo. We Shall Not be Moved March. Faces in the Crowd.

The evidence is refutable, upon Mr. Obama being elected in 2018, Mitch McConnell (R. Kentucky), then Senate Minority leader, publicly affirmed, "I

BLACK HISTORY EVERYDAY
PART TWO

intend to make Barack Obama a one-term president." Hardly a Republican spoke out against this outrageous intent. However, on CNN's Piers Morgan, Morgan Freeman the actor, condemned the statement as being "blatantly racist."

Black History Everyday - Part Two Photo. Faces and signs in the crowd for the 50th Anniversary March on Washington.

Black History Everyday - Part Two Photo. Faces and signs in the crowd for the 50th Anniversary March on Washington.

FREDERICK MONDERSON

Unbeknownst to all, though some clear-sighted thinkers postulated the view, and working with others as the newly formed "Tea party" comprised of Republican activists, in and outside government, these individuals orchestrated a systematic campaign of sabotage to undermine every legislative initiative Mr. Obama proposed, particularly the Affordable Care Act (ACA) mischaracterized as "Obamacare." This very effective obstructionism earned Republicans the title "Party of No." Yet, Obama passed **Lilly Ledbetter Act** and several far-reaching initiatives that benefitted the American people.

Sometimes it is not good to broadcast one's intentions. After Mr. McConnell's boast, President Obama, placed all his adversaries on the hood of his car to keep an eye on them as he drove off to tackle the nation's challenges he inherited. And so, ignored the "Good ole boys" as he affirmed, "Politics is a contact sport!"

Beside his elegance of mind and nobility of spirit, what set Mr. Obama apart from his challengers, as reported was his enormously driven work ethic fueled by an unmatched intellectual capability that dwarfed all as Gulliver to his challengers or the giraffe to the tortoise. So, Mr. Obama addressed Wall Street stagnation, bank bankruptcies, housing industry foreclosures and decline, rising unemployment rates, collapsing national infrastructure, all aided by strong economic and fiscal

BLACK HISTORY EVERYDAY
PART TWO

policy regulation. In the Movie *Gladiator*, the king spoke of "busy bees" meeting in the dark of night. And so, Senator Mitch McConnell conspired with his collaborators from their "under-ground cell." Still, to many there was no doubt the original admonition and charge had changed in any meaningful way. Nevertheless, Mr. Obama kept turning out hits after hits after hits, despite the "Party of No's" full court legislative press to "Not give the Black guy a win!" As such, as Denzel Eli would ultimately confess, "Bruised, but it still will do!"

Come Mr. Obama's 2012 Presidential re-election, on October 6, 2013, *The New York Times* newspaper published a "big write-up" about the plot against the Obama Presidency. The article named Ed Meese and high-ranking Republicans, some 20-heads of Republican managed NGOs and individuals in and outside the legislative government who were involved. Mr. McConnell was named as a "plotter" who, for fifty years in politics had engaged in such behaviors. CNN later did a feature where the faces of the Anti-Obama "Cabal" were shown and this "Coup and Conspiracy" then became fully fleshed out. No one did anything. No one, especially Mr. McConnell was charged or prosecuted.

We are then forced to consider whether the Muller Report and its findings against Mr. Trump and his campaign was legitimate FBI investigation of a possible Russian conspiracy or Republican behavior against Mr. Obama and his administration which was

FREDERICK MONDERSON

a domestic and treasonous act against the American government and people. No one is talking about opening an investigation as to what Republicans did to Mr. Obama.

Black History Everyday - Part Two Photo. Faces in the crowd at **CEMOTAP**.

33. THE RISING TIDE OF COLOR BY DR. FRED MONDERSON

When Lothrop B. Stoddard wrote his *Rising Tide of Color* there was more than a racial and negative component to the message he conveyed. Recently, when Prince Harry married Megan Markle, Reverend Al Sharpton in prophetic fashion pronounced the "end of white supremacy" though American practitioners were not paying attention. Dr. Leonard

BLACK HISTORY EVERYDAY PART TWO

James, a scholar possessing a profound global vision and understanding emphasized, in his **Methodological Plan of Historical Evolution**, that **internal and external factors** and the significance of **antecedent and precipitate causes** project states and individuals along the continuing pageantry of human experience. Nevertheless, persons with keen insights recognize individuals who seek to "hold back the dawn" even "stop the sun from rising" relative to the social and intellectual, even political ascendency of Africans, whether at home or abroad thereby understand how such methods operate.

Black History Everyday - Part Two Photo. **We Shall Not be Moved March**. Faces in the Crowd.

FREDERICK MONDERSON

Evident from four years ago in Brazil, Africans were well-represented among the various teams of the **FIFA World Cup** soccer matches in that country. Though the African nations' teams were eliminated early in the contest, still Africans were very well-represented among winning European teams especially England, France and Germany. Four years later in Russia, 2018, the dominance of Africans on these same teams again reinforces Rev. Sharpton's contention regarding the "end of white supremacy" and those not listening or observing should really take note.

France, as the **2018 World Cup** winner against Croatia, is the perfect and underscored example of this contention, that in a way highlights the immigrant connection which not simply brings diversity but enrichment of the culture in question. The African players on the French team, Paul Pogba, Ngolo Kante, Kylean Mbappe, Nzonzi, Matuidi, Mendy, Umtiti and others were fantastic in carrying France to be world champions. Mbappe especially at 19 years old, has "forever etched his name in the history books." Much more important, however, that France would win is sweet, rich and ripe in its manifestation for a nation that has suffered so much from terrorism over the last two years and that immigrants or sons of immigrants would help in this way is even more joyful. In that vein, the current negative projected view of immigrants flies in the face of Donald Trump who sadly paints those "wretched" fleeing persecution with a broad, filthy

BLACK HISTORY EVERYDAY
PART TWO

brush. In another and historical context, as Germany pounded French manhood in World War I, French President Georges Clemenceau dispatched the French Deputy Blaise Diagne to recruit soldiers in French West-Africa. He Diagne returned with 100,000 recruits that helped save the day for France. The world gathered at Versailles, France, to discuss terms of the Peace Treaty ending the war. In America, the African-American scholar Dr. W.E.B. DuBois, dubbed the "Father of Pan-Africanism," and in view of the condition of Africa and Africans across the world, decided to call the "First Pan-African Congress." This idea was anathema to America and colonial, imperialist, nations and so, a venue for the Conference was nor easily forthcoming.

Black History Everyday - Part Two Photo. Faces and signs in the crowd for the 50th Anniversary March on Washington.

FREDERICK MONDERSON

Black History Everyday - Part Two Photo. Faces and signs in the crowd for the 50th Anniversary March on Washington.

However, DuBois' "Hole-card" was Blaise Diagne whose efforts were significant on behalf of France. When the French Deputy approached him, Clemenceau, perhaps to the chagrin of America and Britain, Clemenceau agreed, saying "Have the conference, but keep it low-key." The Congress did meet, followed by several others in America and elsewhere culminating in the **Fifth Pan-African Congress** in Manchester, England, after World War II in 1945. Because of the significance of this Congress, Africans were empowered with marching orders to return and struggle to decolonize the continent. The success of this effort materialized in Ghana becoming Independent 12 years later on March 6, 1957. In a way, such actions can be

BLACK HISTORY EVERYDAY
PART TWO

considered an early **Rising Tide of Color**, for it motivated many who subsequently led Africa, from Nkrumah to Mandela, to rid the continent of the scourge of colonialism and racism.

Black History Everyday - Part Two Photo. We Shall Not be Moved March. Faces in the Crowd.

Much more significant, adding the many players of African ancestry across the spectrum of sports underscores not just exhibition of talent; but, again, the erosion of "white supremacy" on a massive scale. In a way, we are reminded of young Tiger Woods winning the Masters Golf Championship and "Old Fogies" complaining "The Black guy is beating us at our own game."

FREDERICK MONDERSON

Interesting that on the eve of the Trump/Putin Summit, after France won the World Cup, the Russian President was there to present the trophy and ribboned medals and shook the hands of members of both teams. The French President Macron not simply shook the hands of his winning team but kissed, on both cheeks each player especially the Black players while winning teams in America refuse to visit the White House to meet with President Trump. Another example of the current extreme aberration; Donald Trump, despite his millions, rose to political prominence by promoting the "Birther" controversy falsity and though achieving the highest office in the land; he yet descended to the lowest level by "footballing" the Obama name. In so doing, Mr. Trump has sought to overturn every legislative even negotiated accomplishment Mr. Obama valiantly secured despite the Republican "Party of No" obstructionism and systematic efforts "to deny the Black guy a win." Nonetheless, and given that words matter, as Michelle Obama appropriately extolled, "When they go low, we go high!"

It's been said, "While Rome burned, Nero fiddled." Similarly, and sad, not a Republican nor any member of Mr. Trump's "base," it seems have an inkling of the injustice in his totally disgusting behaviors. As revealed, while Mr. Trump insulted and demeaned the German President, in comparison, hundreds of thousands of German citizens had turned out to give Mr. Obama the "rock star" treatment. England seemed a carbon copy of Germany and while

BLACK HISTORY EVERYDAY
PART TWO

"Mighty Michelle" floored the British and the Queen, Melania could not save the tarnished "Trump baby" who was told, "Go home," you are "Below par! Resist!"

What's alarmingly troublesome, the "base" which regards Donald Trump as "the best thing since sliced bread" does not realize or choose to see or believe the world thinks of their hero as a "zero." They certainly don't hear Lt. Col. Ralph Peters call Mr. Trump's actions, a "disgrace" a "betrayal of the country and its national interest." John McCain called it "shameful." Others held "Russia hit the lottery with Trump" and such terms as "despicable," "shameful," "tragic mistake," "treasonous," "high crimes and misdemeanors," "unbecoming," and "Trump has no shame," representing a "defining moment of the Trump Presidency." Still, President Obama is too decent a person to laugh at Mr. Trump. Thomas Friedman, who thought "The Chinese believed Mr. Trump a chump," and given "Rocket Man" "played Trump," Friedman believed it "unbecoming" and that, in his many actions, Trump "destroys the norms and institutions of this country." Even Michael Anton, a strong Trump supporter took a stand and said, "I can't defend Trump today." Meanwhile, in his ongoing efforts, as Trump goes "low" on Obama, the former President stays "high" with a 53 percent approval rating at the end of his service and is regarded as the most well-liked of contemporary

FREDERICK MONDERSON

Presidents. While Republicans raised hullabaloo about a supposed "lie" Mr. Obama made regarding the Affordable Care Act, they have been silent about Mr. Trump's "13,000 lies and false statements." Are Republicans public servants or legislative cultists? While Mr. Obama consistently flashed that captivating smile, Mr. Trump perennially smirks perhaps anticipating history's treatment of his odious behavior.

The most potent asset a Black public servant has is his integrity and while Mr. Obama demonstrated nobility of sprit and possessed a terrific work ethic of honesty and integrity, despite the avalanche of negativity directed towards him, there were no scandals associated with his administration. Mr. Trump's tenure, not quite three years in, has been inundated with turnovers, nepotism and scandal. Now, who's the better man? Obama, by a longshot.

If "a win is a win," when is "a rocket launch not a rocket launch?" This year 2019, "Rocket man" has launched more than a dozen rockets, and President trump is talking about "Love letters!" Now he is facing impeachment. Added to this, Tom Ridge believed Mr. Trump's behavior, particularly after his disgusting criticism, denigration, humiliation of America's greatest leaders, Britain and Germany, and now in Helsinki his actions are "beyond disappointment." So, "after a bad day for America" in retrospect "the Black guy finally gets a win" for his civility, intellect, noble spirit and being the

BLACK HISTORY EVERYDAY
PART TWO

complete opposite to is successor in the Office of the President.

Black History Everyday - Part Two Photo. Faces and signs in the crowd for the 50th Anniversary March on Washington.

Black History Everyday - Part Two Photo. Faces and signs in the crowd for the 50th Anniversary March on Washington.

FREDERICK MONDERSON

Black History Everyday - Part Two Photo. Torchbearers who carry "The Light" Sonny Carson lit!

BLACK HISTORY EVERYDAY
PART TWO

Black History Everyday - Part Two Photo. We Shall Not be Moved March. Faces in the Crowd.

34. THE VOTING RIGHTS ACT
BY
DR. FRED MONDERSON

Perhaps it was Voltaire who said, regarding Friday the 13th, "Lets crush the accursed thing!" This is certainly the attitude we should take in viewing the ramifications surrounding the **Voting Rights Act** pertaining to Blacks or African-Americans in this great nation. As such, the **Voting Rights Act** (1965) that expired in 2007 further stigmatizes Blacks in this great democracy and the "accursed thing" should be "crushed." A contrasting reality is that a Russian or a Chinese immigrant whose country

FREDERICK MONDERSON

has nuclear weapons pointed at us; whether they will fire or not; can come to this country, work hard, maintain an integrity and qualify to become a citizen and win the franchise or right to vote. Equally too, we went to war against Germany, the French, Japan and these countries' immigrants can also become citizens and win the right to vote. The **Voting Rights Act** affects none of these people once they acquire citizenship (natural or naturalized); residency (at least one month in an area); age (18 or older); registration (sign up to vote and choose a party or remain independent) and can thus participate in the General Election, Special Elections and Primary Election. However, Black Americans whose ancestors slaved to build this country, defended this country against the warlike machinations of these same belligerents, today are still the victims of discrimination, bigotry, institutional racism, racial profiling, under-employment, even police killings and brutality and more, have had a long struggle to pull the lever in these elections. It must stay fresh in our minds that the President of the United States George W. Bush, in his **Second Inaugural Address**, in 2005, called for an end to racism in America. All of this helps to explain the road we have traveled, what we have experienced especially at the hands of "Gerrymandering," where we are and the distance ahead. Let us not forget the obstacles along the way and those yet to be encountered.

BLACK HISTORY EVERYDAY
PART TWO

There have been property ownership and religious requirements, poll taxes, sex discrimination, the effects of the **Three Fifths Clause** (1787) and the **Dred Scott Decision** (1857), which was challenged by the Civil War Amendments. Yet still, **Plessey V. Ferguson** (1896) with its separate but equal philosophy and the **Grandfather Clause**, outlawed in (1915), ruling had to wait for the **Brown V. Board of Education** (1954) and the **Civil Rights Act**s of 1957, 1960 and 1964.

As such then, some reflection needs to focus on Voting Rights in the United States of America, particularly as it pertains to African-Americans.

1. Prior to the Civil War in 1860 only the privileged could exercise the right of franchise and this excluded mostly all blacks, those enslaved, freed as well as poor whites. Women were naturally excluded.

2. The end of the war brought what came to be called the **Civil War Amendments**. The **Thirteenth Amendment** freed the enslaved (1865); the **Fourteenth Amendment** gave citizenship to persons born in America and this meant that Blacks were thus covered; the **Fifteenth Amendment** gave the right to vote to all males

FREDERICK MONDERSON

and hence Black men were allowed to vote. However, the Southern states, just emancipated from the albatross of slavery soon were yet able to reassert their odious political behavior through a phalanx of dubious means. That, in spite of the role blacks played politically in **Southern Reconstruction** advocating universal male suffrage and free public education for the Freedmen. Blacks were elected to the national government as [Representatives and Senators] .... However, in the climate of Reconstruction, the **Radical Republicans** fought President Andrew Johnson's veto of the **Freedman Bureau Act** and the first **Civil Rights Act of 1866** that pronounced all Americans citizens, reinforced by the **Fourteenth Amendment** that repudiated the **Dred Scott Decision** and provided a shield against Southern states "**Black Codes**," was a significant achievement for it insisted on "equal protection of the laws" and "due process of law."

The **Civil Rights Act of 1875** guaranteed equal accommodations in public places (hotels, railroads and theaters). Poor enforcement of this law led to the backlash of **Jim Crow** laws and practices. Harold C. Syrett in *American Historical Documents* (1965) tells, the Supreme Court in 1883 declared this act of Congress **unconstitutional "on the grounds that the Fourteenth**

BLACK HISTORY EVERYDAY
PART TWO

Amendment did not forbid discriminatory actions of private individuals but only of states."

Irving Gordon in *American Studies* (1980) pointed out, politically: (1) Southern states required payment of a poll tax which discouraged blacks mostly poor, as well as impoverished whites from voting. (2) Southern states established difficulty and unfair literacy requirements, which effectively barred blacks, mostly little educated, from voting. (3) To preserve the vote for illiterate whites, some states enacted a "grandfather clause," exempting from literacy requirements persons whose grandfathers had been eligible to vote before the Civil War. (4) The Democratic Party in the South denied membership to blacks and thus kept them from voting in party primaries. This had the effect of disenfranchising blacks, since Democratic nomination in the South, until well into the 20th Century, was equivalent to election. By 1900 most Southern blacks did not vote and had negligible political influence.

The **Civil Rights Movement** spearheaded the effort to not only desegregate but also to win the right to vote. The **Civil Rights Act of 1957** forced the Federal government to respect the voting rights of blacks across the nation in that this act of Congress "created a bipartisan commission to investigate infringement of civil rights because of race, religion, or national origin. A civil rights division was

FREDERICK MONDERSON

established in the Department of Justice and authorized to seek injunctions against violations to voting rights." However, enforcement of such acts required extensive legal action that was cumbersome and time consuming. Yet still, the door began to be pushed ajar slowly. The non-violent protests ma infesting as "sit-ins," "freedom rides," and sustained economic boycotts all culminated in the **1963 March on Washington**. Dick Gregory said, Dr. King's speech was not about a "Dream" but about poverty, economic deprivation, employment, poor people, discrimination, etc., but the media and others co-opted it and emphasized naming it the "I have a dream speech."

The **Civil Rights Act of 1960** - "authorized federal courts to appoint referees if, in suits brought under the **Civil Rights Act of 1957**, the courts decided that Negroes had been deprived of voting rights because of race. In such cases, the referees were empowered to issue voting certificates, legally binding on state officials. The act required state officials to permit Justice Department officials to examine voting records and imposed federal penalties for obstructing federal court orders and crossing state lines to escape prosecution for bombing or arson."

The **Civil Rights Act of 1964** (1) Voting - The law prohibited election officials from applying different standards to black and white voting

BLACK HISTORY EVERYDAY
PART TWO

applicants and declared, as evidence of literacy, a sixth-grade education. (2) Public Accommodations - The law forbade discrimination in most place of public accommodation: hotels, motels, restaurants, lunch counters, retail stores, gas stations, theaters and sports arenas. (3) Public Facilities - The law prohibited discrimination in government-owned or operated facilities such as parks, swimming pools, and libraries. (4) Federally assisted Programs - The law authorized the federal government to withhold financial aid from the state and local programs involving discrimination. (4) Employment - The law prohibited discriminatory practices by most employers, employment agencies, and labor unions. To promote voluntary compliance, the law created an **Equal Employment Opportunity Commission**. The Twenty-fourth Amendment of 1964, aimed at five Southern states particularly, outlawed the use of poll taxes as a requirement for electing federal officials.

3. The **Voting Rights Act of 1965** was President Johnson's response to violence on the part of the Ku Klux Klan to deny voting rights to Alabama Blacks. Out of 15,000 eligible Black voters only 335 were registered because of intimidation and illegal practices. This spawned the **Selma to Montgomery March** to focus attention on the problem. The **Voting Rights Act of 1965** declared:

FREDERICK MONDERSON

(a) In any state or county where less than half of the voting-age population was registered or had voted in 1964, all literacy and other qualification tests were suspended. This provision applied immediately to the five southern states and parts of two others. (b) The Attorney General was empowered to send federal examiners to any county practicing voting discrimination. These registrars were authorized to register all would-be voters who met the state's age and residency requirements. This provision replaced the time-consuming court processes required by previous laws. (c) The Attorney General was empowered to file suits challenging the constitutionality of state poll taxes. This provision affected four Southern states.

As a result, the **Voting Rights Act of 1965** and the **other Civil Rights Acts** helped increased the number of eligible southern blacks from 25 percent in 1957 to 65 percent in 1972. This voting strength enabled blacks to be elected to state and local offices and forced white candidates to appeal for black votes.

Hence, the **1964 Civil Rights Act** "prohibited election officials from applying different standards to black and white voting applicants and declared a sixth-grade education was evidence of literacy. The **Voting Rights Act of 1965** suspended all literacy and other qualification tests in any state of

BLACK HISTORY EVERYDAY
PART TWO

county where less than half of the voting age population was registered or had voted in 1964. The **Voting Rights Act of 1970** forbade all states from requiring literacy as a requirement for voting."

What is interesting is that all gains blacks made by amendment, legal statue or court proceedings aided minorities, women, children, disabled, and even persons accused of crimes. This brings us to the rights of prisoners. All across this nation Black men and women are being incarcerated and losing the right to vote.

In 1982, President Ronald Reagan signed the renewal of the **Voting Rights Act** for 25 years that stood to expire in 2007. If we marshal our political strengths and advocate appropriately in alliances with liberals and people of like persuasion in legislatures across the nation, perhaps we can finally lay the **Voting Rights Act** in the Smithsonian Institution as a historic relic of a people's long struggle for equality, respect and right of self-determination.

FREDERICK MONDERSON

Black History Everyday - Part Two Photo. "True peace is not merely the absence of tension. It is the presence of justice!" ML King.

Black History Everyday - Part Two Photo. Comedian and activist, iconic Richard "Dick" Gregory, the "Bear Hunter."

BLACK HISTORY EVERYDAY PART TWO

> Black and brown people in the United States often are presumed dangerous and guilty when they have done nothing wrong. Our history of racial inequality has created conscious and unconscious bias that has resulted in racial discrimination against people of color by law enforcement and the criminal justice system. Police shootings of unarmed men, women, and children, racially biased and excessive sentencing of people convicted of crimes, and abusive prison conditions make mass incarceration a dominant issue for the poor and people of color.
>
> Hank Willis Thomas (b.1976)
> *Raise Up*, 2016
> Bronze

Black History Everyday - Part Two Photo. The Message!

> In the 17th and 18th centuries, 12 million African people were kidnapped, chained, and brought to the Americas after a torturous journey across the Atlantic Ocean. Nearly two million people died during the voyage. The labor of enslaved black people fueled economic growth in the United States, where an ideology of white supremacy and racial difference was created to justify slavery and make it morally acceptable.
>
> In the 19th century, the demand for enslaved labor grew despite calls for the end of the international slave trade. A thriving plantation economy in the United States and the forcible taking of land from Native people generated the Domestic Slave Trade where over a million enslaved people in the North were trafficked to the South. The population of enslaved people in the South grew dramatically and black people suffered brutal abuse and mistreatment throughout this region. Nearly half of all enslaved people were separated from their children, spouses, parents, or siblings during the Domestic Slave Trade.

Black History Everyday - Part Two Photo. Read the statement!

35. MARCUS MOZIAH GARVEY BY DR. FRED MONDERSON

Today the world knows Marcus Garvey, while the people who conspired against him, for the most part, have gone down in oblivion and the influence he wielded helped fan the whirlwind of African independence movements following World War II.

FREDERICK MONDERSON

The timelessness of his ideas still inspires young people, Pan Africanists and conscious thinking individuals who can gain from his experiences, trials, tribulations, triumphs, failures, betrayals and vision. Except for those who lived before his time, all great Black men of the 20th Century were either influenced by Garvey or by someone whom Garvey influenced. Those modern men who have impacted upon their time unquestionably benefited from the ideas of Marcus Garvey.

A perusal of the **Table of Contents** of the book *The Philosophy and Opinions of Marcus Garvey* shows how wide was the breadth of the man's thinking, a man essentially self-taught at a time when education for Africans anywhere in the world was a hard-won sacrifice. He wrote about "Propaganda, slavery, force, education, miscegenation, prejudice, radicalism, government, evolution and the result, poverty, power, universal suspicion, dissertation on man, race assimilation, Christianity, the function of man and traitors."

Then there is "Present Day Civilization, Divine apportionment of earth, universal unrest in 1922, world disarmament, causes of wars, the fall of governments, great ideals know no nationality, purpose of creation, purity of race, man know thyself, a solution for the world peace in 1922, god as a war lord, and the image of god." Even further, "the slave trade, Negroes' status under alien governments, the Negro as an industrial makeshift, lack of co-operation

BLACK HISTORY EVERYDAY
PART TWO

in the Negro race, white man's solution for the Negro problem in America, the true solution of the Negro problem, white propaganda about Africa, the three stages of the Negro in contact with the white man, Booker T. Washington's program, belief that race problem will adjust itself a fallacy, examples of white Christian control of Africa, the thought behind their deeds, similarity of persecution, shall the Negro be exterminated? Africa for the Africans, the future as I see it." Finally, "Emancipation Speech, Christmas Message, Easter sermon, Convention speech and statement on arrest." These words have been so piercing and influential they were instrumental in galvanizing Kwame Nkrumah as he chaired the **5th Pan-African Congress** in Manchester, England after World War II and in his struggles to free Ghana and assist in decolonization in Africa.

In this country, Raymond Hall in *Black Separatism in the United States* (1978: 66) wrote offering a synopsis of Garvey and his movement. "Marcus Garvey was the UNIA's sole architect. The movement's values, in essence, reflected only slight differences from those of mainstream America. Lewis makes the point, however, that Garvey's ideological creation is paradoxical. Garvey's militant call for Black Nationalism might be too quickly called extremely radical, but its content and emphasis, all reflected 'the conventional American world view.' That is, in exhorting Blacks to be proud of their blackness and black historical achievements,

FREDERICK MONDERSON

'Garvey was merely turning the white American's racial chauvinism on its head.' His ideas of justice and world order were based on the nation-state concept, which most Americans would embrace. His economic philosophy, like Washington's and most Americans,' was bourgeoisie." Finally, "except for its emphasis on the return to Africa, the only 'radicalism' in Garvey's thought (was) his basic assumption that black men could and would manage their affairs in the same manner as did white men."

Marcus Moziah Garvey

Assessing some aspects of Garvey's economic philosophy, Hall believed while Garvey influenced many, others also in turn influenced him. He wrote: "Clearly, Garvey proposed to bring to fruition Washington's goal of 'economic separatism' in urban America. Washington had been concerned about economic separatism - or Black independence - in the rural South, and Garvey applied his philosophy to urban America, with the Back-to-Africa label as an added incentive. He knew that black people had already had large doses of economic self-

BLACK HISTORY EVERYDAY
PART TWO

determination from Washington and of Back-to-Africa from Bishop Turner, Blyden, and others; he therefore had to combine the two with dynamic variables. Perhaps he saw that it was necessary to augment economic independence and Back-to-Africa with race chauvinism, pride in one's racial heritage, glorification of the African past, confidence in oneself, and other ego-bolstering tactics."

W.E.B. DuBois, scholar!

Vincent Bakpetu Thompson in *Africa and Unity: The Evolution of Pan-Africanism* praises Garvey for the many slogans he coined in seeking African unity and progress. These included: "Africa for the Africans," "Renaissance of the **BLACK RACE**," "Ethiopia Awake," "Look for me in the eye of the storm," "Man love your brother," "Up, you mighty race, you can accomplish what you will." His "**One God, One Destiny**" sought to unite Africans and determine the road ahead. As a compliment to his "One destiny" belief Garvey declared: "Therefore, let justice be done to all mankind, realizing that if the strong oppress the weak, confusion and discontent will ever mark the path of man, but love, faith and charity toward all, the reign of peace and plenty will be heralded into the world and the generation of men shall be blessed." Yet still, he did believe passionately: "No one knows when the hour of Africa's redemption cometh. It is in the wind. It is coming. One day, like the storm it will be here. When that day comes all Africa will stand together. Any sane man, race or nation that desires freedom must first of all think in terms of blood. Why, even the Heavenly Father tells us that 'without the shedding of blood there can be no remission of sins?" Then how in the name of God, with history before us, do we expect to redeem Africa without preparing ourselves - some of us to die."

He continued further: "Wake up Ethiopia! Let us work towards the one glorious end of a free, redeemed, and mighty nation. Let Africa be a bright star among the constellation of nations." Even more, the declared objectives of Garvey's Organization were stated thus: "To establish a universal confraternity among the race; to promote the spirit of pride and love; to reclaim the fallen; to administer to and assist the needy; to assist in the development of independent Negro nations and communities; to establish a central nation for the race, to establish commissaries or agencies in principal countries and cities of the world for the representation of all Negroes; to promote a conscientious spiritual worship among the native tribes of Africa; to

BLACK HISTORY EVERYDAY
PART TWO

establish universities, colleges, academies and schools for the racial education and culture of the people; to work for better conditions among Negroes everywhere." Finally, Thompson summed up Garvey's program with its four principles that are hallmarks of the Pan-African movement today, "first, the common destiny of all Africans and the need for continental unity as a prerequisite for dealing with the numerous problems; second, the 'Negro or African Personality'; third, the repudiation of all foreign rule and control and the eradication of all its vestiges which are retarding the grown of African man; and, fourth, social change including cultural regeneration and reactivation of the world's cultures."

Clearly a visionary, Garvey hoped to create an African world state that mirrored the universalism of the Catholic Church. He argued that: "Our union must know no clime, boundary or nationality. Like the great Church of Rome, Negroes the world over must practice one faith, that of confidence in themselves, with **One God, One Aim, One Destiny**... the founding of a racial Empire whose only natural, spiritual and political limits shall be God and Africa at home and abroad."

Certainly, his influence has been immeasurable and his name became enshrined in motifs as schools, parks, and even streets today bear the name of this Pan-African and international icon who helped get us here today. However, while we can give Garvey great

FREDERICK MONDERSON

grades for his efforts in mobilizing "400,000,000 Negroes" around the world we ought to pay some attention to the mistakes he made, trusting in others who betrayed him, meeting with the Ku Klux Klan, underestimating the power of Europeans who controlled those 400,000,000 Negroes through colonialism and the role of Ethiopia and Liberia as pawns in Global white supremacy, imperialism and power politics. His **Black Star Line**, with traitors aboard and their mismanagement, was an alligator that bled the **UNIA**, his return to Africa through the Liberia experiment was un-researched and betrayed, the "Negroes in America" who conspired and had him arrested are all causes of his failures. Nevertheless, no matter what happens, when the people believe in you, your ideas, vision or name never dies and this is why we celebrate and give Marcus Garvey such high marks today, August 17. On his arrest he remarked, "You have caged the lion but his cubs are running free out there!" Those cubs have indeed made their mark! God Bless Marcus Garvey and his timeliness as his ideas, efforts and charisma helped Black people to see the light at the end of the tunnel! Happy Birthday Marcus Moziah Garvey!

BLACK HISTORY EVERYDAY
PART TWO

Black History Everyday - Part Two Photo. The "Garden" entrancing the **Equal Justice Initiative Memorial**, adding tranquility and beauty to the harsh reality of Lynching in the American South, 1870-1950.

FREDERICK MONDERSON

Black History Everyday - Part Two Photo. Jean Jacques Dessalines, President of the Republic of Haiti.

Black History Everyday – Part Two Photo. The Garden that greets the visitor to the horrible evidence of lynching in the South.

BLACK HISTORY EVERYDAY
PART TWO

Black History Everyday - Part Two Photo. Dr. Fred Monderson "Walking with the Ladies who started the Civil Rights Movement by Walking!'"

Black History Everyday - Part Two Photo. Brooklyn Activist Sonny Carson kept images of Black men hanging from trees in his office but this is the actual count of many victimized in that harsh brutality perpetuated in the "Lynching States."

FREDERICK MONDERSON

Black History Everyday - Part Two Photo. Lest we forget!

Black History Everyday - Part Two Photo. The Names, the Names of the victims of Southern racial violence chronicled by the Equal Justice Initiative Remembrance Project.

BLACK HISTORY EVERYDAY
PART TWO

Black History Everyday - Part Two Photo. More of the Names, the Names of the victims of Southern racial violence chronicled by the Equal Justice Initiative Remembrance Project, 4040 and counting!

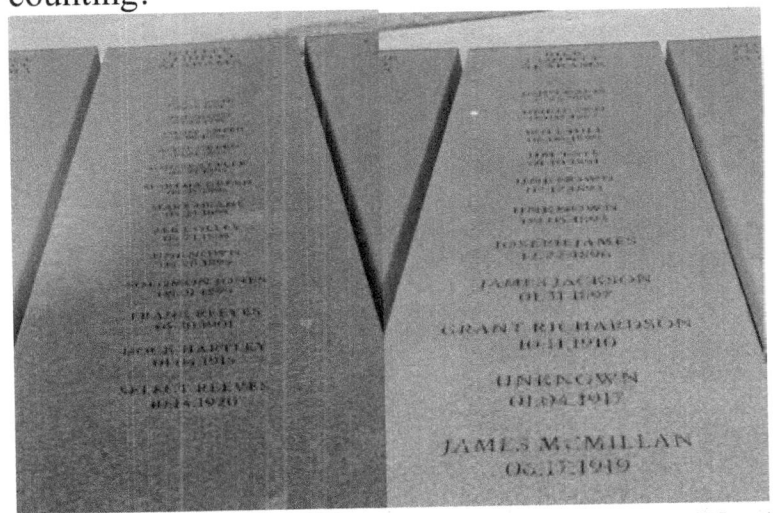

Black History Everyday - Part Two Photo. Still more of the names of lynching victims chronicled by the equal Justice Initiative Remembrance project to a number of 4040 and others still unknown.

www.ingramcontent.com/pod-product-compliance
Lightning Source LLC
Chambersburg PA
CBHW060358230426
43663CB00008B/1310